yright © 1983, 1986 by William P. Fletcher

AMUT BOOK

rights reserved

part of this book may be reproduced in any form
hout permission in writing from the publisher.
lished by Dodd, Mead & Company, Inc.
Madison Avenue, New York, N.Y. 10016
stributed in Canada by
cClelland and Stewart Limited, Toronto
anufactured in the United States of America
esigned by Sofia Grunfeld
n earlier version of this book was published in 1983 under the title *Talking Your Roots*.
irst Edition

2  3  4  5  6  7  8  9  10

*Library of Congress Cataloging-in-Publication Data*

Fletcher, William P.
   Recording your family history.

   Includes index.
   1. Oral biography.   I. Title.
CT22.F56   1986      920'.0028       86-13598
ISBN 0-396-08886-4
ISBN 0-396-08887-2 (pbk.)

# RECORDI...
# YOUR FAM...
# HISTORY...

*A Guide to Preservin...*
*Oral History with*
*· Videotape · Audiotap...*
*· Suggested Topics and Ques...*
*· Interview Techniques*

## WILLIAM FLETCHE...

Dodd, Mead & Company
New York

# Acknowledgments

Without the help of my friends and family over the past eight years I could never have even come close to finishing this book. I'd like to express my thanks to everyone who ever talked to me about this book and the ideas associated with it. If I have left anyone out, please forgive me—eight years is a long time.

I'd like to thank my father, Paul Fletcher, without whom I could never have organized the initial printing of this book, my mother Alice Fletcher, my brother Jerry, who encouraged me for years, and my brother Tom. In addition to the members of my family, I'd like to thank the following friends: Michael Askarinam, Terry Baugh, Dick and Eileen Balzer, Franni Bertolino, Barbara Bien, Ed Bowers, Conrad and Peggy Cafritz, Larry, Roberto, and Pat Catanuso, Chip Coblyn, Debbie Davis, David, Ian, Lisa, and Madie Delmonte, Billy Duggan, Gary Felder, Bob Fener, Martha Gladden, Ron Goldfarb, Rob and Cheryl Katz, Mary Lynn Katz, Hari Har Kaur, Annemarie Higgins, Richard Lew, Willie Lewis, Joel Mackower, Janet Minker, Skip Minker, Lori Mintz, Doug and Susan Miller, Mary Forte Magyar, Don Parker, Diana Parker, Jennifer Phillips, Patty Prender-gast, Emory Rollins, Gail Ross, Dr. Paul Schafer, Pam Schillig, Dr. Sidney Shankman, Dan Snyder, Julie Walters, George Warehime, Matt Wagner, Erica Werner, and Wendy Wheaton.

# CONTENTS

*For inquire, I pray thee, of the former age,*
*And apply thyself to that which their fathers*
  *have searched out*
*(For we are but of yesterday, and know*
  *nothing*
*because our days upon earth are a shadow):*
*Shall not they teach thee, and tell thee,*
*and utter words out of their heart?*

The Book of Job

*The weight of this sad time we must obey;*
*Speak what we feel, not what we ought to*
  *say.*
*The oldest hath borne most; we that are*
  *young*
*Shall never see so much, nor live so long.*

King Lear

*Go to old Nestor, master charioteer,*
*So we may broach the storehouse of his mind.*
*Ask him with courtesy, and in his wisdom*
*he will tell you history and no lies.*

The Odyssey

*"Grandpa, tell me 'bout the good 'ol days . . ."*

The Judds (Country song, © 1986)

# Introduction

❦❧❦❧❦❧

This book is designed to help you conduct an autobiographical oral history—a "Life History Interview"—with an elderly relative or friend, and preserve it on audio- or videotape for future generations. It's fun, interesting, and easy to do, and it creates a unique emotional legacy for you and for the younger members of your narrator's family.

Such a project meets a deep need of most older persons to tell their story for posterity, and it fills an equally strong need in younger people to hear and know about the past and to find their place in the continuity of their family's experience. And the experience for you, the interviewer, in conducting these sessions, is priceless. Feelings and stories you may never have touched on or heard about will come up in these sessions, in a context that has great meaning for you and for the other members of your family. If you undertake such a project with a parent or grandparent or other relative, you will never regret it.

What is a "Life History Interview"? It is a series of audio- or videotaped personal interviews with an elderly member of a family, told to a (usually) younger member of the family, or told to a professional interviewer. To make the interview situations informal, comfortable, and familiar, the interviews are usually conducted at the narrator's own home. The purpose of this book is to enable you to carry out such interviews yourself, much more easily and in a more comprehensive way than if you just tried without preparation to turn on your recorder and ad-lib with your narrator for an hour or so.

Most of this book, as you can see by leafing through it, consists of suggested questions that will help your narrator talk personally about his or her life. The questions are organized in three broad categories:

(1) *Typical life cycle and "life crisis" events*, such as memories of grandparents, memories of adolescence, courtship and marriage, births and development of children, work and career experiences, family life, middle age concerns, retirement, and aging.

(2) *Historical events and your narrator's experience of them*, such as the world wars, the Great Depression, the Atomic Age, Vietnam, impression of presidents, and the rapid technological changes of the twentieth century.

(3) *Personal values, experiences, and life philosophy*, such as religious experiences and attitudes, opinions on child rearing, attitudes about the modern world, musical and artistic values, and high and low points in your narrator's life and what he or she has learned from them.

In addition, a large number of special topics are developed in this book that you can present to your narrator to help bring out other personal characteristics and inner feelings. These special topics include observations about the "sexual revolution," how your narrator got through the hardest times in his or her life, feelings about the tremendous changes in modern technology, "closest brush with death," feelings about death and dying, strange or unusual life experiences, the most famous people ever known, and many other stimulating topics for discussion.

Why does the idea of a Life History Interview strike such a responsive chord in so many people? What do widespread feelings about the value of personal and family history say about the condition of our society and culture?

If you look beneath it, our interest in "roots" and in Life History Interviewing represents an intuitive response to a deeply felt need for a sense of personal and family continuity. We live in a hectic, rapidly changing, highly mobile world, where families have become physically and emotionally disconnected because of high geographical mobility, rapid technological change, generation gaps, historical and present-day waves of immigration, residential seg-regation of the generations, and a cultural and commercial focus on youth.

As a result of all this, millions of people yearn to reconnect in some way with the continuity of their family's experience. This feeling of continuity was once taken for granted when three or four generations of a family lived close together, interacted, and passed on their traditions, values, stories, patterns of belief and feeling, and historical experiences to each successive generation. Now, much of it has been lost.

Conducting a Life History Interview gives you a chance to do something about this loss, both by intensifying the communication that does occur, and by preserving personal and family histories for future generations. The problem of intergenerational com-munication is very great in the modern world; it is difficult enough in stable, conservative societies, so it's no wonder that it's difficult in ours. This book is a tool to help all the generations of a family talk to one another. It also gives you an excuse to begin talking about some important things with older relatives, and perhaps to get to know them better.

Only thirty-five years ago, with the invention of audio- and videotape recorders, it became possible for an ordinary person, just by talking informally with another person, to pass on a unique legacy to enrich future generations. Perhaps one person in ten thousand will ever actually write an autobiography, but virtually everyone can talk one, in his or her own words, to a sympathetic and interested listener. This book is the means for you, that in-terested and sympathetic listener, to help your parents or grand-parents tell their life stories.

# EQUIPMENT

You can use either audiotape recorders or video cassette re-corders to tape the interviews you are about to do. Audiotapes and audiotape recorders are more readily available, are more fa-miliar, and are considerably less expensive than video equipment. They capture the sound of your narrator's voice and record his or her stories, and will last indefinitely. Videotape and videotape recorders capture more expression and more dimensions of your narrator's personality, and are more fun to use, but they are more expensive.

## Audiotape Recorders

Because you are recording within the limited range of the human voice, you do not need any very expensive equipment. You don't want the cheapest recorder you can find, but on the other hand, you don't need anything close to the top-of-the-line model. A middle-price-range cassette tape recorder will do just fine. Try to get one with built-in "internal noise control," which is a special circuitry that diminishes clicks and whirrs on your tape made by the moving parts of the recorder itself. Check to be sure the tape recorder has a microphone, either built-in or as a separate unit.

Use 90-minute cassettes, and, when buying tapes, buy a fairly top-quality brand. (Not so much for super high fidelity, but so the tapes won't break or tangle up.) Always take at least two blank tapes with you—if the session goes well and your narrator isn't tired, you may want to extend the session beyond a couple of hours.

When you are conducting the interview, be sure to keep an eye on the tape as it approaches the end of a side. Some audio recorders don't have a signal to tell you when the tape has run out, and you can miss recording important information if you don't realize that the tape has run out and needs to be turned over.

Keep a pen handy during the interview, and as one tape is used up, immediately write on its label the date, place, person's name, the interview title, and maybe a few themes discussed on the tape. If you are right in the middle of an important thought when the tape ends, just pop a new tape in and go on; but always remember to write the date, place, and name of the narrator on the tape label before you leave at the end of the session. It's easy to mix up tapes and get them out of sequence.

## Videotape Recorders

You should definitely record at least one of your sessions on videotape. You can rent the equipment easily (look in the Yellow Pages under Videotape Recorders—Rentals). It's very easy to do, and it's clearly the trend of the future—more and more people have the equipment in their homes, and within a few years it is likely that every TV set will have a little slot to insert video cassettes. You will want to have recorded at least one of your interview sessions with this visual dimension. With video, you record everything you record with audio, but you get to see your narrator, too. Perhaps the best way is to do a mix—a few sessions on audiotape and a few on videotape.

When you inquire about rental rates for video equipment remember that the best deals are usually over the weekend. If you are planning an interview around a visit to or a visit from a relative, ask about variations on different days of the week.

Video equipment has now advanced to the point where it's easy to set up and use. The sales and rental staff at the video store can show you how to hook up the camera and recorder to your TV, and you can be recording within a few minutes. All videotapes are in color, and are from two to four hours in length.

To videotape an oral history interview you will need a video cassette recorder (VCR), a VCR camera, a tripod for the camera, and a television. The newer models combine the camera and recorder in one portable instrument. There are basically two different formats or types of video cassette recorders and tapes in widespread use in the United States now—Betamax format and VHS format. They're both equally good, but you can't play Betamax tapes on VHS equipment, and vice versa. So take your pick. It's very simple and not very expensive to have a Betamax tape transferred onto VHS or the other way around if you ever want to use the other format. Don't worry about it—your priority is to get something done *now*. Your priority should always be to do something before it's too late; worry about the finer points of technology later. This technology changes so rapidly anyway that within ten or twenty years you will probably arrange to have what you record now transferred to the next generation of video equipment.

Get a tripod for your camera. You can't aim the camera, hold it steady, and do the interviewing, too. Remember, you are the one you want your narrator to relate to, not your equipment. You must maintain emotional contact and not become infatuated with your equipment. Set up your camera and tripod off to one side, and sit facing your narrator. Focus it and turn it on, and then more or less forget about it. You don't have to worry about turning tapes over with videotapes—they are continuous. The important interaction is between the human beings involved, not between the equipment and your narrator. Occasionally, you can reach over and zoom in for a close-up of your speaker, but video technique is nowhere near as important as asking thoughtful questions and listening carefully to your narrator's responses.

## *Check Your Equipment*

Always check to see if your equipment is working properly before beginning an interview to avoid the miserable experience of discovering afterward that your machine did not record it. The best way to do this is simply to record a few minutes of small talk before the interview, and then play it back to make sure everything is working properly.

# INTERVIEWING TECHNIQUES

If possible, interviews should be conducted in the home of the narrator. The reasons for this are simple: it is more relaxed and comfortable for your speaker, it reinforces the idea that your narrator is the central focus of the project, it is likely that familiar surroundings will help the free flow of memories, and it eliminates any inconvenience in traveling for your narrator. It also reinforces the attitude of respect you want to develop for the stories you are about to hear and record. You have been invited to hear your narrator's life story, just as you've been invited as a guest into his or her home.

If you aren't able to conduct the interviews in your speaker's home, let him or her select the location. Ask your narrator to pick a time and place that's convenient and comfortable. You want a relaxed setting where your narrator feels in control and is the emotional center of attention.

Set up the equipment to one side so that you can maintain eye contact and so that the equipment is not a barrier between you. You don't have to sit directly across from your narrator. Just choose an easygoing situation, one that feels natural to the two of you. If you're using audiotape, set up the recorder on a table or on the floor in front of you so you can monitor the tape from time to time. With video, set up the equipment off to one side so it doesn't interfere with the emotional contact between the two of you.

## *Avoiding "Mike Fright"*

Many people suffer from "mike fright," or anxiety over being recorded. A simple way to relax a speaker who freezes at the idea of having to "say something" or to "perform" is to use the "immediate playback technique."

The first thing to do, as soon as you enter your narrator's house, is to look for an electrical outlet. Say something like, "I just want to make sure this is working properly." Then plug the tape recorder into the outlet and turn it on. Then, finish setting up for the interview while the recorder is running. Make small talk about the weather or the house or anything at all while you arrange chairs and so on. After you have chosen where to sit and opened up the book, say something like, "I'm just going to play this back and see if it's working . . . ," rewind the tape, and play back what has just been recorded during the previous couple of minutes.

For many older people, this is interesting in and of itself. It may be the first time they have ever heard their own voice on a recorder, and if you are using videotape, it will certainly be the first time they have seen themselves on television. People are usually delighted and surprised to hear or see themselves, and the ice has been broken before they even have a chance to get nervous. You can now begin the interview, having finessed your narrator's tape recorder anxiety by matter-of-factly playing back the first few minutes of your interview situation.

The technique of immediate playback works especially well with videotape recording. When you arrive at your narrator's house, immediately find the TV, hook up your camera and recorder, focus it, and turn it on. Your narrator's face will appear on the TV as the recorder starts working. To most people who grew up before World War II, the first time they see themselves on TV is a delightful and surprising experience. Even for those of us who grew up with TV, it's still a thrill to see ourselves on camera; but to older people, it is astonishing. The first few minutes of your first tape are usually exclamations of: "Is that me?!" "Oh, my goodness, is that me on television?!!?" and so on. This is great stuff—keep it, do not erase it. Once you are sure everything is working properly, start your interview. You'll see, videotaped interviews are more fun than audiotaped ones. That's not to say that the audiotaped ones are not valuable; again, it's the emotions and the interaction between you and your narrator that are most important. But do try to make the effort to record at least one of your sessions on videotape.

## Trust Your Instincts

Always remember this rule: Trust yourself as an interviewer. You have already gone so far as to buy this book, and you have made all the arrangements to begin interviewing. Therefore, you must have strong feelings about what you are doing and why you want to do it. Trust those feelings and they will provide you with the most important direction for your interviews. You are the key to engaging and maintaining contact with the person you are interviewing. Don't get too involved in interviewing techniques—the best technique is to be interested in what your narrator has to say.

## *Listen and Wait*

Always remember that you are interviewing your narrator, so try not to have a conversation with him or her. Your job is to listen carefully and sensitively, and to be curious about what your narrator wants to say. Try to say as little as possible yourself; in fact, practice waiting instead of interrupting when you start to feel slightly uneasy or uncomfortable because of a pause in your narrator's conversation. A five- or ten-second silence is perfectly acceptable. Count silently to ten, and wait for your narrator to break the silence with another thought. Learning to wait silently long beyond what would be tolerable in a normal conversation is a rewarding skill, for it allows your speaker to talk in more detail and depth about his or her feelings and experiences.

Often you can repeat back the last few words or last sentence of what your narrator has just said in order to continue along in the same vein. For example, suppose in response to a question about "the hardest time in your life and how you got through it," your narrator has been talking about his or her spouse's death. He or she might say something like:

"I don't know how I did get through that year. It was my friends—good friends—and the kids. They kept me going. . . ." Then, a long silence. You could wait for five to ten seconds, and then perhaps you could say:

"Your friends, and the kids, kept you going?"

Your narrator will pick it up and talk further about what it meant to come back from ultimate grief with the help of friends and family.

## *Be Easy on Yourself*

Try not to demand too much of yourself as an interviewer. These interviews are supposed to be enjoyable and fun. Absolutely anything you record will be of intense emotional value to you and your narrator and to the rest of the family. Just try it—turn on your recorder, ask a question, and listen. You can't do a bad interview.

The greatest act of creativity and courage is to overcome your own resistance to starting these interviews with your loved older relative. Part of this resistance has to do with our understandable wish to deny that our parents or grandparents will not always be with us. It's more comforting to think that there will always be a chance to do a Life History Interview "some other time." We want to deny our narrator's and our own mortality. Don't let your fears and wishes about death interfere with your clear intuition that you can help a relative or friend create a unique emotional legacy for you and for the younger people of his or her world.

## STARTING THE INTERVIEWS

Remember the immediate playback technique to get the machine introduced and to break the ice before your speaker has a chance to get nervous, especially when you meet for your first session.

Then, once the equipment is working properly and you and your speaker are comfortable, tell your narrator you are turning on the tape recorder, and turn it on. Always begin an interview by establishing the time and place, and the person you are talking to. (See "Family History," p. 15.) You may say something like, "This is November 9, 1983, and I'm in Fairfax, Virginia, USA, talking with Mr. John K. Jones." Then move right into the first few questions of the first interview: "How old are you now?" "Where and when were you born?" "Where was your mother born?" "Where was your father born?" and so on. Before a minute has passed, you have begun to record, you have set your narrator's mind at ease (these questions are easy to answer and are more or less what someone expects an interview to be like), and you have begun to have your speaker talk to you and not to your machine. Relax, listen, and keep going with the questions and topics you have selected that interest you.

After the first interview, when you begin a new taping session, it is often a good idea to review briefly the last session by asking your narrator if he or she has remembered anything else about the topics and people discussed. Use your sense of the situation when asking this—if you feel that it might interrupt a trend of mood or thought in the direction of the interview you are planning, don't ask it. But, as an introduction to a new session, you can usually ask, "Since we last talked, has anything else come to mind that we didn't mention in the last session?" If your narrator doesn't have anything to add, go on to the questions and topics of the day.

## Taking a Break

About an hour and a half into an interview, you and your narrator will probably want to stop and take a break if you plan to have a two- or three-hour session. Stand up, stretch, and have a cup of coffee or a glass of water. It can sometimes be a good idea to leave the tape recorder running during a break. Often very important spontaneous personal comments will come through after the directed questions have been asked and you are just relaxing. This is especially true in the first interview when the tape recorder is still something unusual and artificial in the interviewing situation.

Be aware of boredom or fatigue on the part of your respondent and yourself. If you are both eager to go on with the interview, then proceed. If not, it is a good idea to schedule the next session for a few days ahead, and let your narrator turn over in his or her mind what has already been discussed.

## After the Interview

If you decide to stop and begin a new session later, briefly go over the general topics of the next session so that your narrator can begin to think about them in the meantime. You could say something like:

> "Next time we'll be talking more about the family: your parents, brothers and sisters, uncles and aunts, and any other important people in the family. Also, we might have time to talk about your childhood and what it was like for you. [Or whatever topics you are planning to discuss in the next session.] Maybe you could think about these memories a bit until we get together again, and I'll see you [day and time] and we can talk some more."

## Label the Tapes and
## Give Them Directly to
## Your Narrator

Once an interview is completed, take the tape out of the recorder, write the name, date, place, and interview title on the label,
and give it directly to your narrator. Ask him or her to keep the
tapes in a safe place until you finish the interviews. Explain that
the point of giving over the tapes is so that no one will hear them
until your narrator feels comfortable about duplicating and dis-
tributing them to other members of the family.

Labeling and giving the tapes directly to your narrator is very
important. It helps build trust, and emphasizes by direct action
the confidentiality that exists between the two of you. You want
to stress that the tapes are for your narrator first, and that you
want him or her to feel completely sure that feelings for privacy
come first where the duplication and distribution of a person's life
story are concerned. Narrators should be able to do whatever they
choose with the tapes, including erasing portions about which they
do not feel comfortable, or keeping the tapes for release only after their death. A request for editing out a portion of a tape that
your narrator might not feel comfortable with does not happen
very often, but your narrator must feel that he or she has this
right.

The payoff for giving the narrator control of the tapes may
come several sessions later, when your narrator trusts you enough
to reveal some deep and truthful feeling, knowing it will not be
treated lightly or played back without permission.

Several weeks after you have completed the interviews, ask your
narrator how he or she feels about the information on the tapes.
If he or she is comfortable with them, you should make at least
one duplicate copy for safekeeping, and several copies for other
members of the family. Look in the Yellow Pages for a recording
studio that can make copies of your tapes.

If you are interested at some point in transcribing the tapes to
produce a written document from the interviews, look in the Yellow Pages under Secretarial Services. Don't worry about transcribing the tapes now; once you have completed the interviews, they
can be transcribed at any time. Transcribing can be fairly expensive, and you will probably want to edit the first draft. A standard
guide to transcribing and editing oral history tapes is *Oral History*

*from Tape to Type* by Davis, Back, and Maclean (see Further Reading, page 307).

## Don't Edit the Original Tapes

Don't edit the original tapes. If you must condense some of the narrative, make a copy first, then do your editing. How can you tell now what may be of value to a listener or viewer in thirty or fifty years? The footage you decide to discard now may include material important to future generations. You should always arrange to make copies of the tapes anyway (after receiving permission from your narrator), so experiment with editing on one of these copies. Look in the Yellow Pages under Recording Service—Sound and Video to find a company that will duplicate your tapes.

# HOW TO USE THIS BOOK TO CONDUCT INTERVIEWS

The best way to use this book is to treat it like a workbook. Skim through each chapter before your sessions, with a pencil in your hand, and mark those questions which are interesting to you. Ask yourself: Which questions do I sincerely want to hear my speaker talk about? Your feelings will provide a genuine emotional quality to the interviews, and the sessions won't be boring to you, your speaker, or a future listener.

*No one conducting a Life History Interview should attempt to ask every single question included here.* Instead, use the book as a general structure for your interviews, and select informally from the large number of specific topics and questions provided. It doesn't tell you exactly what to do at each and every point in your interviews. Rather, use it in conjunction with your own good judgment, and trust your feelings about what you are doing and why you are doing it.

Always remember that there is no such thing as a "bad" interview. Anything you record now will be priceless to you and your family in ten or twenty years from now. If you ask only one in ten of the questions suggested in this book, that's more than enough to guarantee a powerful emotional legacy, more personally valuable to you and your family than a trunkload of photographs or letters, or even a written autobiography.

## The Order of Conduct of the Interviews

This book contains twelve chapters, each addressing a general subject area that lends itself to many questions and lines of exploration. The "Family History" chapter is a good place to start, partly because the questions and topics are not deeply personal or threatening in any way. People find it easy to describe and talk about their grandparents and parents. The more personal, introspective, or sensitive topics usually begin to emerge in later interviews, when the initial novelty of being recorded wears off and after rapport has been built between you and your narrator. Some of the "Childhood" topics will overlap those in the "Family History" session, and other sessions' topics may come up spontaneously at times where they do not appear in the book. Remember that no session will ever be completely self-contained and predictable, so trust your intuition when following the flow of your narrator's reminiscences.

The "Childhood" and "Youth" sessions can follow "Family History" easily. These sessions will sometimes overlap to some extent topics previously discussed, but they provide a general chronological orientation for your first meetings. In the "Childhood" sessions and significantly more in the "Youth" sessions, you will want to start asking questions from the "Historical Events" chapter. (See the introduction to the "Youth" chapter for a discussion of this point.) Historical events always strongly influence the outlook of the generations that experience them. To understand your narrator's life and values, it helps to know the historical context of his or her childhood, adolescence, and young adulthood.

The "General Questions, Unusual Life Experiences, and Personal Philosophy and Values" chapter works best after you have created a comfortable rapport with your narrator. Many people begin to ask questions from this chapter after the second or third session, although some people find it interesting to ask some questions from this chapter during their first recording session. It is a good idea to show your narrator the book, and let him or her leaf through it. Often, some of the topic headings will stimulate memory and get your narrator to make spontaneous comments about some of the different topics. Leafing through the "Personal Philosophy and Values" chapter will also help to get your speaker oriented in a more introspective way, and later, when some of these topics begin to come up in your interviews, they are not a surprise since your narrator knows what to expect.

Questions about middle age, aging, and old age, and the session where you ask your narrator to talk about his or her children and grandchildren, are easily integrated and balanced by questions from the "Historical Events" chapter and the "Unusual Life Experiences" chapter. The later sessions will find you moving back and forth between life cycle topics (such as questions about children, grandchildren, and aging) and historical and philosophical questions. Just as the path of a person's life becomes more complex and complicated as he or she grows older, so too an autobiographical interview becomes more complex and must rely more and more on your ability to try to develop certain ideas or themes as they have evolved in your narrator's life story.

The truth of the matter is that beyond the first two or three sessions, a Life History Interview always becomes more freewheeling. So trust your own curiosity, relax, turn on your recording equipment, and enjoy yourself.

# Family History

༺⟨◈⟩⟨◈⟩⟨◈⟩༻

Family History is almost always the best session to start with when you begin a Life History Interview. It is the session where your narrator is asked to talk about what he or she knows about the family, its members, and its traditions, so that younger family members will know something about the kind of people their ancestors were.

The Family History interview has two broad purposes. One is to elicit from your speaker as much information as he or she can remember about where the members of the family came from and lived, what they did, and what some of their personal characteristics were. The other purpose is to help build rapport and communication between you and the person being interviewed, so that later, in sessions where more introspective and personal topics are introduced, there will be enough trust and sensitivity built up between the two of you that some real and honest communication can take place.

In part, the directness and systematic approach of the questions in this session make the topics easy to talk about, and usually the questions about parents and grandparents evoke warm memories that help to create an easy feeling about the first session. People beginning the interviews are often not sure what a Life History Interview is, even though you will have talked about it before you take out your recording equipment.

Always start out in the same way—turn on the recorder and

establish the time, place, and the person you are talking to. Say something like: "This is Saturday, November 14, 1982, and I'm talking to Mrs. Alice Miller in Baltimore, Maryland, USA." It is important to make this introduction routine because people listening to or viewing your tapes twenty or thirty or more years from now will want to know where you were or when the interview was conducted. These tapes may be around for a very long time, and what seems obvious to you now may not be obvious at all in the not too distant future.

Start out by asking the first four or five questions in a very matter-of-fact way, pretty much as they appear in the text. "How old are you now?" "Where were you born?" "When were you born?" et cetera. Then go on to the questions about where your speaker's parents and grandparents were born. This immediately gets you started, and it conforms to most people's ideas about what an interview is supposed to be like. These questions seem almost like the ones the census taker would ask. They are non-threatening and don't demand any kind of "performance" from your narrator. Before you know it, your speaker is telling you all sorts of interesting things about the family members and his or her memories of the family's history.

There are some things to remember when doing the Family History interview, and some of these points apply to other interviews as well. First, you should always prepare a bit by skimming through the chapter and marking the questions you are most interested in asking your narrator. You can't ask every single question—it would take far too long. But many of them will make you curious: What did your great-grandfather do for a living? What did he look like? Was he scholarly and introspective, or an outgoing man of action? Was he physically strong? Does anybody in the present generations of the family resemble him in looks or personality? Let your own curiosity and genuine interest be your guide. These questions, and your interest in them, will help to stimulate your narrator's recollections.

Before the interview, you might want to jot down a few notes about stories that you have already heard from your narrator. Most of us have heard many stories from our grandparents and parents. They are favorite stories, and can be about anything at all: how an ancestor escaped from the police; Civil War experiences passed down in the family's folklore; colorful personality stories, such as the time grandfather got drunk and started a fight at the volunteer firemen's picnic. Get these "already known" stories down on tape in your narrator's own words.

Finally, you will find that one interview about the past may stimulate your narrator to do a lot of thinking and may raise a lot more questions in your narrator's mind. After the interview is over, he or she may research the questions that he or she couldn't answer. You may then want to schedule another session or part of a session to follow up on some of these family history topics, make additions, and clarify recollections. You might even have a brother or sister or friend of your narrator sit in to help add impressions and information. As another way of dealing with this "stimulation of memory effect," I often start each successive session with the question: "Did anything else come to mind since we last talked, or did we leave anything out last time?" This provides the opportunity to address something important that might have been remembered in the meantime.

But for now, turn on your recorder, check to see that it is working, announce the time, place, and person being interviewed, and start out.

## *Family History*

### AGE, BIRTHDATE, AND BIRTHPLACE

How old are you now?
When were you born?
Where were you born?

### WHERE PARENTS AND GRANDPARENTS WERE BORN

Where was your mother born?
Do you know what her maiden name was?
Do you know where your mother's mother (your grandmother on your mother's side) was born?
How about your mother's father? Where was your grandfather (on your mother's side) born?
So, then, your mother's side of the family came from what country(s)? Or, from what part of this country?
Where was your father born?
Do you know where your father's mother (your grandmother on your father's side) was born?
What about your father's father (your grandfather on your father's side)? Do you know where he was born or where he came from?

So, your father's ancestors came from where? What country, or what part of this country?

## STORIES ABOUT WHY THE FAMILY EMIGRATED TO AMERICA

Do you remember hearing any stories about why your ancestors—either on your father's or mother's side of the family—came to America? [For most black Americans, the answer here will be "slavery."]

Let's take your father's side of the family. Do you know what caused them to pick up and emigrate from the "old country"?

How about your mother's ancestors? Do you remember ever hearing any stories about what led them to leave the "old country" and come to America?

## WHERE THE DIFFERENT BRANCHES OF THE FAMILY SETTLED DOWN IN AMERICA

After your ancestors arrived in this country, where did they settle down?

Does either branch of the family have a regional character? Are they more Southern, or Western, or Eastern, or Midwestern?

Would you say they were more city, or more rural people?

# Grandparents

Let's take some time to talk about your grandparents. Can you tell me anything about them? What do you remember or know about them, on either side of the family? [wait, allow narrator to answer]

## MOTHER'S PARENTS

Let's start with your grandparents on your mother's side. Can you tell me something about them?

Do you remember hearing any stories about how your grandparents met each other? How they first got together and subsequently married?

## GRANDMOTHER (MOTHER'S SIDE)

Can you tell me something about your grandmother on your mother's side? [wait] Do you remember anything else about her?
[If narrator can't remember, follow up with]:

What kind of person was she? What was her personality like?

What did she look like?

How many children did she have? (How many aunts and uncles do you have on your mother's side?)

What were some of her positive qualities? Perhaps there are some special skills or abilities that you remember?

How about some of her more negative qualities?

What social class would you say she was from?

How important was she to you? Do you think she had much of an effect on you?

Did she pass anything on in the family's traditions—either in material possessions or in some characteristic way of looking at life or doing things?

Do you know what she died of?

And, do you know where she was buried?

## GRANDFATHER (MOTHER'S SIDE)

What can you tell me about your grandfather on your mother's side of the family? [wait for response]

What kind of work did he do?

What kind of a person was he? How would you describe his personality?

Can you remember any specific incidents or memories associated with him? For example, good times you had with him, or any other specific memories about you and him? Does anything come to mind?

What did he look like?

Can you think of something about him that was especially distinctive or characteristic? Something that really stood out about him?

What was he like emotionally? Quiet or loud? Happy or more melancholy? Was he funny? Was he a stern man, or more easygoing?

Do you think he passed on in the traditions of the family any special personality characteristic or way of doing things or way of looking at life?

Do you think you have any of his qualities in you?

Do you know how he died, and where he was buried?

## FAMILY HEIRLOOMS FROM MOTHER'S PARENTS

Are there any family heirlooms or property that came down from your grandparents on your mother's side of the family?

Where are they now? Who in the family has them?

## FATHER'S PARENTS

Now, tell me something about your father's parents—your grandparents on your father's side. [wait]

Do you remember hearing any stories about how they met each other and came to be married?

## GRANDMOTHER (FATHER'S SIDE)

Tell me something that you remember about your grandmother on your father's side of the family. [wait]

Can you remember anything else about her?

What kind of a person was she? How would you describe her personality?

What did she look like? Describe her for me.

Do any memories come to mind of things you did with her? Any specific memories or places you went, or of things you did together?

Did she work outside the home? Or was she mainly a housewife and a mother?

What social class would you say she was from?

How important was she to you? Do you think she had much of an effect on you?

In what ways? Do you think you have any of her traits in you?

Tell me a story about her that would characterize her—something that she did, or her response to something that happened to her.

Was there anything about her that was unusual or especially distinctive?

What was she like emotionally?

Do you think she passed on in the traditions of the family any special personality characteristics or special ways of looking at things?

Do you know how she died, and where she was buried?

## GRANDFATHER (FATHER'S SIDE)

And finally, tell me something about your father's father, your grandfather on your father's side of the family. [wait]

Can you remember anything else about him?

What kind of work did he do?

Was he successful, or prosperous in his work?

What kind of person was he? Can you describe some of his personality characteristics?

What did he look like?

Do you think you have any of his characteristics in you?

Did he pass on in the traditions of the family any special personality traits or ways of looking at life that you are aware of?

I am thinking, for example, of maybe a stubbornness, or maybe an optimistic, cheerful outlook, or something characteristic like that.

Do any incidents or memories about him stand out especially in your mind?

Tell me about what you are remembering right now.

How important was your grandfather to you? Do you think he had much of an effect on you?

Do you know how he died, and where he was buried?

## FAMILY HEIRLOOMS FROM FATHER'S PARENTS

Were there any family heirlooms or property or traditions that came down from your grandparents on your father's side of the family?

Where are they now? Who in the family has them?

## ANY OTHER STORIES ABOUT ANCESTORS

Can you think of anything else about your ancestors? Any stories that were told about the [mother's family name] family, or about the [father's family name] family that we haven't mentioned?

Do you know of any "black sheep," notorious characters, or "horse thieves" on either side of the family?

How about stories about "ladies' men" or "womanizers," or stories about beautiful women in your family's history?

Any stories about royalty in the family's history?

Any stories about famous or infamous relatives on either side of the family, for example, a "distant cousin" who might have done something especially important? [wait]

Was there anyone you ever heard of in the family with any unusual psychic abilities or special powers? Such as a gift for healing, or perhaps some power of ESP, or "fortune telling" or "second sight"?

Who was that, and what was he or she said to be able to do?

Do you think any of these abilities have been passed on in the family?

## *Parents*

Now let's talk about your parents. Take some time now, and tell me something about them. [wait, allow your narrator to finish his or her initial comments about parents before asking additional questions]

## HOW PARENTS MET AND FELL IN LOVE

Do you remember the story of how they first met and fell in love?

Tell me that story. Did they ever tell it to you?

Did they ever talk much about the circumstances around which they came to get married?

What did they talk about? What was their courtship like?

## MOTHER

Let's spend the next several minutes talking about your mother. Do you know where and when she was born?

## MOTHER'S CHILDHOOD

Where did she grow up?

What was her childhood like? Did she ever tell you much about it?

## MOTHER'S LIFE BEFORE SHE MARRIED

What did she do before she married your father? Did she ever talk about this part of her life?

Do you know if she worked before she married?

Was she previously married before she married your father?

## COURTSHIP

What was your parents' courtship like? Did your mother ever talk about it?

What did she say about her courtship with your father? Can you remember any stories she told about herself or about him at that time in her life?

Do you know how long they knew each other, or went out with each other, or were engaged, before they got married?

## MOTHER'S CHILDREN (YOUR BROTHERS AND SISTERS)

How many children did your mother have?

Can you briefly name her children (your brothers and sisters), and which was the eldest, the next, and so on?

## DESCRIPTION OF YOUR MOTHER

What did your mother look like? Can you describe her?

When you remember her, how do you remember her looking? How old is she, what does she look like, in the picture of her that you have in your memory?

Do you have any actual photographs of her? Or does anybody in the family?

Did your mother have any scars or birthmarks that you remember?

[If birthmarks]: Are there any birthmarks similar to hers that you know of anywhere else in the family? Like among any of her children or grandchildren?

[If scars]: How did she get the scar? Did she ever tell you about it?

## A STORY TO CHARACTERIZE YOUR MOTHER

Tell me something about your mother that would characterize her. A story about her or an anecdote that reveals something about the kind of a woman she was. [wait]

What special story about something she did or about the way she was stands out in your mind?

What thoughts are you thinking right now? What are you thinking about her right at this moment?

## SOCIAL CLASS, EDUCATION

What social class would you say your mother grew up in?

How much education did she have?

## MOTHER: WORK, HOMEMAKER

Did she work outside the home, or was she mainly a homemaker?

[If mother worked outside the home]:

What kind of work did she do?

Was it unusual for a woman and mother at that time to work for a wage outside the home?

Why do you think that was?

Do you think you learned something about what women were capable of doing in the world of work from your mother's career that helped you in your life?

Why do you say that?

[If mother was primarily a homemaker]:

What kinds of things did your mother do around the home?

Was she a good cook?

What dish that she made was your favorite?

How did it taste?

Can you make that dish?

Take a minute now and describe the recipe for me. How do you go about making it?

## MOTHER'S TALENTS AND INTERESTS

Was she good at crafts of any kind? Like making toys or clothes, for example?

Was she artistic? Or musical?

Did your mother have any hobbies?

>   What were they?


## BEDTIME STORIES

Did she tell you bedtime stories when you were little?

>   Do you still remember any of them?

>   Could you tell me one of them now? Or part of one? Who were the characters in her stories, and what would they do?

>   Did you ever tell any of these bedtime stories to your kids?


## MOTHER'S CIVIC INVOLVEMENTS

How about her civic responsibilities? Was she active in the community, or in the schools?

>   In what ways? What did she do?


## SKILLS LEARNED AND TALENTS INHERITED FROM MOTHER

What skills do you think you learned from her?

Which of her talents do you think you inherited?


## MOTHER'S PERSONALITY, EMOTIONAL CHARACTERISTICS

What were some of her emotional qualities? Can you describe her personality a little more? [wait]

>   Was she a loving and warm person? Or did her personality have a strict and severe side to it? Or both?

>   Did she ever lose her temper that you remember?

>>   Can you remember one time when she got really mad at you?

>>   What had you done?

>>   How did it all end up?

>>   Did she have a good sense of humor?

## BEST AND WORST THINGS ABOUT HER

What were some of her best personal qualities?
And what about the bad things about her? Can you think of any of her negative qualities?

## EMOTIONAL QUALITIES YOU INHERITED FROM HER

Which of her emotional qualities do you think you inherited from her?
In what ways do you think you are very much like your mother, and in what ways do you think you are the most different?

## MOTHER'S CHILD-REARING ATTITUDES

How would you characterize her attitude toward raising her children?
   Was she strict or more easygoing?
   What do you think were some of the main values she tried to teach her children?

## MOTHER'S ATTITUDE TOWARD SEX AND SEXUALITY

What was your mother's attitude toward sex and sexuality, in your opinion?
   Would you say she was more of a "prude" about sex, or was she more open, natural, and communicative about it?
   Did she communicate those attitudes to you, do you think?
   Did she ever give you and your brothers and sisters any "sex education," or talk about sex or marriage when you were growing up?
   How were young men and women expected to behave when you were growing up? What would have been your mother's attitude toward premarital sex or teenage sexuality?
   Why do you think she felt that way?

## ANYTHING UNUSUAL ABOUT YOUR MOTHER

Was there anything really unusual about your mother? [wait]
   Why do you say that?

## DISAPPOINTMENTS/TRAGEDIES IN YOUR MOTHER'S LIFE

What disappointments do you think she suffered in her life?

Was there any great sadness, or tragedy, or regret that she had suffered in her life that you know of?

How did she cope with, or come to terms with, sadnesses and disappointments?

Was she the type to dwell on her misfortunes, or was she more the type who picks up and goes on in spite of hardships?

## MOTHER'S RELIGIOUS BELIEFS

Do you know if she had a strong religious faith or feeling?

Did she believe in God?

Did she pray?

What religion was she raised in, and what religion did she practice?

## MOTHER'S HEALTH

How was your mother's health generally?

Did she have any severe illnesses or injuries while you were growing up?

How do you think that affected you and the rest of the family?

## MOTHER'S DEATH

How and when did she die?

Tell me about her death. [wait]

Where is the cemetery where she is buried?

How hard was it for you to accept and get over your mother's death?

Before she died, did you ever talk to her about her attitude toward death and dying?

What was her attitude?

Do you think she believed in any kind of afterlife?

Do you think you share your mother's attitude toward death and mortality?

## THE MOST IMPORTANT THING YOU LEARNED FROM YOUR MOTHER

What do you think was the most important thing you learned from your mother?

## HEIRLOOMS FROM MOTHER

Did she leave any personal belongings or heirlooms that you still have, or that another member of the family has?

## ANYTHING ABOUT YOUR MOTHER I DIDN'T ASK?

Is there anything else important that I forgot to ask about her? Anything that we left out about her? [wait]

## FATHER

Now let's go on and talk in the same way about your father. Tell me something about him. [wait for initial comments]

Where did he come from? Where did he grow up?

Do you know where and when he was born?

## FATHER'S CHILDHOOD

What was his childhood like? Do you remember his telling you anything about his early years?

Did he talk much about his parents, or his boyhood, or about what his life was like when he was growing up?

What do you remember?

## WHAT FATHER LOOKED LIKE

What did he look like?

When you remember him, how do you remember him looking? How old is he, and what does he look like, in the picture of him that you have in your memory?

Do you have any actual photographs of him? Or does anybody in the family have one?

## FATHER'S WORK

What was your father's occupation? What did he do for a living?
What kinds of work did he do as a young man? Did he ever tell
you about some of his first jobs?
What other kinds of work did your father do when you were
growing up?

## SOCIAL CLASS AND EDUCATION

What social class would you say he grew up in?
How much education did he have?

## FATHER'S LIFE BEFORE HE MARRIED

What did he do before he married your mother? Did he talk much
about that part of his life?

Was he previously married?
Did he ever tell you about any of his adventures or about his
life as a bachelor?

How and where did he live, and what did he do before he
married your mother?

## FATHER'S COURTSHIP OF YOUR MOTHER

What was his courtship of your mother like? Did he tell any stories
about when they were going out together that you remember?

How did he meet and fall in love with your mother?
Any funny stories that you remember him telling about his
courtship of your mother?

## A STORY TO CHARACTERIZE YOUR FATHER

How would you characterize your father? Can you think of a story
about him that illustrates something about the kind of man he
was? [wait]

What special story stands out in your mind about him? Something you did with him, or something you know about him that
he did?

What thoughts are going through your head right now? What
are you thinking or remembering?

any sex education or talk to you about sex or marriage when you were growing up?

What would your father's attitude have been toward teenage or premarital sex?

## BEST AND WORST THINGS ABOUT FATHER

What were some of your father's best personal qualities, as you remember him?

What about bad things about him? What were some of his more negative qualities?

## BEDTIME STORIES TOLD BY FATHER

Do you remember any of the bedtime stories that he used to tell you when you were little?

What were they about? Who were some of the characters? Do you remember?

Did you ever tell any of these bedtime stories to your kids?

## FATHER'S HEALTH

How was your father's health in general?

Did he have any severe illnesses or injuries while you were growing up?

How do you think that affected you and the rest of the family?

## FATHER'S DEATH

How and when did your father die?

Tell me about his death. [wait]

Where is he buried?

How hard was it for you to accept and get over your father's death?

Before he died, did you ever talk with him about his attitude toward death and dying?

What was his attitude?

Do you think he believed in any kind of an afterlife?

Do you think you have the same attitude that your father had toward death and mortality?

## MOST IMPORTANT THING YOU LEARNED FROM YOUR FATHER

What do you think was the most important thing you learned from your father?

## HEIRLOOMS FROM FATHER

Did he leave any personal belongings or heirlooms that you still have, or that another member of the family has?

## ANYTHING I LEFT OUT ABOUT YOUR FATHER

Is there anything else that I forgot to ask about him? Anything that we left out about the kind of a man he was? [wait]

# Other Family Members

## UNCLES AND AUNTS

Let's go on now with any other members of the family. Were there any favorite uncles or aunts who were important to you when you were growing up?

Tell me their names, and something about them.

What did they do?

In what ways were they important to you, or in what ways did they influence you?

Were your parents' families close? Were your mother and father close to their brothers and sisters?

## COUSINS

Were there any cousins that you remember who were important to you, or who are important to you now?

Tell me something about them.

In what ways were they important to you when you were growing up?

Did you see them often?

Did you have a favorite cousin?

Who was he/she, and what was he/she like?

What are some of the things that you remember doing together? Do you have any funny stories about things you did?
How did your cousins do in later life? Are you in touch with
any of them, or with their children?

How could somebody in the family trace them or their children and contact them now? Do you know where your cousins and their families are now?


## BROTHERS AND SISTERS

How about your brothers and sisters? [wait]

How many brothers and sisters did you have?

What were, or are, their names, and what was their position in
the family (oldest, next to oldest, and so on)?

Did you help to take care of any of your brothers and sisters when
they were small, or they you?

How did you feel about that, and how do you think it might
have affected you or them in later life?

Do you remember any funny stories about things that happened
when one or the other of you was supposed to be taking care
of the other one(s)?

Can you take some time now and tell me something about each
of your brothers and sisters? [wait, let your narrator frame his or
her own answers. Then, if appropriate, go on to ask about each,
filling in their names on each question]:

What was _____ like when you were all growing up together?

Tell me a funny story if you can think of one, about something
_____ did?

What did _____ look like? Can you describe him/her?

What special skills, abilities, or talents did _____ have?

What was _____ 's personality like? How would you describe
him/her emotionally?

What did _____ go on to do in later life?

Is _____ still living?

[If not living]: When and how did he/she die?

Did he/she have any children, that is, your nephews and nieces?

What are their names, and where are they? Are you in touch
with any of them?

[Repeat above questions for each brother and sister, if appropriate.]

Which brother or sister were you the closest to?

Why do you think ____ was your favorite?

What was it about him/her that you especially liked?

Do you think you were alike in many ways, or was it your difference that attracted you?

Is there a special memory about you and ____ that stands out in your mind now after all these years?

Are you still in touch with your brothers and sisters?

## OTHERS IN AND AROUND THE FAMILY

Was there anybody else associated with your family who was important to you when you were growing up? A nursemaid, for example, or a special family friend who had an influence on you? Tell me about them if you can remember.

What was the influence that they had on you and your family, in your opinion?

## SUMMARIZE THE BRANCHES OF THE FAMILY

Can you briefly summarize what you know about the branches of the family, in case in the future someone wants to look up his or her distant relatives? Their names, where they live, or what they do for a living?

Do you know of any family still in the "old country" that a person could get back in touch with?

## END OF INTERVIEW, SCHEDULE OF NEXT SESSION

Okay, thank you for talking with me. Next time we'll be talking about your childhood and your memories of your first school experiences. Let's set a time and date to get together and talk again.

# Childhood

CRISPACRISP

This interview focuses in on your speaker's childhood, roughly from ages one to eleven or twelve. Many of the questions developed here will already have been touched on in the Family History interview, but this chapter focuses more on the speaker himself or herself as a child, and less on knowledge about ancestors.

Part of what you want to do in this interview is help your speaker build a picture of the world in which his or her formative years were spent. For older people, the world they grew up in was a very different place from what it is now. Childhood entertainment, family values, education, travel, medicine, and many other aspects of life have changed tremendously. This interview helps evoke a picture of that childhood world. It can be especially important to the younger members of the family, as might be expected. Kids today find it hard to imagine a world of horse transportation, with no TV, no video games, or even no radio, and an attitude that "father knows best." You, as interviewer, must act as an agent for some of the interests and feelings of the younger members of the family. The results of this session can help younger family members begin to establish a sense of family continuity, and it helps them to stretch their minds to imagine the changes that their grandparents' and parents' experiences encompass.

Psychologically, for your speaker this interview is fun and usually filled with powerful, warm, and funny memories. Again these questions are not emotionally difficult to talk about and not threatening in any way. And, when your narrator shares these memories with you, it contributes to the rapport necessary for an honest Life History narrative in the sessions to come. In general, this chapter is a systematic approach to the age-old question that grandchildren ask grandparents and children ask parents: "What was it like when you were kids?" The childhood interview also sets the stage for later "life cycle" sessions and questions centered around different times in your narrator's life, and for later questions about how values and outlook changed from the formative years into and through adulthood.

As you can see, there is a wide range of questions here. Questions about doctors and home remedies and scary diseases are interesting in contrast to today's scientific medicine. The questions about holiday ceremonies at home are good ones to paint a picture of family life fifty or seventy-five years ago. The "best and worst years" questions help your narrator to reflect on important turning points in his or her life, and they set the stage for similar later questions about crucial formative experiences in your speaker's life. The other questions are self-explanatory.

As before, look through this chapter and mark the questions that you would like to hear your narrator talk about. The first question, "Earliest Memory," gets you started and sets the period in time. Try to remember your own childhood as you ask these questions to get a feel for the kind of picture you want your narrator to create.

So, to get started, turn on your recorder, check to see that it is working properly, announce the date, place, and person being interviewed, and either ask one of the optional questions (see text), or ask, "What's the earliest thing you remember . . . ?"

## OPTIONAL INITIAL QUESTION

Since we last talked, did you remember anything else about your parents, brothers and sisters, or grandparents that we left out last time?

## OPTIONAL QUESTION

Did you have any interesting dreams since we last talked?

## NARRATOR'S SENSE OF MOST SIGNIFICANT EVENT OR EXPERIENCE OF YOUTH

In this interview, we want to focus in on your childhood—from when you were born until you were eleven or twelve years old or so. Before we get into specific questions, I'd like you to think about what you think was the most significant event or experience of this period of your life. How would you answer this question: "What was the most important event or experience of your life between the ages of one and twelve?"

[At this point you must use some judgment. If your respondent seems talkative on this subject, and if your curiosity about it seems natural, then go ahead and ask some follow-up questions now. Then, after you have elaborated on this topic, you can go back and pick up with the topics and questions that follow. If the event or experience your narrator mentions fits better into your plan for the interview, or if it is addressed in the questions below, you can just make a comment about how interested you are in the subject, and how you plan to touch on it later on. Then go ahead with the interview and elaborate on the topic mentioned when it comes up again in the course of discussing your narrator's childhood. Trust your own curiosity and judgment whether to elaborate on the subject now or later.]

## EARLIEST MEMORY

We're talking about your childhood—from the time you were born until you were eleven or twelve years old or so. What's the earliest thing you remember? Maybe just a fragment of a memory? [wait]

Why do you think you remember that?

How old were you then?

Where were you living at that time?

What kind of a neighborhood was it?

Was that the neighborhood you grew up in?

## STORIES ABOUT NARRATOR AS A BABY

Do you remember any of the stories they told about you as a baby?

Where were you born? In a hospital?

Do you know how much you weighed?

Did they say anything about what you looked like?

Do you know if you were nursed or bottle-fed?

## BIRTH OF SIBLINGS

Do you remember when any of your brothers or sisters were born?

Do you remember how you felt at having a new baby around the house?

How about caretaking? Did you help out taking care of the new baby?

Later on, did you continue to help raise your younger brothers and sisters?

How do you think your caretaker role affected you or them in later life?

Did you ever resent having to help raise your younger brothers and sisters?

What about the other way around? Which of your brothers and sisters helped to raise you when you were little, and how did that affect you in later life?

Did you and your brothers and sisters grow up feeling pretty close? Would you say you were a close family?

## NEIGHBORHOOD AND PLAYMATES

Take some time and describe what the neighborhood was like that you grew up in. [wait]

Was it an urban area, or rural?

What were some of the significant local places around the neighborhood? Schools? Parks? Vacant lots you played in? Alleys? The corner store? Old houses or barns or other places you played?

Who were your neighbors, and where did they live?

Do you remember any of the games you played or the things you did with them?

Did you stay in touch with them, or do you know what happened to your playmates in later life?

## STORIES ABOUT BROTHERS AND SISTERS

Do you remember any funny stories about mischief or trouble you got into with your brothers and sisters when you were little?

How about arguments and fights? Can you remember any memorable arguments or fights you got into with your brothers and sisters?

What were your parents' attitudes toward you and your brothers and sisters fighting?

## DISCIPLINE

How were you disciplined when you acted up or did something wrong? [wait]

Were you spanked or hit?

Do you remember a memorable spanking you got?

What had you done?

Were you "sent to your room"?

Did your parents talk to you, or was there physical punishment,. or a combination of the two?

If there was physical punishment, how old were you when it stopped?

Do you remember a specific time when your parents no longer hit you? Or when you refused to let them?

Who was the one who mostly carried out the discipline? Was it your mother or father? Or was it divided between them?

## THE HOUSE YOU GREW UP IN

Describe the house you grew up in. Can you picture it in your mind now? [wait]

Did you have your own room?

## RELIGIOUS TRAINING AS A CHILD

What religion were you raised in?

Was religion important to you in your formative years?

Describe the religious atmosphere in your home. How intense was it?

Who would you say was more religious, your mother or your father?

Could you say a little more about that?

## FIRST SCHOOL EXPERIENCES

Tell me something about your first school experiences. [wait]

> Did you go to a kindergarten or nursery school when you were little? Can you remember your first day at elementary school? What happened?
>
> What was the name of your elementary school? Do you remember?
>
> What subjects did the children study in school when you first started your schooling?

Were you especially good at any particular subject?

> Did that talent stay with you throughout your life?

Does any single grade stand out especially in your mind?

> Why that grade?

Does any teacher that you had during elementary school stand out especially in your mind?

> Why does he/she still come to memory?
>
> In what ways do you think he/she had an influence on you?

Which of your elementary school teachers did you have a crush on?

## SELF-DESCRIPTION AS A CHILD

What were you like as a child? How would you describe yourself then?

> How have other people described you as you were then?

## HAPPY CHILDHOOD MEMORIES

Do you think you had a happy childhood?

What are some of your favorite memories of your childhood?

## CHILDHOOD CHORES, GAMES

Did you have any chores around the house that you had to do?

> What were they? Describe some of the chores that you had to do around the house on a typical day.

Were you good at sports or games?

Can you remember some of the games you played?

Can you picture in your mind one of those games now? Who are the other kids who are playing with you? How did you play that game?

## CHILDHOOD BEDTIME STORIES

When you were little, did your parents ever tell you bedtime stories before you went to sleep? [wait]
    Can you remember any of them, and tell one or part of one now?
    Did you ever tell the same stories to your children?

## DREAMS AS A CHILD

Did you have any important or memorable dreams as a child?
    Do you remember any of them?
What's the earliest dream you remember?

## AMBITIONS AS A CHILD

Do you remember any of your childhood ambitions—what you wanted to be when you grew up?
    What did you say to grown-ups when they asked you "What do you want to be when you grow up?"
        Whatever happened to that ambition?

## ATTITUDE TOWARD DOCTORS IN YOUR YOUTH

What were people's attitudes toward doctors when you were young?
    Did they go to them for every little thing? Or did they take care of a lot of ailments at home?
Did you ever want to be a doctor?
    Whatever happened to that ambition?

## HOME REMEDIES

What were some of the home remedies that your mother or grandmother used when you got sick? Do your remember any of the treatments they used?
    Did they ever use mustard plasters or asafetida bags? What about herbal teas, like chamomile tea or linden tea? Or roots?
    What were some of the other things they did and told you to

do in order to promote good health, or get better when you were sick?

Did anyone you ever heard of in the family have a reputation as a healer? Was anyone thought to be good at curing certain ailments?

Who was that? What do you know about him/her?

## CHILDHOOD MEMORIES OF DOCTORS AND DENTISTS

Do you have any childhood memories of doctors and dentists?

Who was your family doctor when you were young?

What was he like? Can you describe him?

How did you feel about him? Did you like him? Or were you scared of him?

What kinds of things did he do? How did he act on a visit to your home?

Do you have any specific memories about times the doctor came, or you had to go to the doctor?

What happened? What was wrong with you?

Any memorable shots you had to have, or accidents you had that resulted in a visit to or from the doctor?

Were there many women doctors around then?

What were people's attitudes toward them?

I've heard that doctors acted differently then from the way they do now. Is that true?

What is the biggest difference, in your opinion?

How about dentists? [wait]

Do you remember some of your experiences with dentists when you were young?

How did dentists perform their services when you were younger?

Do you remember any memorable visits to the dentist's office?

Tell me what it was like.

I've heard that dentistry was a lot more painful in the old days. Is that true?

## LOST TOOTH RITUALS IN CHILDHOOD

Did your family have a practice of putting a child's lost tooth under the pillow, and rewarding him or her with a "visit from the tooth fairy" when you were little? Or something similar?

What did the "tooth fairy" leave behind when you lost a tooth?

Did you do the same for your kids when they were little?

Where do you think that custom came from?


## CRAZY PEOPLE, NEIGHBORHOOD CHARACTERS, AND CRABBY NEIGHBORS

Did you know any "crazy people" when you were little, or did you hear any stories about crazy people?

Were there any people in your neighborhood who acted a little funny?

What did they do? How did they act?

What's the craziest thing you ever heard of anybody doing when you were growing up?

How about just eccentric people? Or neighborhood characters? Do you remember any of them from your childhood?

Who were they, and what were they like?

Were there any real crabby neighbors who didn't like kids? Any really cranky people whom you still remember?

Who were they, and what were some of the things they did?

What did the kids used to do to harass them?

What were some of the stories that the neighborhood kids used to tell about them?


## STRANGE OR UNUSUAL EXPERIENCES

Did anything strange or unusual happen to you when you were young? [wait]

Did you ever feel different or special in any way from the rest of your family or friends?

In what way?

Why do you think you felt that way?

What did it mean to you?


## CHILDHOOD ILLNESSES

Did you suffer any serious illnesses or injuries during your childhood?

What happened? How did it turn out?

Do you think that had much of an effect on you in later life?

## DISEASES PEOPLE WERE AFRAID OF

What were some of the diseases that people were scared of getting when you were a child?

Did you know anybody who got diphtheria or typhus?

What about TB or polio?

Were there any others that people were especially afraid of?

Did you hear as much about cancer back when you were young as people do now?

Why not?

What about heart attacks? Did people seem to die of heart attacks and heart disease back then as much as they do now?

Why do you think that is?

## MEMORABLE CHARACTERS OF YOUR HOMETOWN

Who were some of the memorable characters of your hometown—like bums, or drunks, or doctors, or eccentric people?

What did he/she look like?

How did he/she act?

How did the children feel about him/her?

## HALLOWEEN PRANKS PLAYED AS A CHILD

Did the kids in your hometown celebrate Halloween?

How did they act? What were some of the things they did?

Can you remember some of the pranks you used to pull when you were a kid on Halloween?

What were some of the great or famous pranks you have heard about being pulled on Halloween?

Did you soap windows? Or wax them?

What about turning over outhouses?

Did you dress up in costumes and go out to "trick or treat" the way kids do today?

Why do you think kids like to do mischief on Halloween? Why do they do things like soap windows, in your opinion?

## CELEBRATING CHRISTMAS AS A CHILD

When you were growing up, did your family celebrate Christmas?

Who would be there?

Did someone go out and cut the tree down, or did your family buy one?

How was it decorated, and who would decorate it?

Was there a special Christmas meal you always ate?

What was it, and who would be all around the table?

Can you remember any especially memorable Christmases?

Why does that year stand out in your memory? What makes it especially memorable?

What kinds of gifts did you give and receive?

Can you remember the most memorable gift you received as a child?

Can you remember the most memorable one you gave?

## CELEBRATING THANKSGIVING AS A CHILD

What was Thanksgiving like when you were growing up? Can you describe an old-fashioned Thanksgiving dinner?

Who came to dinner, or where did your family go for dinner?

Think back and describe who would be there around the table and what it was like for you on that holiday.

Describe the meal itself. What would the women of the family prepare for Thanksgiving dinner?

Was it a religious occasion for your family?

Would you say a prayer? Who said the prayer?

## CELEBRATING NEW YEAR'S EVE

What was New Year's Eve like for you as a holiday when you were growing up?

Did you stay up and make a lot of noise at midnight the way people do nowadays?

Do you remember a lot of drinking and celebrating and "New Year's resolutions"?

## EASTER

What about Easter? Were there any memorable family traditions around Easter?

## THE 4TH OF JULY

What was the 4th of July like as a holiday when you were growing up?

Where did you and your family go, and what was it like on the 4th of July?

## OTHER HOLIDAYS FROM ANCESTORS' CULTURES

Were there any other holidays that your family celebrated? I'm thinking of holidays or special days that might have been carried over from European customs that hadn't been changed yet into the American holidays.

What were they?

How did your family celebrate them?

What were the meanings of these holidays or special days as you understood them?

## THE JEWISH CEREMONIAL CYCLE

[Ask in similar fashion about the Jewish ceremonial calendar, if appropriate. Ask your narrator what each holiday was like for him or her as a child, who was there at the celebration, memorable holidays, and special family traditions around the holidays, such as traditional meals, and so on.]

## FAMILY VACATIONS

Do you have any memories of memorable family vacations that your family took when you were little?

Where did you go, and what happened on that trip?

Did your family have a summer place where you used to go every year?

Where was that?

What was it like there then?

Have you been back there since?

Can you describe some of the changes that have taken place there since you went there as a child?

What's the best time you remember on a vacation with your family as a child?

### FAMILY ENVIRONMENT: READING, MUSIC, DANCING, SINGING

What kinds of things did your family have around to read when you were growing up?

Do you remember any magazines that your family subscribed to?

Was reading emphasized in your family?

What are some of the books you remember reading as a child?

Do you remember the first book you ever read?

Was the Bible read very much around your home?

How about music? What kinds of music did your family listen to or play when you were growing up?

Was anyone in the family good at playing the piano, or singing?

What kinds of songs do you remember?

Who was the best amateur musician in the family?

Did you study any musical instruments?

Did you like to play? Or did your parents have to make you practice?

What about dancing? What was your parents' and your family's attitude toward dancing?

And singing? Did your family sing together when you were growing up?

What were some of your favorite songs then? Do you remember any of them?

Who had the best voice in the family?


### A TYPICAL SUNDAY

Think back to a typical Sunday [Saturday for Jewish narrators] in your family when you were growing up. Can you just reminisce a bit and tell me what an average Sunday was like in your home? For example, when did you get up, what did you do, when and what did you eat, who prepared the food, did you go to church, when was the "big meal" of the day, who was there, what did you do for entertainment, what went on in the afternoon and evening, and so on, until you went to bed? Can you just take your time and describe that to me?

## FAMILY PETS

Did you or your family have any favorite pets when you were growing up?

Tell me about your pet.

Did your pet ever do anything noteworthy or famous, for example, bark and wake up the family in a fire, or scare away a prowler, or something like that?

Tell me that story.

## GEOGRAPHICAL MOVES IN CHILDHOOD

Did you make any geographical moves during your childhood?

Where did you and your family move to?

Why did you move?

How did the move affect you? Were you upset by moving? Or did you enjoy the new people and experiences? Or both?

## DEATHS IN CHILDHOOD

Did any people who were important to you die during this time of your life?

How did they die? What happened?

How important to you were these experiences in your later life, in your opinion?

Why do you say that?

How did you react to their death when you were a child?

## BEST AND WORST YEARS FROM ONE TO TWELVE

What were the best and the worst years of your life from ages one to twelve? [wait]

Why do you pick those years? What happened in them?

## ANYTHING IMPORTANT I DIDN'T ASK ABOUT YOUR CHILDHOOD

Is there anything important that we haven't mentioned about you as a young child?

## THANK YOU—NEXT INTERVIEW

Okay, thank you. Next time we'll be talking about your "youth." By that I mean from about twelve to about twenty years of age or so. Maybe in the meantime you could just let yourself reminisce about your junior high school and high school memories, your adolescence and your growing up physically, your first jobs, first boyfriends/girlfriends, how you started to grow up and think about leaving your parents' home, and so on. Let's set a date and time now to get together and talk again.

# *Youth*

&#9766;&#10048;&#9766;&#10048;&#9766;&#10048;&#9766;

This chapter covers events from the onset of adolescence through the teenage years and early twenties. Because it encompasses a great deal of time and experience, it has been separated into two parts. Part 1 covers the teenage years; Part 2 covers college, the military, first job, and courtship and marriage.

Part 1 is divided into five smaller sections: School Memories; Teenage Activities and Styles; Entertainment and Interests; Dating, Courtship, and Sex; and Teenage Conflicts. Part 2 deals with events after your narrator left home or finished high school.

It is the goal of this session to capture the tone and content of your narrator's teenage and adult years so that younger relatives can make meaningful comparisons with their own lives and draw emotionally closer to their older relatives.

This is not a session for your narrator to talk only about the trials and tribulations he or she faced growing up. It is also a session to record fond and funny memories—teenage love or high school and college antics. Some of these memories can be both painful and funny—many are of incidents that may have caused your narrator to think at the time, "I'll look back on all this someday and laugh."

The historical times in which your narrator grew up are as important as life cycle and personal events. Historical events have a tremendous influence, especially during a person's youth and young adulthood. It is very important to be aware of this and to

51

ask about the currents of social, cultural, and historical change that influenced your narrator as a maturing young person. Consult the "Historical Events" chapter while planning this interview to see what might have been going on in the world as your narrator grew into adulthood. For example, if your narrator grew up in the Great Depression of the 1930s, this may go a long way toward explaining how he or she chose to live in the years that followed. Or, if your narrator was a young man in 1939, caught up in World War II, he may have been making choices about flying a B-52 or being an infantryman instead of making marriage or career choices.

As before, read through these questions with an attitude of trust in your own interests and curiosity, and mark those which are interesting to you. Some of these questions can help to reveal powerful feelings, such as the ones about changes in attitudes toward sexuality in the modern world, or the ones about conflicts with authority. Many of them also reveal warm, sensitive, and funny stories and memories, especially the ones on courtship and marriage. "The first time you ever saw your spouse" is a must question. Almost everybody can tell you exactly when and where they first saw or met their spouse, can remember their first impressions, and can describe a certain "spark"—something out of the ordinary—that first caught their attention.

So, skim through this chapter, look through the "Historical Events" chapter for things that happened during this time period in your narrator's life, and get started.

# TEENAGE YEARS

## *Introduction to Youth Interview*

This time we want to talk mostly about your youth, from the time you were about twelve or so until you were about eighteen to twenty-one. That would cover things like junior high and high school, your growing up, your first work experiences, teenage years and concerns, dating and courtship, and perhaps leaving home—whether for a job or to college or to get married or to join the military. Anything important or interesting that happened in your life during these years I hope we will get around to talking about.

## MOST SIGNIFICANT EVENT OR EXPERIENCE OF YOUTH

Just to start, before we get into too much detail, what would you pick out as the most significant event of your life during this period, from about age twelve to about twenty?

[At this point, you must again use some judgment. If your speaker seems talkative on this subject—whatever it is—go ahead with some more questions. Trust your own sensitivity and curiosity here. If it looks like the subject will fit in with the general topics of this interview (which you have already reviewed), you can make a comment about how interested you are in that event (it may be marriage, death of a parent, an illness, or any number of things) and pick it up again a little later on as the interview progresses. If the topic that your narrator mentions is not in this section, you can look ahead and find the topic where it is dealt with so that you will have some questions to ask. But just continue to be curious and to trust your intuition about which questions to ask.

If your narrator does say something like, "Oh, I don't know, I suppose it would be my marriage . . . ," you can take that subject up as it appears in the flow of the interview.

You can follow the initial question with a comment like: "I just wanted to know what you felt was the most important thing about this period of your life before we started in with the more detailed questions."

Now, go on to the questions that interest you in the pages that follow.]

## YOUR TENTH BIRTHDAY

Do you remember your tenth birthday?
   What do you remember about it? Anything special?
   Where were you living then?
   Who else was living in your household when you were ten?
What was your life like when you were ten?

## BECOMING A TEENAGER

What about the beginning of your teenage years? Do you remember turning thirteen?

Was there anything special attached to being a teenager then? Nowadays, teenagers are almost a separate group, with their own styles, music, money, and so on. Were teenagers such a separate group when you were growing up?

Can you say anything more about that?

## School Memories

Think back now to some of your memories of junior high school and high school, and tell me what it was like for you going to school then. [wait]

### JUNIOR HIGH

What do you remember about your junior high school? [wait]
  What was the name of your junior high school?
  How large was it? Do you remember, for example, how many people were in your class?
  Describe the building itself. What did it look like from the outside, and on the inside?

### HIGH SCHOOL

What do you remember about your high school? [wait]
  What was the name of the high school you attended?
  How large was it? Do you remember, for example, how many people were in your graduating class?
  Describe the building itself. What did it look like from the outside, and on the inside?
  What year did you graduate from high school?

### TEENAGE FRIENDS

Who were your best friends? Your group? What were the names of the "gang" you hung around with?
  Can you remember some of the things you used to do together?
  Tell me about their personalities. Were there any real "characters" among them?
  Who was the craziest one among your crowd? Tell me about him/her.

Who went on to be the biggest success?

Have you stayed in touch with any of your teenage friends throughout your life?

Describe some of the other "in-groups" or "cliques" that formed among your schoolmates. Did your group have any rivals?

Would you say that you were a member of the most prestigious "in-group"? Or were you and your group of friends not considered to be among the social "elite," the social "higher-ups"?

## FUNNY MEMORIES OF JUNIOR HIGH AND HIGH SCHOOL

When you think back on some of the crazy or funny things that you did, or that happened to you in junior high or high school, what comes to mind? [wait]

Tell me what you are thinking right now.

Tell me a funny story about something you did in junior high or high school.

What's the craziest thing you ever did in high school?

Why did you do it?

How did it turn out?

## MEMORIES OF JUNIOR HIGH AND HIGH SCHOOL TEACHERS

What are some of your memories of the teachers you had in junior or senior high school? Do you still remember any of them? [wait]

Do you remember any teachers who were strange characters? Like teachers who wore really funny clothes, or who had strange habits, for example?

Tell me about some of them. What were they like?

Who would you say was the teacher who had the most influence on you? [wait]

Why was he/she the most influential teacher you had? What did you learn from him/her?

What about teachers who had a negative influence? Did you ever have an especially mean or incompetent teacher whom you had a lot of trouble with, or who had a negative influence on you?

What happened?

How did that affect you, and what did you do about it?

What was it about this teacher that you especially could not stand?

How did it work out in the end?

## WORST TROUBLE YOU GOT INTO IN HIGH SCHOOL, PRANKS PLAYED

What's the worst trouble you got into during your high school years?

Does any specific instance of trouble you got into come to mind now? Something that you did that got you into trouble?

What happened?

Why did you do it?

How did it all work out in the end?

What about pranks? Did you and your friends ever play any pranks?

Whom did you play the prank on?

What did you do? What happened?

Why did you do it?

## TEACHERS' NICKNAMES

Do you remember any of the nicknames that you had for any of your teachers? [From my high school days: "Bird Legs" Ageter, "Death Breath" Demerest, "Boogers" Nolan, to name a few.]

## ADOLESCENT AMBITIONS

When you were a teenager in high school, what did you want to be? What were your ambitions then?

Why do you think you chose that? What about it appealed to you?

What happened to those ambitions in later life? How many of them came true?

Would you say that you did or didn't achieve what you wanted to achieve when you were young and full of ambition?

Or would you say that your ambitions just changed?

In what ways did they change?

## FAVORITE SUBJECTS, GRADES IN HIGH SCHOOL

What was your favorite subject in high school?

Why was that your favorite?

What about your best subject? Did you have any particular talent for math, for example, or for writing, or drawing?

Do you still have that skill now?

How about grades? Would you say you were a poor, average, or above-average student?

Did you ever flunk anything? I mean, get an "F" on your report card?

Why did you fail? What happened?

What did your parents say when you brought home your report card?

## HIGH SCHOOL GRADUATION, PROM, YEARBOOK

When did you graduate from high school?

Do you remember anything noteworthy about the graduation ceremony? Like who spoke at it, or a prank somebody played?

Was there a big party to celebrate graduating?

What happened? Do you remember the party?

Did you get any special graduation gift from your family that you remember now?

Did you go to your high school prom?

What was that like? Do you remember?

Whom did you go with?

Did you think of the end of your high school days as a sad time? Did you think of having to say good-bye to many of your friends forever? Or were you more glad to be getting out, glad it was over?

Do you still have your high school yearbook?

Where is it, in case somebody in the family would like to see it?

Did you have a nickname in high school?

What did you expect to do with your life when you finished high school?

## Teenage Activities and Styles

Let's talk some more about you as a teenager and try to describe in more detail what it was like to be a young person when you were growing up.

## CLOTHING STYLES AS A TEENAGER

How did the average teenager dress when you were in high school?

Do you remember some of the clothing styles that were "in" when you were that age?

Picture in your mind one of your typical outfits, and describe how you looked when you got dressed for school.

Do you remember any reaction from the older people to your clothing styles when you were young? What did your parents think, for example?

## HAIR STYLES

Can you describe the hair styles that everyone wore then? How did you wear your hair?

Did all the other girls/boys wear their hair that way, too?

How about the [opposite sex of narrator]? How did they wear their hair?

Do you remember whether or not the older people got upset about long hair, or hair parted in the middle, or about bobbed hair on the girls?

When you were a teenager, was there anything to compare with what we saw in the 1960s and 1970s, when young people grew their hair very long and men grew beards and so on? Or in the 1970s and 1980s when some of them dyed their hair, cut it in Mohawk styles, or shaved their heads?

Why do you think young people attach so much importance to their hair styles?

## YOUR APPEARANCE AS A YOUNG PERSON

What did you look like at this time in your life? Can you describe yourself as a teenager?

Were you considered attractive or good-looking?

How did you feel about your appearance?

At the time, what did you consider your "worst feature"?

And what was your "best feature"?

Were looks very important to you then? And how important are looks to you now?

## TEENAGE FADS, DRESS STYLES, AND SLANG

What were some of the fads and styles among young people when you were a teenager? [wait]

Describe the dress styles. What did young people wear?

What about slang expressions? What were some of the slang expressions that the young people used? For example, today a young person might say "bad," or "far out," or "gag me with a spoon," or some such expression. What were some of the slang expressions when you were young?

Did people really say things like "I'll be a monkey's uncle," "twenty-three skidoo," and so on?

## WERE YOU MORE OF AN ATHLETE, OR A SCHOLAR?

Would you say you were more of an athlete and sports-lover as a youth, or were you more of a scholarly type who liked to read and study?

[If an athlete]: What were your best sports?

How good were you? Did you ever set any records or win any important events?

[If a scholar]: What were your favorite subjects and favorite books?

Do you still have these characteristics today—toward study or toward physical activity?

Name some of your favorite books from when you were a teenager.

How about your debating teams or academic clubs? Do you remember any of those that interested you when you were young?

Did you participate in them?

## SOCIAL CLASS AS A TEENAGER

What social class would you say your family was when you were a teenager?

What did your father do at the time for a living?

Do you remember any specific incidents when you became aware of class differences? I'm thinking of a time when you were made to feel that you weren't as good as other people because of your class position. Or the opposite—when you felt that you were better than other people because of your family's money and possessions?

How did you feel about that?

How do you think your social class background affected you then?

How do you think the social class you grew up in affected you in later life?

Was there any one family whose wealth dominated the town you grew up in?

Who were they, and how did they behave?

Were you friends with any of that family? Or were you in a completely different social circle?

## IMPORTANCE OF SOCIAL CLASS

How important in life do you think a person's social class is?

Why do you say that?

Do you think it makes much of a difference for the important things in life what social class a person is born into?

What are the important things in life? The really important things? [wait]

## HEROES AND IDOLS IN ADOLESCENCE

Who were some of your heroes during your teenage years?

Can you remember any singers or actors, political figures, or literary, artistic, or poetic figures whom you especially admired?

[If your narrator responds to one of these categories, let him or her finish. Then continue.]

What was it about him/her/them that you found especially appealing at that time?

Do you still admire those qualities in people?

Who were some of the heroes of your generation?

Why were they considered so admirable by the young people then?

Do you think young people in general have a tendency to hero-worship to some extent? And if you think so, why do you think it's so important for young people to have heroes?

What about people you knew, perhaps teachers or influential people in your community? Do you remember any influential persons whom you especially admired and tried to pattern your life after?

Tell me about that person.

What do you think it was that you admired so much about him/ her?

What is your impression of that person now? Are you still as impressed?

## Entertainment and Interests

What kinds of things did you do for entertainment when you were a teenager? I know, for example, that they didn't have TV or video games then, so what would you do for entertainment? [wait]

### SPORTS

Were there any sports that you especially liked, or were especially good at?

What were the most popular sports that you played in your youth?

Were baseball, basketball, and football the biggest sports then, as they are today?

What sports did girls play?

Were there organized athletic programs in the high schools for girls?

What sports were girls expected to play?

### RADIO

Did you sit around and listen to your favorite shows on the radio?

What were your favorite shows, and who were your favorite performers?

Do you remember the first time you ever heard a radio?

What did you think of it at the time?

What did the first radios look like?

Who were some of the great performers of early radio?

### MOVIES

When you were young, did you go to the movies?

Do you remember going to your first movie?

Was there a special time when you would usually go? Like Friday or Saturday night?

What was it like going to the movies then?

How much did they cost? Do you remember?

## LECTURES, POLITICAL RALLIES

Did speakers and lecturers come around to give presentations to people as a form of entertainment?

What were these like? What kinds of subjects would you go to hear a speaker talk about?

Do you remember a particularly moving speaker whom you heard in your youth?

What about political rallies? What was it like when politicians came to town?

Who's the most famous politician you remember seeing in your youth?

What happened? Tell me about it.

## RELIGION, REVIVALS, RELIGIOUS EXPERIENCES

What about religion? Was religion very important to you in your youth?

Would you call yourself a religious person at that time in your life?

What do you mean by that?

Were you active in your church when you were a teenager?

What were some of your activities?

Were your parents active in the church?

What was your church like then? Was it mostly preaching, or was it more of a social center where people went to get together?

What about the young people? Was church a place where you went to get together with other people your age? Or was that more something that you did at school, or with friends or relatives?

How would you describe a typical Sunday? [Substitute Saturday for Jewish narrators.]

For example, when would you get up, what would you wear, how would you get to church, what would your family do afterward, and so on?

How about religious revivals? Do you remember any old-fashioned revivals when you were a youth?

Did you ever go to a revival?

What was a revival like? Can you describe one and tell what went on and what it felt like?

Did you ever have a "religious experience" or "conversion" experience during this time in your life?

What happened? Can you tell me about it and what it meant to you?

## A RELIGIOUS CEREMONY AT PUBERTY

In your religion, did you have a confirmation or a kind of religious ceremony when you were about twelve years of age?

What was that ceremony called?

What was its purpose? What did it mean?

What did you have to do in order to go through it? Did you have to study or recite scriptures or learn other things about your religion?

How did you feel after you had gone through it?

Do you feel that you understood the purpose of what you were doing at that age? Or were you still too young to be fully aware of what the ceremony was supposed to be all about?

Did your children go through a similar ceremony when they got to be around twelve years of age?

Why did you want them to go through it?

Do you think it did them any good?

Why do you think that?

## MUSIC IN YOUR FAMILY

Did you or anyone in your family sing or play any musical instruments?

Who was that, and what instruments did he/she play?

Who had the best voice in your family?

Do you still remember any of the songs you used to sing?

Can you sing any parts of them now, just for fun? A song that you remember singing in your family from your youth? Or maybe a song that your mother or father used to sing?

## DANCING

Did you like to dance as a youth?

What were some of the dances that the young people did when you were a teenager? What were they called?

Did you know how to do all the latest dances?

Where did the young people go if they wanted to go dancing? To nightclubs? Bars? Or school- and church-sponsored dances?

Do you remember the first time you ever danced with a girl/boy?

Were you nervous? What happened?

What was the general attitude in your family toward dancing?

## SCHOOL TEAMS

Did your school have any athletic teams that you played on or went to cheer for when they played games?

What was the name of your school team, and what was the name of your school's biggest rival?

Do you remember any memorable games?

Did your team ever win any regional or state championships?

How about debating teams or academic clubs? Do you remember any of those that interested you when you were young?

## READING

What kinds of things did you like to read as a youth and teenager?

What were some of your favorite books that you read in your youth?

Does it seem to you that young people read a lot more when you were young than young people do today?

Why do you think that is?

## GIRLS' SPORTS ACTIVITIES

[For females]: Were there many athletic opportunities for girls when you were growing up? I mean team sports and the like?

What were the girls' sports and games that you played?

Was it considered to be not quite "feminine" for girls to be athletic when you were growing up?

What were girls expected to be like?

What were you like?

Were there things like athletic scholarships available for girls when you were growing up?

What do you think of the changes in the laws that require schools to offer equality of opportunity to both sexes in athletics?

What do you think of some of these cases where girls play against boys on the same athletic teams, and so on?

Why do you think that?

Do you think girls who are athletic are as feminine as girls who are not athletic?

Why do you say that?

## YOUR JOB AS A TEENAGER

Did you have a job when you were in high school?

What did you do?

About how much did you earn? Do you remember?

About how many hours a week did you work?

## HOUSEHOLD RESPONSIBILITIES/CHORES

When you were a teenager, what were some of your responsibilities around the house? Were you allowed to run around and play after school, or did you have to come home and do chores and help out?

Did you have to help take care of younger brothers and sisters?

Did you have regular chores?

What were they?

Which chores did you most hate doing?

Why?

Do you think it's good for a teenager to have a job, or do you think those years should be more of a time to have fun, to experiment, and not to have much responsibility?

Why do you say that?

## ALLOWANCE, SPENDING MONEY, FINANCIAL INDEPENDENCE

When you were a teenager, did your parents give you an allowance to spend each week? Or were you expected to earn your own money?

If they did give you an allowance, do you remember how much it was?

When did you become financially independent from your family?

## Dating, Courtship, and Sex

What were boy/girl relationships like when you were growing up? Take some time now and look back on dating when you were young. How were boys and girls expected to behave, and how did they behave? [wait]

### WHERE BOYS AND GIRLS WENT TO MEET WHEN YOU WERE GROWING UP

Where did the young people go to meet one another and get together when you were growing up?

Did the church or school sponsor social activities or dances?

Did the young people have a favorite sandwich shop or place where they could go to meet?

Do you have any specific memories of places like that that are going through your mind now?

### FIRST DATE

Do you remember your first date? [wait]

Tell me about it.

Who was it with, where did you go, and what did you do?

Do you remember how you felt at the time? Were you nervous?

Was your first date chaperoned?

### FIRST KISS

Do you remember the first boy/girl you ever kissed?

How was it?

## FIRST BOYFRIEND/GIRLFRIEND

Who was your first boyfriend/girlfriend?

What was he/she like?

What did he/she look like? Can you describe him/her?

How long were you "sweethearts"?

What happened to your relationship? Did you break up?
Why?

What happened to him/her in later life? Do you know?

## DATING BEHAVIOR

What was the expected behavior on dates when you were young?
[wait]

Did the boy have to meet the girl's parents first? Where would
you go on a typical date? What time did you have to be home?
And so on.

What about the family car? Was it common for the boy to be
able to use the family car for a date?

Was the girl ever allowed to invite the boy to do something?
Or was it always supposed to be up to the boy to do the asking?

How different were dating patterns then from what you know
about dating patterns of young people today?

If you think there have been changes, do you think those changes
are for the better or for the worse?
Why?

## A STEADY BOYFRIEND/GIRLFRIEND

Did you have a steady boyfriend/girlfriend during your high school
years?

How serious was your relationship?

What was his/her name?

What did he/she look like? Can you describe him/her?

What did you like most about him/her?

Do you know what happened to him/her in later life?

Was it fairly common for people of your age back then to pair up
and have a steady boyfriend or girlfriend? Or was teenage courtship and dating not as well developed as it seems to be today?

About how old were your high school friends when they married? What was the typical age of marriage when you were growing up?

## PHYSICAL MATURITY

About how old were you when you began to "grow up," to become physically mature? Were you "mature for your age," about the same as, or later than your friends in your physical development?

Do you remember how you felt about this at the time? Sometimes young people worry about this.

## SEX EDUCATION AND THE FACTS OF LIFE

Were people back when you were growing up more secretive about sex than they are today?

Was it pretty much a "forbidden" subject? I've heard that most people didn't talk about it as openly as they do today. Was sex something that was just not mentioned very much?

Why do you think that was?

Do you remember your parents giving you any talks about the facts of life? Or about sex education?

Which parent talked to you? Do you remember what he/she said?

Nowadays, kids learn about sex from their parents, friends, TV, the movies, magazines, in school, and so on. When you were growing up, how did you learn about the facts of life? Was there anybody you could go to to talk about it?

What do you think about the way kids learn about sex today?

Why do you think that?

Do you think there is a better way?

Do you think there's too much sex information and sexual imagery around today? Or do you think it's a good thing to have a society that is more open about sexuality?

Why do you say that?

Was there any talk about birth control or planned parenthood when you were growing up and learning about sexuality?

Do you remember hearing the name of Dr. Margaret Sanger?

What did people think of her and her programs for "planned parenthood"?

What did you think of her?

## PEOPLE'S ATTITUDES TOWARD SEX WHEN YOU WERE YOUNG

What were people's attitudes toward sex when you were growing up? [wait]

What was the general attitude toward sexual activity among teenagers?

Did you agree with that attitude?

Did most people agree that sex was something to be reserved for marriage, and that premarital sex was wrong or dangerous?

Did you agree with those attitudes?

Why, or why not?

Was there a "double standard"? One for boys and another for girls?

What was the double standard?

What did you think of the double standard?

Why did you think that?

Do you think there was any reason for the double standard?

Do you think it made any sense?

Why?

What about VD? Was venereal disease a frightening possibility when you were growing up?

Were there any prostitutes in your town? Or was there a "red light" district in your town?

Did you ever see it? What was it like?

Did you ever know a woman who was a prostitute?

## WHY ATTITUDES TOWARD SEX WERE MORE STRICT IN YOUR YOUTH

Why do you think people's attitudes toward sex were more strict and more tied to marriage than they are today? [wait]

Do you think it has something to do with the availability of birth control and sex education today?

Do you think the willingness of people today to talk more about sex, birth control, and so on is a change for the better or for the worse?

Why?

## PREGNANCY AND ILLEGITIMACY

Did any girls in your high school get pregnant?

How did the people react to it? Was the girl considered to be "ruined"? Was her reputation ruined?

How did you react to it? How did you feel about her?

Did any of your friends get pregnant?

How did you react? What did you think?

Was abortion ever considered then? Or did people "have to get married" in such a situation?

This is definitely an area where attitudes have changed in the modern world. Do you think that the changes are for the better or for the worse?

Why?

## YOUNG PEOPLE'S ATTITUDES TOWARD SEX TODAY—THE SEXUAL REVOLUTION

Many people say that one of the biggest changes in the modern world is in attitudes toward sex—the so-called sexual revolution. Do you think it is true that young people's attitudes toward sex are very different today from your generation's sexual attitudes?

Why do you say that?

What is the difference? Is it just in talk, or behavior, or both?

Do you think this is a change for the better or for the worse?

Why?

## Teenage Conflicts

### TYPICAL CONFLICTS, BIGGEST CONFLICTS

Take some time now and think about some of the conflicts that you remember having with your parents or other authority figures when you were growing up. Do you remember any conflicts you had with authority when you were growing up? [wait]

I am thinking of things like your parents not liking some of your friends or not liking some of the clothes you wore, the music you listened to, or your values. I'm also thinking of things like conflicts over your personal freedom, political or religious beliefs, or school, marriage, or career plans. What can you tell me about yourself with respect to things like this when you were young? [wait, allow your narrator to answer. Then follow up with the topics developed below that interest you.]

## BIGGEST TROUBLE YOU EVER GOT INTO AS A YOUNG PERSON

What would you say was the biggest trouble you ever got into as a young person? [wait]

What happened? Can you tell me the story?

How did it end up?

Did you learn anything useful from it?

Were you ever sort of "wild" or "rebellious" as a teenager? [wait]

Were you ever suspended from school, or did you ever play "hooky" or anything like that?

Tell me what happened. Tell me a story of something you did that was considered "wild" when you were a teenager.

Were you ever paddled by a teacher while you were in school?

What happened? What had you done, and how did you feel about it?

Nowadays it's against the law to paddle a kid in school. What do you think of that change?

## BIGGEST POINT OF CONTENTION BETWEEN YOU AND YOUR PARENTS

What would you say was the biggest point of contention or disagreement between you and your parents when you were growing up? [wait]

Was there any issue that you just never could see eye-to-eye on?

Was it ever resolved? Or did you just go your separate ways as you got older and became more independent?

In retrospect, do you have a better understanding of parents' point of view? Or do you still disagree?

## PARENTS' ATTITUDE TOWARD DISAGREEMENTS WITH THEM

Were you able to sit down and talk things over with your parents, or was it not permitted for you to contradict or question their point of view? Was it a matter of your parents saying "this is it because I say so!" or was it more a matter of your being able to talk it through with them?

How did you feel about your parents' attitude?

Do you think you adopted the same attitude or a different one with your own children when they were growing up?


## THE CROWD YOU WENT AROUND WITH, YOUR FRIENDS

Were there ever any conflicts with your parents over any of the crowd you liked to hang around with? Did they disapprove of any of your friends?

What happened? Why do you think they wanted to influence your social life in this way? And how did you feel about it at the time?

What would have been your parents' reaction if you had been friends with somebody from a different race than yours?

Did you have any close friends who were [black/white—opposite of narrator] when you were growing up?

Did you stay friends? What happened to him/her in later life?


## TEENAGE DATING

Did your parents ever forbid you to date someone of whom they disapproved?

Why did they say they disapproved?

What did you feel about it at the time? And how do you feel about it now?

What happened? How did the conflict finally work out?


## YOUR LIFESTYLE

What about your lifestyle—your taste in music, or your clothes, or the way you wanted to wear your hair? Do you remember any conflicts or arguments or even joking disagreements about any of these kinds of things?

What happened? How did the conflicts work out?

What were some of the clothing, music, and hair styles that seemed to get on the older generation's nerves?

Why do you think they objected to these things?

## DRINKING, SMOKING, AND DRUGS

What about drinking and smoking? Were you allowed to drink and smoke?

When was the first drink you ever took? What happened?

What about the first time you ever smoked tobacco?

Do you have a "classic" story about your smoking for the first time and getting sick?

What would your mother and father have done if you had been caught smoking or drinking at home? What would have been their reaction, and what would have been the punishment?

What about other drugs? Did any young people at that time have the opportunity or the desire to take other drugs?

Did you ever hear about or know anybody who took drugs when you were a youth?

This problem of young people and drugs is a big change in the modern world. What do you think causes it? [wait]

Do you think drugs are worse than drinking?

Why?

## SCHOOL PERFORMANCE, ATTITUDES TOWARD TEACHERS

What about conflicts with your parents over your performance in school? Or over "discipline" problems in school?

What grades were you expected to get, and what grades did you in fact usually get?

What attitude were schoolchildren expected to have toward their teachers? Were you expected to obey them and not to give them any trouble?

There seem to be a lot of problems in the schools nowadays. Do you think young people's attitudes toward teachers and authority are different now?

How are they different? Is there more or less "respect for authority" in the classroom, in your opinion?

What do you think of this change? Is there a good side and a bad side to it?

Was there ever a time when you got bad grades, or had trouble at school, and you got into hot water with your parents?

What happened?

Why did you get bad grades during that time?

Were you ever something of a "rowdy" or a "cut-up" at school?

Why do you say that? What do you remember about yourself then?

Can you remember a specific incident when you acted up or did something a little wild?

## FIGHTING, VIOLENCE

Did you ever get into fights in or after school, or in your neighborhood?

Tell me a memorable story of a fight you got into.

What were your parents' attitudes toward fighting? Did they strongly disapprove? Or was there an attitude that you had the right and duty to defend yourself?

Do you have any "classic" stories about yourself "standing up to a bully" and fighting back?

Tell me that story.

How important is physical courage in life?

Can you say a little more about that?

Do you believe that it is sometimes necessary to stand and fight, or are you opposed to violence and believe in "turning the other cheek" and pursuing peaceful means of resolving disputes?

Why do you say that?

Can you give me an example from your life that has led you to believe as you do?

## JOB/CAREER PLANS

Were there any conflicts over your getting a job?

What was that all about? What was your point of view, and what was your parents'?

What about your ideas about the career you wanted to take up? Did your parents try to influence your choice of "what you wanted to be when you grew up"? Or did they just want you to do whatever you wanted?

What was your point of view, and what was theirs?

What happened? What did you do about it?

## POLITICAL AND/OR RELIGIOUS BELIEFS

What about your political or religious beliefs and your parents' beliefs? Do you remember any differences or disagreements as you were growing up and starting to think for yourself?

What were some of the issues about which you and your parents disagreed? Do you remember?

Young people often think that their parents are too "square" or conservative. Did your parents seem too conservative to you on the burning political or social issues of the day?

What was going on in the world during that time? Did you differ with your parents on any of these issues? [Check the Historical Events chapter for this time in your narrator's life for possible issues where your teenaged narrator might have differed with his or her parents.]

## DECLARING YOUR INDEPENDENCE

Was there ever a time when you insisted on doing something you felt to be important or right despite your parents' wishes? Does any specific incident stand out in your mind?

Tell me that story.

How did it turn out?

Do you think a time like this comes to almost all young people, when they have to do what they think to be right no matter what other people might be telling them?

Could you say a little more about that?

## YOUTH'S CONFLICTS WITH THE OLDER GENERATION

Some people say that in earlier times, young people did not have as many conflicts with their parents as young people do today. In their opinion, young people used to obey their parents and other authority figures more than they do today. On the other hand, it is also said that conflicts between the generations happen in every historical time and with every generation. Which of these opinions do you think is more true? [wait]

Why do you say that?

Which of these two opinions was more true in your case? Did you experience a period of conflict or disagreement with your parents or other authority figures when you were growing up?

What do you remember about that time in your life?

What were you like then? Can you describe yourself as you were then?

## GENERATION GAP

Would you say there was anything like a generation gap between you and your parents when you were growing up? A "generation gap" is when the young and the old cannot communicate well together because they don't have much common ground to share with each other. Was there anything like that between you and your parents when you were coming up?

Was there a generation gap between you and your children?

How much of this do you think has to do with rapid changes, like new inventions, the mass media, and so on?

Could you say anything more about that?

## HIGH SCHOOL FRIENDS, HIGH SCHOOL CLASS REUNIONS

Who were the people closest to you when you finished high school?

What happened to some of them in later life?

Do you still keep in touch with any of your high school friends?

Who is that?

Why do you think you stayed in touch with him/her, and you lost contact with all the others? What was special about your friendship?

Have you ever gone to one of your high school class reunions?

When was the last one you attended?

Who turned out to be the biggest surprise from your high school class?

## WHAT THE WORLD LOOKED LIKE WHEN YOU GRADUATED FROM HIGH SCHOOL

What did the world look like when you graduated from high school? What did the world look like to a high school graduate in 19 ____ ? [fill in date]

What did you expect to accomplish with your life then?

## WHAT YOU DID AFTER YOU LEFT HIGH SCHOOL

What did you do after you left high school? [wait]

What was expected of young people on graduation from high school then? Was it normal for young people to leave their parents' home and begin to fend for themselves? Or was it acceptable then to stay at home for a while? Was college a common option? Or the military? Or marriage?

# COLLEGE, MILITARY, JOB, MARRIAGE

These four topics developed below are the options that a young person might have chosen on graduation from high school. Depending on what your narrator says, go on to the section that is appropriate.

This might be a good place to take a break, and either schedule another interview or just relax, stretch, and have a cup of coffee. Check to make sure your recording equipment is working properly.

## *College*

### WHERE AND WHEN ATTENDED

Where did you go to college? And what year did you graduate?

Why did you choose to go there and not someplace else?

When you entered college, did you have something definite that you wanted to study? Or did you expect to pursue studies toward a general education?

### LEAVING HOME

Do you remember when you left home to go away to school?

How did you get to college? How did you travel?

Do you remember the trip itself, and the first few days at college?

Was this the first time you'd ever been away from home for any length of time?

How did you feel at first? Do you remember?

Where did you stay? Describe your accommodations when you

first went to college. What was your room like? Whom did you
room with?

Do you remember any of the first friends you made?

## MONEY

How had you arranged to pay for your education?

Do you remember what it cost to go to school then? For tuition
and for room and board?

Did you earn the money yourself, or have a scholarship, or a loan,
or did your family help you out? Or a combination of these?

What about jobs? Did you have any part-time jobs to make ends
meet in college?

How long did you work each day?

## FRATERNITY/SORORITY

Did you join a fraternity or sorority?

Which one did you join?

Why did you pick that one?

Can you remember any of the crazy things you had to do when
you were initiated into your fraternity/sorority?

Did people really eat goldfish, get paddled, wear ridiculous clothes,
and the like?

What other silly things did they do?

Why did they do those things?

Do you remember it as a fun time for you?

## COLLEGE MAJOR

What was your major field of study in college?

Why did you choose that?

What was it about you and your personality that led you to choose
that as your major field of study?

## WERE YOU A GOOD STUDENT?

Were you a good student? Or average? Or poor?

What kind of grades did you usually get?

What was your academic ranking in your college class when
you graduated? Do you remember?

## WERE YOU MORE OF A SCHOLAR, ATHLETE, OR FUN-LOVING STUDENT?

Would you say you were more of a scholar, more of an athlete, or more of a fun-loving, social college student?

Why do you say that?

## ADJUSTMENT TO COLLEGE LIFE

In general, did you enjoy your college years? Was it easy or difficult for you to adjust to life away from the home and community you had grown up in?

Why do you say that?

What was it about the way you were raised that made it easy or difficult for you to adjust to college life?

## HOW COMMON WAS IT FOR YOUNG PEOPLE TO GO TO COLLEGE THEN?

How common was it for young people of your age to go to college? Was it the "expected" thing to do in your family and in your circle of friends?

About what percentage, would you guess, of young people in your generation went to college? Were you definitely in the minority?

What about women? Did as many women go to college in your generation as they do now?

Why was that? If they didn't, why didn't they, in your opinion?

## BEST FRIENDS IN COLLEGE YEARS

Who were your best friends in your college years?

Tell me something about them. Describe them and their personalities and their appearance then.

Tell me some of the fun things you remember doing with them. What were you like as a group together?

## COLLEGE ANTICS

Tell me some of the crazy or funny things you remember doing when you were in college. [wait]

What's the silliest, dumbest thing you remember doing when you were in college? [wait]

What were some of the things that students did in your generation when they wanted to let off a little steam and "raise hell"?

Did they do much drinking?

Do you remember any memorable nights when you and your friends had a little too much to drink?

I've heard about something called a "panty raid." Did you ever hear of such a thing?

What was a "panty raid"?

Do you remember ever going on one? Or seeing one?

What happened?


## POLITICAL ACTIVITY

Was there much of an atmosphere of political involvement on the campuses of your generation?

Why do you say that? What was happening then?

Were there organizations of different political groups on the campuses representing left-wing or right-wing issues?

Do you remember any of these, and do you remember what you thought of them?

Why did you think that?

In general, how intensely involved were the students of your generation in the political issues of the day?

How involved were you?

Why?

What about "demonstrations"? College students today always seem to be ready to demonstrate about some issue or other. Did your generation do that?

What were some of the demonstrations about?

Were you involved, and if so, in what way, and why?

## IMPORTANT POLITICAL ISSUES OF THE TIMES

What were some of the burning political issues of the day that you remember from your college years? [Consult the Historical Events chapter for the dates of your narrator's college years to ask about specific political issues of the day.]

Were you involved in any of these issues?

Which ones, and why?

What do you think it was about you that made you identify with those issues and organizations instead of others?

Do you think you still have some of those values and personality qualities? Or do you think your opinions and values changed dramatically in later life?

What caused you to change your political values, if you think you did?


## DRUGS OR ALCOHOL IN COLLEGE

Did many of the students of your generation take drugs? I mean drugs other than alcohol?

Did you ever hear about drugs? Or about drug addicts when you were in college?

What about drinking? What was the attitude then toward college students and drinking?

Do you remember whether or not you took your first drink in college?

Can you describe the circumstances, and what happened?


## SPORTS

Were you an athlete in college? Were you active in any sports or on any college teams?

Which sport?

What was your best sport?

Were you on the college team?

Did you set any records? Or do you remember an especially big game or big play you made that you can still brag about?

## THEATER OR MUSICAL ACTIVITIES

Were you active in any drama productions or any other artistic or musical activities?

What kinds of theater or music?

What roles do you remember playing in dramatic productions?

Tell me something about it. What was it like for you?

What were some of your favorite roles and your favorite plays?

Why were these your favorites?

Did you have any talent?

Where in the family did you get your talent for or interest in dramatic productions? Do you think you inherited any acting or performing abilities from anybody in the family?

Who was that, and what was he or she like in this respect?

What about musical talent? Did you sing or play in a band in college?

What instrument did you play?

What kind of music did you play?

Did your group have a name?

Does anything memorable come to mind about your musical experiences?

## MUSIC LISTENED TO IN COLLEGE

What kind of music did your generation listen to when you were in college? Who were some of the great musical artists of your generation?

Do you remember ever seeing any of these musicians at concerts?

What was it like? Tell me of a memorable musical performance by a great artist that you remember from your college days.

In your opinion, who was the greatest musician or group of musicians for your generation? Who best expressed musically the mood of your generation?

Why do you choose him/her/them? What was it about his/her/their music that appealed to you?

What was it about the times that his/her/their music expressed? [wait]

Can you say a little more about that?

## INFLUENTIAL PROFESSORS

Were there any especially influential professors that you still remember?

Who was that? What was it about him/her that you especially admired?

What did he/she teach you that you carried into later life?

## DESCRIBE YOURSELF DURING YOUR COLLEGE YEARS

How would you describe yourself during your college years? [wait]

Why do you say that?

How have others described you as you were then?

## PERIODS OF DEPRESSION, TURMOIL, OR BEING UPSET; SADDEST MEMORY

Do you remember times during your college and student years when you were very depressed or upset? Did you go through periods of emotional turmoil or crisis at this time in your life?

What was happening with you then? What was going on, and what do you think brought it on?

What did you do about it?

How long did it last?

Do you think you were just "going through a stage," or was it something more than that?

Why do you say that?

Do you think college or young adulthood is a time of life when a person can expect to go through more emotional ups and downs than other times in life? Or is it a time no different from other times of change and adjustment in a person's life?

Why do you say that? Can you talk a little more about that?

What's the saddest memory you have from your college years? [wait]

What happened, and how did you react to it?

If you did go through a time of significant emotional change and turmoil during this time in your life, can you talk about it a little more?

Viewed in the context of your whole life, how important was this period to the development of your personality?

Why do you say that? Can you elaborate on this a little more?

From your perspective now, what can you say about the value of going through periods of turmoil like these? For example, do you think growth and maturity are often achieved after a period of turmoil, crisis, and decision? Or do you think this is a myth, and that maturity does not have to be painfully achieved?

Can you say a little more about that?

## BOYFRIENDS/GIRLFRIENDS

How were your relationships with the opposite sex? Tell me a little about your boyfriends/girlfriends during your college years.

Did you have a steady boyfriend/girlfriend?

Were you "in love"? Or did you think you were?

What's the difference?

How did you meet him/her?

What did he/she look like?

What did you like most about him/her?

What happened to him/her later on in life?

Did you date a lot in college?

Were you ever pinned or engaged in college?

To whom? What was he/she like, and what happened to your relationship?

Would you say that you were popular with the opposite sex?

Do you still ever think about someone you loved or were involved with back then?

Who was that? And why do you think you still remember him/her?

What about feelings of insecurity or loneliness, or feeling out of place? Do you remember feeling like that in relation to the opposite sex? Or do you remember yourself as being pretty self-confident?

Why do you think you felt this way?

If you had insecure feelings, what did you do about them? Do you remember?

## COLLEGE GRADUATION

Did you graduate from college?

[If "no"]: Why didn't you?

Did you ever regret this in later life?

What year did you graduate?

What was your degree?

Do you remember who attended your graduation ceremony? And how you felt then?

## HOW THE FUTURE LOOKED AT THAT TIME

How did the future look to you when you graduated from college? [wait]

Were you concerned about the world—the political situation, your job prospects, the threat of war, or war itself? What did the future look like to a recent college graduate in 19 ____ [year of graduation]?

What were your plans for the future at that time?

How well did your plans turn out, as it happened?

## GRADUATE OR PROFESSIONAL SCHOOL

Did you go on to graduate school?

What did you study in graduate school?

How did you decide to study that? What went into your decision?

How did you pay for graduate or professional school?

What else was happening in your life then, and how did your graduate studies fit in with that?

In what ways was your life different as a graduate or professional student from what it had been as an undergraduate? Could you talk a little about yourself as a graduate student?

Do you remember some of your friends from those days?

How tight was money for you then?

Do you have any memorable stories about your poverty when you were a student?

Did you have a part-time job? Or more than one?

What did you do?

How about your studies? How hard did you have to work, and were you a successful student?

## ADVANCED DEGREE

Did you receive an advanced diploma?

What degree did you earn, and when did you earn it?


## SPECIAL EXPERTISE IN YOUR FIELD

What was your special area of interest or expertise within your field?

Did you write a thesis or dissertation?

What was it on? Do you have a copy of it anywhere?

Did you retain an interest in the subject in later years?

Did you ever work or teach in your field?


## INFLUENTIAL TEACHERS IN GRADUATE SCHOOL

Can you remember any especially influential teachers when you were in graduate school?

What qualities in him/her did you most admire, and what about them influenced you the most?

What's the most important thing you learned from him/her?


## HOME LIFE AS PREPARATION FOR COLLEGE

How would you say your earlier home life had prepared you for college?

From whom in the family did you get your intellectual values and your desire to be successful in college?

Did anyone else in your family go on to get a college education?

[If "no"]: What do you think was different about you? Why did you have these values and others in your family did not?

[If "yes"]: Who was that, and where did they go to college?

How successful were they?


# *Military*


## EXPERIENCE

Tell me about your experience in the military. [wait]

What led up to your decision to go into the military services?

## DRAFTED OR ENLISTED

Were you drafted? Or did you enlist?

[If drafted]:

What was your attitude toward being drafted at the time?

Were you philosophically or politically opposed to serving in the military?

Why, or why not?

What was the world situation at the time you were drafted? Was the country at war or was war impending?

How did you feel about that?

Were you the kind of person who was involved in the political issues of the day? Did you have strong patriotic feelings and definite ideas about what policies the government should have been following? Or would you say you were more uninterested and unaware politically?

Why do you think you felt as you did?

Were you the type whose attitude might be expressed as "my country right or wrong"? Or were you more critical and independent in your thinking?

Why do you say that?

What were some of your feelings about war at that time? Did you have any "isolationist" feelings or "pacifist" feelings? Or did you accept your being drafted and view it as your duty?

Did your family have a tradition of military service? For example, had your father been in the military, or had there been any stories about your ancestors' military exploits or ancestors' feelings about armies and war?

Tell me what you know about the military traditions of your ancestors.

[If enlisted]:

Why did you enlist? [wait]

What were your feelings about the world situation at that time? Did you expect that you might have to see combat?

What were your feelings about that?

Were you the kind of person who believed "my country right or wrong"? Or were you more critical than that and had decided for yourself that you wanted to enlist in the service?

Did you have to overcome any "isolationist" or "pacifist" feelings in yourself before you enlisted in the military?

> Can you say a little more about that? What went into your thinking about those issues?

## WHY NOT COLLEGE?

Why didn't you go to college? Why did you go into the military instead of continuing your education?

> Did you ever regret that choice?

Would you have been able to go to college if you had wanted to?

## PARENTS' REACTION TO YOUR JOINING THE SERVICE

When you joined the military, do you remember your parents' reaction? What was your mother's reaction, for example?

> And what was your father's attitude?

## PEOPLE'S ATTITUDE TOWARD THE MILITARY

What was the general attitude in society toward the military at that time? [wait]

> Were the military and military service held in high esteem? Or did the military not have such a high position in people's eyes then?
>
>> Why do you think people felt that way toward the military?

## ISOLATIONIST, ANTIWAR, OR PACIFIST SENTIMENTS

Were you aware of "isolationist" arguments in the political atmosphere of the times that influenced you?

Was there anything like the "antiwar" movement that rose up against the Vietnam War several years ago? Or was society generally more in support of the government when you went in the service?

What about peace demonstrations or other isolationist or antiwar activities going on when you were going into the service? Were you exposed to such ideas at that time?

> If you were exposed to such ideas and demonstrations, what did you think of them?
>
>> Could you say a little more about that?

If people's attitudes were different from people's attitudes toward the Vietnam War, why were they different, in your opinion? What accounts for the differences between the popular support for the different wars?

## PROWAR ACTIVITIES

Do you remember any agitation or debates in support of the Americans getting involved in the wars that were threatening when you went into the service? Do you remember any "prowar" activities and ideas then?

Were you influenced by these ideas?

In what ways? Did you agree or disagree?

Why?

## THE ARMY AS A BREAK WITH THE PAST

Do you think that going into the military was a significant break with your past? For example, we have all heard the slogan, "Join the Army and Become a Man." Was your joining the military an important psychological break from your way of life up to that time, a way for you to "leave the nest," so to speak?

Why?

Was the military an important turning point in your life?

Why do you say that?

## MILITARY TRAINING

What branch of the military did you enter?

Where and how were you trained?

Do you remember your basic training?

Where was your basic training?

What was it like? Can you describe it?

What's your most vivid memory of your basic training?

What were you trained to do? What was your specialty?

What weapons were you trained to operate?

Which weapon were you most familiar with and most skilled at?

What was your rank when you finished basic training?

## WHERE STATIONED DURING MILITARY CAREER

What happened when you finished basic training? Where were you first sent?

Briefly tell me the different places you served while you were in the military—where you went, how long you stayed there, where you went next, and so on.

## COMBAT

Did you ever see combat?

Tell me about some of your combat experiences. [wait]

Where and when did you see combat?

What battles were you engaged in?

Where exactly in the development of the fighting did your action come? What was your role, and the role of your unit, in the battle as it developed?

Were you ever wounded?

What happened? How did it happen?

Can you describe in as much detail as you remember what happened and what went through your mind at the time?

How were you evacuated, and what did you go through during your recovery?

During this time, is there any one person who stands out in your memory as the one who helped you the most?

Who was that? And how did he/she help you to get through this time in your life?

Did you ever kill anybody in the war?

Can you tell in as much detail as you can remember what happened?

What were your feelings at the time? Can you remember what you thought and felt?

Are these war memories still painful to you? Or have you come to terms with what happened to you and what you had to do in the war?

How long did it take you before you were able to think about your war experiences and come to some resolution of your feelings about them? Did it take you years to get over your war experiences? Or were you pretty much able to put your war years behind you and get on with your life?

Do you ever think about war experiences now?

What do you usually remember?

What is it like for you when you think and talk about it?

How do you feel right now? How does it make you feel to talk about your experiences to me now?

Do you think that your recounting some of your experiences here and now might be of some value to a future member of the family who might be faced with coming to terms with similar feelings as a result of some future war?

Could you say a little more about that?

Do you ever dream about any of your war experiences?

Did you ever have dreams—perhaps recurring dreams—about any of your war experiences?

What do you think those dreams mean? Or meant?

## CLOSEST BRUSH WITH DEATH IN THE WAR

What was your closest brush with death during the war? [wait]

What happened, and how did you feel afterward?

Did you ever think about that brush with death afterward? Or do you ever still think about it?

What did you think? What do you think it taught you?

## YOUR UNIT, BEST FRIENDS IN THE SERVICE

Who were the people in your unit? Can you still remember them and describe them? What were they like?

What did you call yourselves? What was your nickname?

Who was your best friend in the service?

Can you tell me something about him, and what happened to him?

Do you have any Army buddies whom you are still in touch with?

Did you lose any of your friends, your Army buddies, in the war?

What were the circumstances? What happened?

Can you remember your feelings, and how you came to terms with them?

## HOW LONG IN THE SERVICE

Exactly how long were you in the service?

Why do you think you still remember the exact number of days, hours, and minutes (if you do)?

## ARMY STORIES

Tell me one of your "army stories" that you are famous for in the family. I mean one of those that you've told so often that people in the family start to groan when you start to tell it.

## BEST AND WORST: MILITARY SERVICE

What was the worst thing about your years in the military?
And what would you say was the best thing about those years?

## MEDALS OR AWARDS WON

Were you awarded any medals or decorations during your military service?
  Which ones were you awarded, and what were they awarded for?
  Where are they now?

## LEAVING THE MILITARY, COMING HOME

Where did you go when you left the service?
How difficult was it for you to adjust to civilian life again after being in the service?
  What do you think was the hardest thing to adjust to after you left the military?
  How had things changed in the years that you had been away from home? Do you remember how you felt?
    In your memory, what was the thing that had changed the most?
Many people have talked about how much of a shock it was for them to come home after a war. They say things like how they walked around in a daze for a year, jumped at loud noises, and so on. Did anything like that happen to you?
  What did it feel like for you when you first came home?
  Do you remember suffering a lot of psychological stress, being depressed, or feeling out of place?
  How long did you feel this way? How long did it take before you began to feel more "normal" about life?

## EFFECTS OF WAR EXPERIENCES ON YOUR LIFE

Is there any way you can describe the effects of these war experiences on your later life? How significant were these experiences to the way your personality developed as you grew older?

Would you have been a totally different person if you had not had the experiences you did?

How did your war experiences change your life? Can you say anything more about that?

What did these experiences do to you emotionally? Can you talk about that?

How did you feel at the time, and how did you come to feel later, about your "fate"—to be caught up in a war and to have the experiences you had?

Have you ever read a book or any literature that came close to describing what it was really like for you and those of your generation during your war experiences? Has any writer captured what it was like, in your opinion?

What book or movie or other artistic expression has come closest, in your opinion?

## DID WAR EXPERIENCES CHANGE YOUR OPINIONS ABOUT FOREIGN POLICY?

In terms of your personal views on foreign policy, military spending, and the government's military posture, did your war experiences (or experiences in the services) change your opinions about war and about the role of the armed forces?

In what ways did your experiences change you? Did you come out of the service with more pacifist beliefs and opinions? Or did you become more militaristic in your views on foreign policy? Did you become more of a "dove" or more of a "hawk"?

Why did you change in that direction, and are you still that way?

## WOMEN IN COMBAT

Recently there has been debate on whether or not women should be drafted and used in combat situations, if necessary. What is your opinion on whether women should be in combat roles?

Why do you say that?

## WHY MEN FIGHT

Why do men do the things they do in war? What motivates them? In your opinion, what makes them face the horrors that they face? How do they, on an individual level, carry on?

How did you carry on?

## THE VETERANS ADMINISTRATION

Do you think that the government and the Veterans Administration have treated you and others of your generation well and fairly as veterans?

What could or should they have done differently in treating you more fairly as veterans?

Have you ever used the VA's hospitals, loan assistance, or educational benefits?

## ANYTHING I FORGOT TO ASK

Is there anything else important about your experiences in the military and their effects on you that I forgot to ask? [wait]

# First Job

## FIRST JOB

Why did you go to work after high school instead of completing more schooling?

Tell me about your first job after you graduated from high school.

How did you get the job?

Do you remember how much it paid? And how many hours a day you worked?

Do you still remember any of the people you worked with?

What were some of them like? Any "characters" you remember?

What about your boss? What was his name, and what was he like?

Did you get along with him?

## FRINGE BENEFITS

Did you have things like health insurance, unemployment compensation, and disability insurance to cover you on your job?

What would you have done if you lost your job?

What if you had been injured and couldn't work? Who would have helped you and helped support you?

## CLOTHING STYLES AT WORK FOR YOUNG PEOPLE

How did you dress when you went to work? Can you picture young people's clothing styles in your mind and describe them now?

What about hair styles? How did you wear your hair when you went to work?

## WHERE LIVING, FIRST PLACE OF YOUR OWN

Where were you living after you finished high school and first started working?

When did you get a place of your own?

What was it like? Can you describe the first place you lived after you started working and moved away from home?

How much was the rent?

Who were your roommates? Whom did you live with?

## TRAVEL, FIRST CAR

How did you get to and from work?

How far did you have to go?

Did you buy a car?

What was the first car you ever owned? Can you remember it and describe it?

When did you buy your first car?

What did you pay for it?

What did you think of the workmanship that went into that car? How would you compare it to the cars of today?

What special features did your car have?

What happened to that car?

## SOCIAL LIFE, MONEY

How did your social life start to change after you left high school, started making some money, and started living on your own?

What were some of your first purchases? Do you remember buying something that you had wanted for a long time? Or helping out somebody in the family with the extra money you were making?

Describe your monthly budget then. Approximately how much were you making, and where did it go?

If you were still living at home, did you give some money to your parents for your room and board or to help out around the house?

Was it a common practice for young people then to live at home and contribute something to help out around the house?

Do you think it's a good idea for grown-up children to live in their parents' home nowadays?

Why, or why not?

## BOYFRIEND/GIRLFRIEND

Did you have a boyfriend/girlfriend then?

Who was he/she?

Can you say a little about him/her? What did he/she look like, what kinds of things did you do together, what kind of a person was he/she, and so on?

What happened to him/her in later life?

What were some of the things that young people did for entertainment where you were living then? For example, what would a "typical date" have been? Where would you and your date go, what would it cost, and so on?

## DESCRIBE YOURSELF DURING THIS PERIOD

How would you describe yourself during this period of your life?

What were you like as a young man/woman starting out in your first job and beginning to be more on your own?

How have other people described you at that time?

In retrospect, would you say this was a happy time in your life? Or was it an unhappy time for you?

Why do you say that?

## HOW FIRST JOB INFLUENCED YOUR CAREER

How much did that first job you had influence the development of your career?

> I mean either positively or negatively. Was the job so boring or distasteful that you began to look around and prepare yourself for another career? Or did you like it a lot, and begin to get better and better at it to the point where your life's work was in the general area of your first job?

What were some of the important things you learned on your first job?

## WHAT YOU WANTED TO BE

Were you one of those people who seemed always to "know what they wanted to be when they grew up"?

Already, in your first jobs, did it seem to you that you knew what kind of work you wanted to do in your life? Or were you one of those who more gradually worked out what the main patterns of your working life would be?

> Looking back now, when did you begin to decide on a career? In other words, when did you finally decide "what you were going to be"?

Were there seeds of your later career development in your early work experiences? Could you see even then what some of the main interests of your career would be?

> Could you say a little more about that?

## HOW THE FUTURE LOOKED

How did the future look to you after you had finished high school and started out on your first real job? [wait]

> Were you concerned about the world? The political situation? Job prospects? The threat of war or war itself? I want to know what in the world seemed important at your age then.

## ANYTHING ELSE IMPORTANT ABOUT FIRST JOB

Is there anything else important about you and your first jobs out of high school that I forgot to ask? [wait]

## Courtship and Marriage

**WHEN MARRIED**

When did you get married?

**HOW OLD YOU WERE**

How old were you when you married?
How old was your wife/husband?

**HOW YOU MADE THE DECISION**

How did you come to make the decision to get married? [wait]
  What do you think were the major things you considered when
  you came to your decison to marry?

**COURTSHIP**

Tell me something about your courtship. [wait]
  Tell me something else about your courtship. [wait]

**THE FIRST TIME YOU SAW YOUR SPOUSE**

Do you remember the very first time you ever saw your wife/
husband—the very first time your eyes met? [wait]
  Tell me about that.
  Do you remember the first time you talked to each other?
    Do you remember what you talked about?
  Did you have any idea at that time how your relationship would
  develop?
  What did you think of him/her at first?

**LOVE AT FIRST SIGHT**

Do you think it was love at first sight?
  Why, or why not?
  Was there anything special about him/her that you noticed right
  away?
  Do you believe in love at first sight?

Why, or why not?

Has it ever happened to you? Or to someone you know?

What do you think people mean when they talk about love at first sight?


## HOW LONG

How long after your first meeting until you met again?

What happened that time?

How long did you know each other before you began to get serious?

How did you know when you began to get serious about each other? Was there an incident of any kind that you remember when you realized that you were getting serious, that you were falling in love?

I'm thinking of something like an incident of jealousy, or a time when you realized that you'd rather be with [spouse's name] than do anything else?

Or did your relationship sort of evolve into a more serious relationship?

Does any turning point really stick out in your memory when you think about your courtship?

What was the turning point of your courtship?

How long had you known each other before you got married?


## INCIDENTS OF JEALOUSY

Do your recall any incidents of jealousy about some rival during your courtship? Either you feeling jealous, or [spouse's name] being jealous of somebody else?

Who was your biggest rival for ____ 's affections?

And who was ____ 's biggest rival for your affections?

Do you remember any funny incidents or misunderstandings over other girlfriends/boyfriends?

Do you remember any not-so-funny incidents or misunderstandings?

Describe your biggest rival. What was he/she like?

## BREAKING UP

Did you ever come close to breaking up?

What was the disagreement or quarrel about?

Did you ever break up for a time and get back together?

What would you say was the most serious quarrel you had while you were courting?

Do you remember the quarrel? What was it about, and what happened?

## STORMY OR CALM COURTSHIP

Would you say yours was a stormy and tumultuous courtship, or would you describe it as a calm friendship, characterized more by a quietly growing love and understanding?

Why do you say that?

What's the stormiest incident you remember in your courtship?

## WHO LOST OUT—WHO YOU (AND SPOUSE) DIDN'T MARRY

Who were some of the other boys/girls you were going out with before you began to get more serious about _____ ?

What was he/she like?

What made you pick _____ over him/her? What did he/she have that the others didn't have?

What about [name of spouse]? Who else was he/she going out with?

What was he/she like? What did you think of him/her?

What did you have that your rivals didn't have? What made _____ pick you over your rivals?

## FUNNIEST STORY ABOUT COURTSHIP

What's the funniest story you tell about your courtship? [wait]

What memories really stick out in your mind when you think about your courtship? Something especially funny, for example, or a big fight you had?

## YOUR DECISION TO MARRY

Why did you decide to marry [spouse's name]? [wait]

Was it difficult for you to make the decision to get married? Did you agonize over it and wonder whether you had made the right decision? Or did you just come to the decison easily, as the thing you really wanted to do?

What were some of the things you thought about when you decided to get married?

Would you say that you never had any doubts when you came to the point in your life to make the decision to marry? Or do you remember doubts and questions and a hard time in coming to your decision?

How did you know you were making the right decision? [wait]

Do you think you were ready for marriage?

Why, or why not?

## MARRIAGE PROPOSAL

Do you remember when you actually proposed to [name of spouse]? Or when ____ actually proposed to you? [wait]

I mean, the actual moment itself? The night he proposed to you [or the night you proposed to him]?

Tell me about it. Where were you, and what did you/he/she say?

Did you/he/she accept right away? Or did you/he/she take some time to decide?

Was it the custom then to go to the woman's father to ask for her hand in marriage? Or was it a matter just between the two people as it pretty much is today?

Did you/he ask her/your father for permission? Or do you remember what happened when you/he asked her/your father?

What happened?

## REACTIONS OF YOUR SPOUSE'S FAMILY TO YOUR PLANS TO MARRY

What was the reaction of your spouse's family to your plans to marry?

Can you talk about that a little more?

How did you feel about and get along with your prospective in-laws?

Which one did you have the most trouble getting along with?

Why do you think that was?

How long did it take before you started to get along with them or before they accepted your marriage and accepted you?

Do you think it is more or less "normal" for there to be, at least initially, tension and conflicts between in-laws, or prospective in-laws?

Why do you think that is?

How did you get along with your mother-in-law? [wait]

Can you talk a little more about that?


## YOUR FAMILY'S OPINIONS OF SPOUSE

What about your family's opinion of [spouse's name]? Did your family like him/her?

Do you remember any problems or opposition?

What did your mother say about him/her?

What did your father say about him/her?

Do you remember their opinions causing any conflicts?

What did you do about it?


## ENGAGEMENT

Were you formally engaged?

How long were you engaged before your marriage?

Do you think long engagements are a good idea?

Why, or why not?

Do you think a long engagement is as appropriate today as it was when you were making plans to marry?

Why do you say that?


## YOUR LIKES AND DISLIKES ABOUT FUTURE SPOUSE

What did you like most about your fiancé/fiancée?

What did you most dislike?

Did you have many interests in common? Or did you seem to be very different people?

Could you say a little more about that?

## WHY YOU FELL IN LOVE WITH HIM/HER

Why did you fall in love with him/her?

    Could you say a little more about that?

## BEING ALONE

Where did you two go if you wanted to be alone? Was that a problem for you?

## ATTITUDE TOWARD SEX

What was the general attitude toward premarital sex at that time?

    Did you agree with that attitude? Did you share those values?

        Why?

Would it have been possible for you to live together without being married, as many young people do today?

    Why, or why not?

    What would have been the community reaction?

    Why do you think things have changed in this regard in the modern world?

        Do you think this is a change for the better or for the worse?

            Why do you think that?

## DESCRIBE YOUR SPOUSE AT THAT TIME

What did [spouse's name] look like at that time? Can you describe him/her?

    Did you think he/she was handsome/beautiful?

    Would you say that his/her appearance was an important factor to you then? Was it an important factor in your attraction to him/her?

If looks was not the most important factor in your attraction to him/her, what was the most important thing that attracted you?

    Can you say a little more about that?

Did you think he/she had an interesting personality?

    Describe his/her personality. What kind of a person was he/she then?

What about his/her sense of humor? Did you think he/she had a good sense of humor?

How important do you think a sense of humor is for the success of a marriage?

Why do you say that?

Did he/she seem stable, honest, and reliable? Or did he/she seem to have a bit of a "wild" streak that appealed to you?

Could you say anything more about that?

Did he/she seem kind, considerate, and thoughtful to you?

How important would you say those characteristics were in attracting you to him/her?

What about financial security? Did either of you have a good job or money saved up?

Of all these things, which would you say was the most important one in your attraction to your future spouse?

Why?

## WEDDING CEREMONY

What was your wedding ceremony like? Tell me about it.

Where was it performed?

Was it a religious ceremony?

Who performed the ceremony?

## WEDDING GUESTS

Who were some of the people in the wedding party? Do you remember?

Who was your best man/maid of honor?

Was it a big wedding or a small wedding? Can you describe it?

## WHAT YOU WORE

What did you wear?

Can you describe your wedding gown in more detail?

Who made it for you? Or where did your dress come from?

## LAST-MINUTE "HITCHES," NERVOUSNESS

Do you remember any last-minute hitches developing before the wedding? I'm thinking of things like losing the ring or being late for the ceremony.

Do you remember being very nervous?
  What did you feel like walking down the aisle?
Who do you think was the most nervous person at your wedding?
Who was more nervous—you or your spouse?
  Why do you say that?

## WEDDING GIFTS

What were some of the gifts you received?
  Do you still have any of them?

## HONEYMOON

Did you go on a honeymoon?
  Where did you go?
Do you remember some of the things you did? [ha-ha]
What did it cost you? Do you remember? What were some of the prices of things on your honeymoon?
What kind of a car did you have?

## A FUNNY OR MEMORABLE STORY ABOUT YOUR HONEYMOON

What's the funniest story you tell about your honeymoon? What's the funniest thing that happened to you on your honeymoon?
What's the most memorable thing that you did or that happened to you on your honeymoon?

## DESCRIBE YOURSELVES AS NEWLYWEDS

Describe yourselves as newlyweds. How did you act?
  Can you remember anything else about how you used to get together as newlyweds?

## DESCRIBE YOURSELF AT THAT TIME IN YOUR LIFE

How would you describe yourself at this period in your life?
  How have others described you?

## HOW THE FUTURE LOOKED

How did the future look to you at that time? [wait]

Were you concerned about where the world seemed to be going? I mean, were you worried about the political situation or the economy? Or about your job prospects? Or about war? I want to know what the world seemed like to a newly married couple then.

In spite of whatever else was going on, you must have had a certain faith in the future, or you wouldn't have gotten married. Would you agree with that?

What did you think the future held for you?

## FIRST HOME AFTER MARRIAGE

Where did you live after you first got married?

Can you describe the first place you lived? Was it a house or an apartment? How many rooms did it have, what did it look like, and so on?

How was it furnished? Where did you get the furnishings?

Do you still have any of the things you had when you set up your first household after you got married?

Do you consider any of these things "family heirlooms"? And, if so, what do you want to have happen to them after you are gone?

## JOBS

Did both of you work?

What were you/was your job at that time?

## HOUSEHOLD BUDGET WHEN FIRST MARRIED

Can you remember what your household budget was then? For example, what did you pay for rent, food, car, and so on?

Do you remember how much a dozen eggs cost? Or a pound of hamburger?

How much did you pay for your car?

How much did a gallon of gas cost then?

## THE FIRST YEAR OF MARRIED LIFE

Describe the first year of married life. What would you say about it? [wait]

Do you think you knew your spouse very well before you got married?

Why do you say that?

Do you remember any particular problems that you had adjusting to married life?

How would you sum up the problems of the first year of married life?

Did you have to change your lifestyle very much after you got married?

How did you have to change? In what ways?

How about your spouse? Do you think he/she had to change a lot, too?

## BEST AND WORST THING ABOUT THE FIRST YEAR OF MARRIAGE

What was the best thing about being married during that first year, compared to your life before you married?

And what was the worst thing about it? What was the hardest thing to adjust to?

# Middle Age

This section presents questions for you and your narrator on some of the concerns of middle age—roughly the years from ages forty to sixty-five. This is a short section, and deals mainly with the theme of change during one's middle years. Middle age has often been characterized as a time of stability, consolidation, and growing maturity. But increasingly, psychologists are finding that the middle years are just as intense, creative, and change-filled as other periods of people's lives. Developed here are questions about midlife crisis, positive achievements of middle age, best and worst years, and other stability-and-change-oriented themes.

## TURNING FORTY

What was it like for you to turn forty? [wait]

> We always hear jokes about people who keep saying that they are "thirty-nine" long after they have really passed that age, as if "forty" were some magical, special turning point to be dreaded and denied. How did you feel when you turned forty? [wait]

> Why do you think some people regard the age of forty as an important milestone in their lives?

How was the beginning of your forties different from the beginning of your thirties? Or the beginning of your fifties or sixties? [wait]

What was the biggest difference about you at forty, compared to you at thirty (besides your waistline)?

## THE SECOND HALF OF LIFE

Many people have said that "the second half of life," that is, after forty, is different from the first half of life. In the first half of life, they say, people are mostly concerned with making a living and surviving and raising their family. But in the second half of life, once many of their earlier goals have been reached, people must find new goals and new meanings for their lives. Do you agree with this idea? [wait]

Some people say that the first half of life is more concerned with achieving material things and physical security while the second half of life is more concerned with meaning, or with more spiritual concerns. Do you agree or disagree?

Why do you say that?

In what sense would you say that you started to evolve new life goals and new meanings in the second half of your life? [wait]

How did the things you found important change after you passed forty?

In what ways did you change? What new values, goals, and activities did you take up?

Could you say more about that?


## QUESTIONING WHERE YOUR LIFE WAS GOING

What about a time of intense self-questioning or self-evaluation during your middle-age years, when you questioned what you were doing and evolved new goals and purposes for yourself? Did you ever go through a period like that? [wait]

What was it like for you? How long did this period of reevaluation last, and what new level of self-understanding did you finally achieve?

Could you say a little more about that?


## SPIRITUAL CONCERNS AND DEVELOPMENT AFTER FORTY

Would you say that you underwent any significant "spiritual" development after you passed forty? [wait]

What do you mean by that? [wait]

Did you become more religious than you were earlier in your life?

Why do you think that was?

Did making money and being a "success" become less important to you after you entered your middle-age years?

Could you say a little more about that?

Do you think your values changed, in the sense that you regarded what makes a person a "success" differently than you did at an earlier age?

What does make a person a success, in your opinion? [wait]


## BIGGEST CHANGE: AGES FORTY TO SIXTY

What's the biggest change you went through in your middle age? [wait]

Did you get a divorce, or quit a job, have a great adventure, or survive a serious sickness? Or something like that?

Can you talk about this a little more? What was its effect on you?


## MIDLIFE CRISIS

Does the term "midlife crisis" mean anything to you? [wait]

What is a midlife crisis, in your opinion?

Do you think anything like a midlife crisis ever happened to you? Did you go through one yourself?

What happened during that time? What were you questioning, and what did you do?

Psychologists say that a midlife crisis happens to many people between the ages of forty and sixty or so. They say it is a period of deep personal reevaluation and change. People often become emotionally upset, and over a period of a few years they may change their values, goals, and their family and work life, before they achieve a new, more stable period. Did you ever go through a period of turmoil and change during your middle years?

What was that all about? Can you describe it, and tell how you were feeling then, and what happened?

What would be your advice to people in their middle years who are going through midlife crises themselves, when they are questioning their past lives and trying to achieve new, more meaningful lives for themselves? Can you tell them something that might be useful to them?

## MENOPAUSE (WOMEN)

Do you remember going through menopause as your childbearing years were coming to a close?

What was that period of your life like for you? [wait]

What were some of your experiences then? Many women talk about it as a time of stress and turmoil. Was that at all true for you? [wait]

Was that time a period of more than usual anxiety or depression for you?

Why do you say that?

Would you say that menopause was any more stressful than any other time in your life? Or was it about the same? Or was it not particularly difficult a time for you at all?

Why do you think that was?

Why do you think some women experience this time in their lives as a time of turmoil and stress?

Can you give some advice from your experience on how a woman can best get through this time in her life?

## FEELINGS OF LOST YOUTH

Some people go through a period during their forties when they seem to be trying to be twenty again. Maybe they're trying to do something they feel they missed. In your forties, did you ever go through a period when you were yearning after your "lost youth"? Or did you go through a time when you felt that it was your "last chance" to do something that you had not done?

Could you say a little more about that?

What was it that you wanted to do that you felt you had not done? What did you feel it was your "last chance" to do?

If you don't remember such feelings in yourself, can you understand why some other people might feel this way when they begin to move into middle age?

Why do you think that sometimes happens?

Did you ever know somebody who seemed to be doing something like that in his or her middle age? Or do you think it might be a myth about middle age that isn't really true?

## STRENGTHS AND POSITIVE SIDE OF THE MIDDLE YEARS

What do you think are the strengths of the middle years? In what ways are the middle years better than a person's teens, or twenties, or thirties?

Can you say a little more about that? [wait]

What opportunities do you have in middle age that you don't have at younger ages?

Do you think the middle years can be more productive, creative, and secure than earlier ages?

Why do you say that?

What had you learned about life by the time you reached your middle years that you could apply to make yourself happier and more secure?

Do you think in some ways that middle age has a bad reputation?

Why do you say that? What are the best things about being middle aged?

## YOUR MOST POSITIVE ACHIEVEMENT

What do you consider your most important achievement during your middle years?

Could you say a little more about that?

Is this the achievement of which you are most proud during this time in your life?

For example, I'm thinking of things like successfully raising your family and seeing your kids educated, or some special achievement in your job. Or the happiness of your marriage. Or even perhaps some new feeling of self-esteem and stability.

Could you say a little more about that?

## COMPARE YOUR FORTIES AND YOUR FIFTIES

If you look at yourself in the decade of your forties, and compare it with your fifties, what do you think are the differences? [wait]

What were the central concerns of your forties, and what were the central concerns of your fifties, as you remember them?

What do you think is the main difference in these two decades of a person's life?

Can you think about this and comment on it a bit more?

How would you characterize your fifties? [wait]

What do you think are the opportunities and strengths of a person in the decade of his or her fifties?

Could you say a little more about that?


## BEST AND WORST YEARS

During this time in your life, from about forty to about sixty, which year was the best, and which was the worst for you? [wait]

Why? Why do you pick those years?

Could you say a little more about what happened during those years?


## THE MAIN TASKS AND CONCERNS OF MIDDLE AGE

What else can you say about these years in a person's life? What does it mean to be middle aged? [wait]

What are the main tasks and concerns of middle age, in your opinion? [wait]

# Old Age

This chapter provides questions to be asked of narrators who have reached a relatively advanced age; that is, about seventy years old or so and older. It finishes the chronological organization of the previous interviews, and brings the narrative up to the present time. The number of persons reaching these ages is changing rapidly in our society, and a seventy-year-old narrator is at a very different life stage from a ninety-year-old narrator. Each question must therefore be evaluated for its appropriateness in your particular interviewing situation, but in general these are interesting questions that can apply to anyone over the age of seventy or so. As a society, we don't know a great deal about what it means to have a large percentage of our population active and involved at an advanced age. It is important to explore the feelings and thoughts of our older people in order to create a viable culture of elderly family members and citizens. The answers to questions such as those presented below can help us all to think of the potentialities and expectations of people in their seventies, eighties, and nineties.

This chapter should be treated as the others have been—scan through it and mark the questions that interest you. Don't worry about asking every question presented here. Just trust your feelings for your narrator and get started.

## YOU AS AN ELDER OF SOCIETY

You are now older than most of the other people in our society. How do you feel about being one of our society's elders?

Does it mean anything at all to you? Do you think of yourself as an elder?

What do you think is the most important thing that the elders of a society can do for the younger people? [wait]

How important is remembering and keeping a sense of how the past has influenced the present?

Do you think younger people listen enough to the things that the older people know and could tell them?

Why should younger people listen to older people?

Can you say a little more about that?

## FINANCES, KEEPING UP WITH INFLATION, SOCIAL SECURITY

How is your financial situation now? Would you say you are economically secure now?

What's the single biggest item in your budget now?

You must have learned a lot of money-saving and money-managing skills during your lifetime. What are some of the ways you economize now, and keep up with inflation?

You were around before Social Security came in. Do you think Social Security is adequate, and that it has fulfilled its promise?

Were you in favor of Social Security when Roosevelt first proposed it?

Do you think Social Security should be increased?

Before Social Security, how did people get along after they stopped working?

Did family take over? Or churches? Or just the older person's savings?

Do you think older people were better taken care of then, before the government got involved?

Why?

Was there an "old folks home" where you grew up?

What was it, and how did it work?

## THE ELDERLY AS A POLITICAL FORCE

How important do you think the elderly are as a political force in our country? [wait]

Do you vote?

Did you vote in the last election?

Do you follow politics very closely now?

What kind of a job do you think the President is doing for elderly citizens?

Could you say a little more about that?

Do you think the government should do more for older people?

What else should be done, in your opinion?

What's the most important change that should be made in the treatment of elderly people in the United States? [wait]

What is the number-one priority law that should be passed for the benefit of older people, in your opinion?

Why do you say that?


## OLDER PEOPLE'S ORGANIZATIONS

Do you belong to any organizations for older people, such as the American Association for Retired Persons?

Why do you belong? Or why don't you?

Have you heard of the more "radical" or activist groups of elderly citizens, like the Grey Panthers?

What do you think of the Grey Panthers?

What do you think they want to accomplish?

Do you support their goals?


## THE TERM "SENIOR CITIZEN"

What do you think of the term "senior citizen"? Is it all right with you? Or do you find it somewhat objectionable?

Why?

How do you think older people should be referred to? For example, should older people be referred to as "the elderly," or "old people," or something else?


## BOREDOM

Do you ever get bored now?

What do you do when you get bored?

Do you have any hobbies?

If you had as much money as you wanted, what would you like to do? If money were no consideration at all . . . [wait]

**LONELINESS**

Is loneliness ever a problem for you now? [wait]

How do you cope with loneliness?

Is learning to cope with loneliness just one of the realities of growing older? Or would you say that you have just as many friends and social activities as you always had?

Could you say a little more about this?

What do you do about the fact that there are more elderly women than elderly men?

Is this a problem for you socially?

Do you find it difficult to meet and socialize with [men/women— opposite sex of narrator] who are about your own age?

Where do you go now to socialize with people your own age?

What about people younger than you? Do you have a lot of contact with people younger than you?

Do you have much contact with your children and grandchildren?

Would you like to see them more than you do?


**"TOO SOON OLD AND TOO LATE SMART"**

What do you think of the old saying, "We get too soon old, and too late smart"? [wait]

Have you heard that saying before? What do you think it means?

In what ways, if any, do you feel that you got smart too late?

Can you say a little more about that?


**YOUR PHYSICAL HEALTH**

How is your physical health now? [wait]

Are there any medical problems that you have to deal with now? Do you have to go through a daily routine of any kind for your physical health?

How well do you think you've been able to cope with this?

Do you do anything to keep physically fit? Like exercise or sports?

What do you do?

## YOUR MENTAL HEALTH AND PSYCHOLOGICAL STRENGTHS

How would you describe your mental health now? How do you feel emotionally most of the time?

Do you think that people get psychologically stronger as they get older because of the life experiences they have been through?

Why do you say that? Could you say a little more about that?

When you are feeling especially low or down on a certain day, what do you do to get out of that mood? How do you get out of a bad mood?

Do you think that just the passage of time itself is enough to get you out of a low mood? Or do you actively try to think certain thoughts, or get some exercise, or take a walk, or do something active?

Which is best for you? Just waiting for the mood to pass, or doing something directly to get you out of it?

## YOUR BIGGEST PROBLEMS OR WORRIES

What do you consider your biggest problems now? What worries you the most at this time in your life?

Could you say a little more about that?

What could or should be done about your problem?

Is there anything I could do to help?

## DOES TIME SEEM TO GO BY FASTER THE OLDER YOU GET?

People often say that the years seem to have flown by so fast. They say that time seems to go faster the older you get, and "before you know it" your children are grown and you have reached an advanced age. Do you feel that way, or have you felt that way?

Why is that?

Why do you think people say that—about "time flying by" and so forth?

Do you think it might be because they regret not having done things that they wanted to do?

What comes to mind that you regret not having done?

Can you say a little more about that?

## HOW YOU ARE DIFFERENT FROM OTHER PEOPLE YOUR AGE

How are you different from other people your age? [wait]

For example, do you do things that other people your age don't do? Or do you see things differently from most other people your age?

What things are those, and why do you think you are different?

Do you have stronger opinions about some things than most of your contemporaries?

What are those?

Would you say you are more conservative or less conservative than most other people your age?

Why do you say that?

What accounts for it? Why are you the way you are?

Do you ever have private, personal visions or meditations about the meaning of life or about your place in the universe? Or about death and what comes after it? [wait]

Can you talk at all about some of your private meditations? Is it possible to talk about thoughts like these?

## THE MOST UNUSUAL THING ABOUT YOU

What would you say is the most unusual thing about you? [wait]

Why do you say that? Can you say a little more about that?

In what ways don't you fit the popular image of "myths" about being ____ years old? In what ways are you not like the way you are "supposed" to be at your age? [wait]

## FITTING IN WITH THE MODERN WORLD

Do you ever feel that you do not fit in very well with some of the things that are happening in the modern world? Or would you say that you feel right at home in the modern world?

Why do you say that?

What makes you feel that you are not up to date? What are the things about the modern world that you don't understand very well?

What about the things that you just don't like very much? What things do you not go along with in the modern world?

## UNDERSTANDING YOUNGER PEOPLE

Do you understand young people today?

Do they seem to be pretty much like the young people of forty or fifty years ago?

If they seem to be different from the kids of your generation or of your children's generation, how are they different? How do they seem different to you?

Do you feel that you have a lot of things in common with younger people? Or do you feel that you really don't have much in common?

Why do you say that? Why do you think that is?

## ARE OLDER PEOPLE SOMETIMES NOT INCLUDED?

Are older people sometimes treated as somehow different, just because they are older? Are they sometimes not paid attention to, or not included in younger people's conversations or activities, just because they are old? [wait]

Have you ever felt something like this happening when you are around younger people?

Why do you think some younger people would treat older people this way?

Do you think this might be an example of "age discrimination"—a situation where people are prejudiced against somebody just because of how old he or she is?

What do you think about age discrimination?

Do you think it works both ways? That sometimes older people would be given privileges and treated better, and sometimes ignored and treated worse, just because of how old they are?

## AGE DISCRIMINATION

What is "age discrimination"? [wait]

Do any specific incidents come to your mind when I mention the topic of age discrimination?

As an older person, have you ever experienced incidents where you feel you were ignored, treated unfairly, rudely, or with disrespect just because of your age? Or times when people assumed you would feel a certain way just because of your age? [wait]

Can you tell me of an instance of this kind of thing?

How did it make you feel, and what did you do about it?

Do you think that age discrimination is the same kind of a thing as race discrimination? That is, someone is denied his or her rights or denied respect because of some physical characteristic or cultural difference?

Can you say a little more about that?

## WHAT CAN BE DONE ABOUT AGE DISCRIMINATION

Do you think anything can be done about prejudice against older people?

What do you think has to happen in our society before young people will fully respect old people? Can you think of any changes that have to take place?

Can you say a little more about that?

## CHANGES YOU'D LIKE TO SEE HELP OLDER PEOPLE

What would you like to see change in our society to help older people more?

What do you think the government should do?

Do you think that people's values and attitudes have to change so that older people are respected more?

How could such a change come about?

How important is it for older people to stay involved or even get more involved in the daily life of their communities and their families?

What changes do you think should happen so that when people who are young now become as old as you are now, they might have it a bit easier, and be happier?

Why do you say that?

When did you retire?

What did it mean to you to retire? Could you talk about retirement a little?

Many people report that they got very bored, or depressed, or felt at loose ends. Did you feel that way?

Based on your experience, what is your advice to someone facing retirement, or who has just retired? What should they expect, and what should they do?

How secure were you financially? Did you have a reasonable pension?

How much did you miss working?


## MANDATORY RETIREMENT

Should people be forced to retire at a certain age whether they want to or not? [wait]

   Why, or why not?

Do you know of anybody this happened to—someone who had to retire, even though he or she didn't want to?

Is mandatory retirement an example of age discrimination, in your opinion?

How important is work, a job, to a person's sense of self-respect and well-being?


## REGRETS OR ADVICE ABOUT RETIRING

Do you ever wish you'd never retired?

   Why, or why not?

Would you advise people to go on working if they can? Or do you think people can be just as happy with more leisure time after they've retired?

What do you think a person should watch out for after retirement to avoid being bored or to avoid withdrawing from the world?


## THE WORST THING ABOUT HOW OLDER PEOPLE ARE TREATED

What do you find is the most annoying thing about the way people treat you now?

   What do they do? Can you say a little more about that?


## WHAT IS REALLY GOOD ABOUT BEING YOUR AGE?

What's the best thing about being [age of narrator]? [wait]

   Can you say a little more about that?

What else can you think of that is really good about being your age? [wait]

What are some of the privileges and prerogatives—the special treatment—that somebody as old as yourself has in our society?

> For example, do you feel free to speak your own mind now whenever you want to whomever you want?

> Do you have a lot of free time to think about things, to meditate on things that you feel deeply about, without being bothered by a lot of distractions?

> What about sleep? Someone famous once commented on the great pleasure of taking a daily nap after he had grown older. Do you agree?

> Any other privileges or prerogatives you can think of?

## PEACE OF MIND

People often expect that older people should have attained a certain peace of mind. Is this true for you? Do you have peace of mind now?

> Did you ever in your life not have peace of mind?

## OLDER PEOPLE AND THE IMAGE OF WISDOM

What about this idea that older people have attained a certain wisdom about life by virtue of their greater life experience. Do you think this is true, or is this just another myth about what older people are supposed to be like?

> Have you attained a certain measure of wisdom based on your life experience? Or do you still make just as many mistakes and do just as many dumb things as you always did?

Isn't it common sense to think that a person would acquire a certain wisdom and acceptance of life just by having lived a long time and having gone through a lot of different experiences?

> Or do you think that some people just never learn?

Do you think old people can be just as stupid as young people, regardless of how much life experience they have?

Have you learned what makes you happy?

> What does make you happy? And how long did it take you in life to learn that?

## MYTHS AND ILLUSIONS ABOUT BEING OLDER

Do you think that most younger people have a false image of what it means to be [age of narrator] years old?

Could you give me an example of what you mean?

What do you think are some of the main illusions that younger people seem to have about being older?

## POSITIVE AND NEGATIVE SIDES OF NOT BEING CAUGHT UP IN THE WORKADAY WORLD

Is there a positive side to not being so involved in the everyday, workaday world? [wait]

Do you value having more time to think and contemplate and do what you want?

Do you agree that one of the advantages of having more time to yourself is that you have more time for meditation and contemplation? Or is it just an opportunity to get bored? [wait]

What can you say about the negative things, like the tendency or danger of withdrawing or of losing interest in the world when you are not so involved in the day-to-day world of a job and so on?

Do you ever feel that way yourself?

What are some other negative things about not being so involved in the workaday world? [wait]

Do you ever get bored or tired of life or lonely now?

If you do get this way, what do you do about it?

## PSYCHOLOGICAL DANGERS OF OLD AGE

What are some of the greatest psychological dangers that people become susceptible to as they grow older? [wait]

For example, I am thinking about things like loneliness, or the tendency of some older people to "withdraw" more and more from the world or to get depressed and lose interest in life. Or the problems of finding people their own age to talk to. Are these realistic dangers for older people?

Why do you say that?

What about this issue of withdrawing? Some older people seem to lose interest in things. Is this really a danger, in your opinion, for older people?

Have you ever felt this way yourself, or known anyone who
did?

Why do some people react that way as they grow older, and
some don't?

What should be done if someone you know begins to act this
way?

## IMPORTANCE OF WORK AND ACTIVITY TO LONGEVITY
## AND HAPPINESS

How important do you think work, activity, or keeping busy are
to being happy, no matter how old you are?

Can you say more about that?

What do you do to keep busy?

Do you keep a pretty full schedule? For example, what are some
of the things you did in the last week?

Recently, someone asked several people in their eighties and nineties whether they thought that work and activity and keeping busy
were crucial to their well-being. They all agreed. What is your
opinion? Do you think keeping busy helps people live longer?

Why?

## IMPORTANCE OF DIET OR GENES FOR LONGEVITY

How important is a good diet to living long and feeling good?

What foods do you think are good to eat if somebody wants to
live a long life?

Do you eat a lot of onions? Recently, somebody with a computer
compared a group of eighty-plus-year-olds' diets with the number of times that they had to go to the doctor. The only food
that came out to compare with lower numbers of visits to the
doctor was onions! What do you think of that?

What about old age running in the family? Some people say that
this is the most important of all if a person wants to live a long
time. They have to have had long-lived parents. What do you
think?

Does old age run in your family?

What's the oldest age anybody you know of in your family lived
to be?

## JOKES YOU'VE HEARD ABOUT OLD PEOPLE

Do you know any funny jokes about old people?

　Tell me one.


## YOUR DREAMS

Do you dream much?

　What do you dream about? [wait]

Tell me a dream, any dream, that you've had lately.

　What do you think it means? [wait]

Do your dreams have any meaning, in your opinion? Are they trying to tell you something?

Have you ever had a particularly vivid or memorable dream that meant a lot to you?

　Tell me about that dream.


## WORRIES OF YOUR LIFE, AND YOUR STRENGTH THROUGH LIFE'S EXPERIENCES

What are some of the main things that you worry about now, or that you have to plan for in your life now? [wait]

　How important is the strength that you can draw on from having
　lived a long time and having faced numerous difficulties and
　crises in the past? Does your life experience make it easier to
　cope with worries and difficulties now?

　Can you say a little more about what you mean?

In other words, what have you learned in your life about how to face up to the stresses and worries of life without giving in to despair?


## RELIGIOUS THOUGHTS AS YOU'VE GROWN OLDER

Would you say that in general you have thought more about religious values or about the meaning of your life as you have grown older? [wait]

　Why?

Have you found more personal meaning in your religion as you have grown older?

　Why do you think that is?

Can you describe what your religion means to you now?

Have you come to any conclusions, or peace of mind, during your times of spiritual meditation? Have you come to believe and feel certain things about the meaning of your life, or about God, or about how well you tried to live your life? [wait]

How well have you lived your life? [wait]

What do you mean by that?

## ARE YOU GLAD TO HAVE LIVED AS LONG AS YOU HAVE?

Are you glad to have lived to be as old as you have? Or do you sometimes think you would rather not have lived so long?

Why?

Can you say more about that?

## GRIEF

Is losing someone any easier to bear at your age? [wait]

Why do you say that?

Who close to you has died in recent years? [wait]

Do you think you might see them again someday? [wait]

Have you accepted the fact of death in a way now that you could not have accepted when you were younger?

Why do you say that?

## IS YOUR LIFE NOW LIKE YOU THOUGHT IT WOULD BE?

When you were younger, did you ever think that you would live to be [age of narrator] years old?

Is your life now like you thought it would be then?

In what ways is your life now different from what you thought it would be when you were younger?

What did you think it would be like to be [age of narrator], and in what ways were you right and in what ways were you wrong about it?

## IF YOU COULD HEAR OR SEE A TAPE MADE BY YOUR MOTHER OR FATHER

If you could hear or see a tape now of your mother and father talking about themselves and their lives, as you are doing here,

what would you especially like to hear them tell about themselves?
Have you told that about yourself in these tapes?

## COMPARE PHYSICAL AND MENTAL CHANGES AS YOU'VE GROWN OLDER

If you had to compare yourself now with yourself, say, forty or fifty years ago, would you say that the changes in you have been more physical, or would you say that they are more psychological and mental?
Why do you say that?
In other words, are you still the same person you were forty years ago, except that your body has gotten older? Or have you changed mentally and psychologically as much as you've changed physically? [wait]
In what ways have you changed? Could you say more about how you've changed, both physically and mentally, as you've grown older?

## WHAT IT IS LIKE TO BE YOUR AGE

What is it like to be [age of narrator]? What does it feel like to be ____ years old?
Can you compare how you feel now to what you felt like when you were, say, thirty years old?
What kind of a person are you now, compared to the kind of person you were when you were thirty?
What would you describe as some of the main changes in your personality since age thirty, as you have grown older and gotten more mature?

## YOUR LEGACY

What will be your most important legacy to those you leave behind? Not just your material goods or money, but also your "mark"—what have you accomplished in life?
What do you consider to be your most important accomplishment in life? [wait]

## SEX

Young people often think that romantic love and sexual attraction stop when people get to be a certain age. Would you say that this is true? Or is it another example of a myth that younger people have about older people?

How important is sex to you now?

How important is sex compared to other things in life now?

Young people often think that sexual attractiveness is the most important thing in life. In general, what you regard as the most important thing in life seems to depend partly on how old you are. At about what age did you find that sexual attractiveness had become less important and other things had become more important to you in life?

## VISITS OF YOUR YOUNGER RELATIVES, AND YOUR INFLUENCE ON THEM

Do your children and grandchildren, nephews and nieces, and other younger relatives come to visit you very often now?

As often as you would like?

Would you like to have more influence on the lives of your younger relatives?

Why? What could you tell them about life?

Do you think you know things that could help them and be important to them?

What things are those?

If you did have more influence on your younger relatives, or on younger people in general, what would you like to tell them and show them?

What would you like them to know about you?

What could you tell them that might be useful in trying to live happy and full lives?

## YOUNG PEOPLE'S FEAR OF OLD AGE

Many young people are very afraid of growing old. They don't know any old people, so they don't know what it means to grow old. They are afraid they will have nothing to enjoy when they grow older. Could you comment on this fear of growing old?

In your opinion, is there really anything to fear about growing old?

Why do you think young people fear growing old?

What can you tell them about it?

Do you think young people fear growing older because they fear dying or being closer to their time of dying? Or do they fear illness?

> Could you comment on these fears? How can a younger person cope with his or her fears about death or illness?

What do older people know that younger people should be learning from them? In what areas is it most likely that an older person would be able to teach a younger person something? [wait]

> What about just knowledge of growing older itself? Since most younger people will themselves grow old, who else are they going to learn what it's like from but someone who's been there?

## PERSONAL POSSESSIONS AND HEIRLOOMS

What personal possessions are especially important to you now?

Are you in charge of any important family heirlooms, like furniture, jewelry, or old diaries and photographs?

> What are these heirlooms? Whom did they belong to, and how old are they?

What do you want to have happen to your most important possessions after you are gone?

## FEELINGS ABOUT NURSING HOMES

What do you think of nursing homes? [wait]

> Does the idea of someday having to move to one upset you? Why?

What do you think would be the best and the worst thing about being in a nursing home?

Do you know anyone now who is living in a nursing home?

> How does he or she like it?

[If narrator is in a nursing home now]: Do you like living here?

> Why, or why not?
>
> What's the best thing about being here?
>
> What's the worst thing?

## STILL CURIOUS AND LEARNING

Are you still curious about things, and are you still learning new things? Or do you have the attitude that you've pretty much seen it all, and that there's nothing new under the sun? [wait]

What's the most interesting new thing you've heard about or gotten curious about lately?

## A TYPICAL DAY/WEEK FOR YOU

What would be an example of a typical day for you now? Or a typical week? [wait]

For example, where do you go? What do you do for entertainment?

Do you read much? What do you read?

Do you watch a lot of TV? What shows do you not want to miss?

Do you have a hobby?

Who are the people you see most? Spouse? Best friend?

Children? How often do you see them? Any nephews or nieces?

Do you see any of your brothers or sisters regularly?

What about neighbors?

## ANYTHING ELSE IMPORTANT ABOUT BEING YOUR AGE

Is there anything else important about growing older or about being your age that younger people might not know?

## HOW YOU FEEL ABOUT THESE INTERVIEWS

How do you feel about these interviews, the tapes we are doing right now? [wait]

What do you think will happen to these tapes?

What do you hope will happen to them?

Do you think these tapes will be your memoirs? Your autobiography?

Would you like to see these tapes written down someday, so that you could be in a book and others could read about your life and about the things you thought were important?

## THOUGHTS ABOUT WRITING AN AUTOBIOGRAPHY/ PRIVATE COMMUNICATION

Before we started making these tapes, did you ever think that you'd like to have written your own autobiography?

Do these tapes serve the purpose? Have you talked about most of the things that you would have written about in your autobiography?

Can you think of anything we've left out?

If there's something you'd like to talk about on this tape privately, I can show you how to operate the equipment, and I'll leave the room. That way, you can say something completely private, and you can keep the tape to be played only when you specify it can be played. [You can show your narrator how to turn the tape recorder on and off. This tape can then be restricted from duplication until a future time of your narrator's choosing. This is an opportunity for a completely private statement by your narrator about anything he or she might choose.]

# *Narrator as Parent*

his section develops questions to help your narrator recall his or her experiences as a parent, and to describe the character and development of his or her children as they grew up. The wording of some of the questions will have to be changed slightly if you are interviewing one of your own parents or grandparents. For example, if the question or topic as it is written refers to the narrator's wife, you of course would change it to "Mom" or "Grandma"; or if the question refers to the other children of your narrator, you would be able to ask it personally about your brothers and sisters instead of asking about "your second child" or "your third child." Just take the basic idea or theme of the question or topic, and ask it so that it applies to you.

The idea of this chapter is to get an impression from your narrator of his or her children at different times in their lives: as children, adolescents, young married adults, and as they are at the present time. The subsections developed here are: questions to be asked of mothers; questions addressed to fathers; questions about children growing up and as teenagers; questions about children's marriages; and observations on children as they are now.

Trust your curiosity and instincts as you have done in the previous interviews. This is not the easiest interview to do with one's own parents. Select the ideas that interest you and mark those questions before you turn on your recorder. Even if you pick out only a dozen questions, you will be able to record some sense of your narrator as a parent, and you will capture some very important feelings that continue to reveal who and what kind of person your narrator is.

Some of the more interesting themes are impressions of the children at different ages, comparisons between childhood characteristics and adult characteristics, teenage antics and behavior, trouble gotten into by children, and memories of children's courtships and marriages.

Only a parent can answer the questions presented here. The answers are invaluable for self-knowledge and for understanding your parents or grandparents and what they tried to do in raising their children.

## Questions for Mothers

### FIRST PREGNANCY

Tell me about your first pregnancy. What was it like for you? [wait]

Can you remember your feelings when you first found out that you were going to have a child? [wait]

What were some of the things you felt and thought about? [wait]

How old were you when you had your first child?

Had you planned to have a baby, or was it more of an accident?

### THOUGHTS ABOUT BABY WHILE PREGNANT

Do you think that a mother's thoughts while she is pregnant affect her child?

What do you mean? In what ways?

For example, do you think that a mother's thoughts while she is pregnant might affect the kind of a personality her child will have or what her child will look like? Or, for example, if a mother listens to music while she is pregnant, will her child be musical?

What did you hope your child would be like? What kinds of thoughts did you try to have for your first baby? Do you remember?

Did you hope for a boy or a girl? Do you remember?

Why did you hope for a boy/girl?

## PRENATAL CARE AND INFORMATION, PREGNANCY EXPERIENCES

Who was the doctor who attended you when you had your first child?

Do you think you had good prenatal care? Did you have good information and did you know what to expect?

 Whom did you rely on for your information? Your doctor? Your mother? Sisters or friends?

What kinds of things did they tell mothers to do then if they wanted to have healthy babies?

 Did you smoke or drink while you were pregnant?

Nowadays, pregnant women do everything they want to, from working to exercising to shopping and so on. When you were having your children, were women expected to go out less, and to stay quiet during the later stages of their pregnancy?

 Why do you think that was?

Do you remember experiencing any food cravings or unusual desires like those women are supposed to feel during pregnancy— like ice cream in the middle of the night? Or do you think such stories are just jokes?


## NATURAL CHILDBIRTH

Was there as much talk about "natural childbirth" then as we hear about today? That's when mothers give birth without anesthesia and practice exercises beforehand. Or some even give birth at home with the aid of a midwife instead of in a hospital with a doctor.

 What do you think of natural childbirth? [wait]

Were there midwives available to mothers when you were having your family? Did you know any midwives?


## STORIES ABOUT GETTING TO THE HOSPITAL

Tell me the story of how you got to the hospital for your first baby. Do you remember that day? Or any funny stories about it?

 Where were you and what were you doing when you first began to feel your labor pains?

 Where was your husband at that time?

How did you get to the hospital?

What hospital did you go to?

How did your husband act? Was he pretty nervous? Or did he act calm and in control?

## LABOR AND DELIVERY, FIRST THOUGHTS ON SEEING FIRST CHILD

How long were you in labor?

Did you receive any drugs or anesthesia?

Were there any complications or problems with the birth?

How did you feel when you first saw your baby? [wait]

Could you say anything more about your feelings and thoughts when you first saw your baby? When they first brought him/her to you?

## COST

Nowadays, it can cost thousands of dollars to have a baby in a hospital. What did it cost when you had your first baby? Do you remember the hospital bill?

How long were you in the hospital? Do you remember that?

## NURSING OR BOTTLE FEEDING

Did you nurse or bottle feed your baby?

Why?

[If nursed]: How long do you think a child should be nursed in order to be healthy? At what age should a child be weaned and trained to eat other foods?

Why do you say that?

Who influenced your decision to nurse or not to nurse your baby? What was the prevailing attitude then about the best way to feed babies?

When you were a baby, do you know whether you were nursed, or were you a "bottle baby"?

## NAMING BABY

How did you decide what to name your baby?

Was [name] named after anybody?

Was it more your choice or your husband's?

Do you remember any of the names you rejected?

Why? What names did you veto?

What would ____ have been named if he/she had been a boy/girl [opposite of actual sex]? Had you picked out names before ____ was born?

## INFANT'S TEMPERAMENT

What kind of baby was [name]? Could you tell his/her disposition right from the start?

Did he/she cry a lot? Or was he/she happy and good-natured?

Did he/she sleep well or wake up a lot?

Was he/she strong or sickly?

Did he/she eat well?

Do you think you could tell, even from that early age, what kind of a person your [son/daughter] would turn out to be?

What kind of a person was that?

Do any funny or special memories come easily to mind right now as you think about ____ as an infant?

Anything else distinctive that you can remember about ____ as an infant?

## PHILOSOPHY OF CHILD-REARING

Did you mostly trust your instincts in raising your children, or did you listen to advice and study books on child-rearing to find out the best way to raise them?

Do you remember any books that you might have read on the best way to raise children?

What were some of the things you were told to do?

Was your philosophy to let the baby cry until feeding time came? Or did you feel that it was important to respond right away to the baby's crying?

Why did you do that? What effect did you want to have on the baby?

What about toilet training? What was your philosophy with regard to toilet training? [wait]

About how old was your child before you started to toilet train him/her?

Do you remember any funny stories about your attempts to toilet train [name]?

Thinking about it now, what do you think is the best way for a parent to go about toilet training a child?

## HUSBAND'S AND WIFE'S ROLES IN CARETAKING

Did your husband help you out much with the baby? I mean in basic caretaking—feeding, changing, bathing, and so on? Or was this pretty much up to you?

Today, fathers are doing some of these tasks instead of leaving them exclusively to the mother. Do you think household and child-rearing chores should be shared? Or are you more in favor of women being the ones who pay the most attention to the home and the children?

Why?

## WHAT A NEW MOTHER NEEDS MOST

From your experience, what does a new mother need the most during the first few weeks after she comes home with a new baby? [wait]

Did your mother come to help you out during the first few weeks after you had your baby?

Do you remember this as being much of a help at the time?

Did you do the same for your daughters?

## SECOND PREGNANCY AND BIRTH

What is your second child's name?

How long after your first child was born did [name] come along?

Tell me about your pregnancy and the birth of ____. [wait]

Did you plan for this baby? Or was he/she a surprise?

Do you remember whether you wanted a boy or a girl?

Why did you want a [boy/girl] this time?

## FEELINGS OF FIRST CHILD

Do you remember how you handled the feelings and curiosity of [name of first child] when you began to be obviously expecting?

How did you explain what was happening and what to expect? Do you remember?

Do you remember any funny stories about it?

## STORIES ABOUT WHERE BABIES COME FROM

Did you have any stories that you told in your family about where babies come from? I mean, did you tell your children stories about the stork, the cabbage patch, and so on? Or did you try to talk about sex and love and pregnancy, more or less "the facts of life"?

How did you explain it to your children?

How much of what you were saying do you think your child understood?

Did you talk at all about God in trying to explain pregnancy and birth to your child?

## THOUGHTS ABOUT SECOND CHILD WHILE PREGNANT

What did you imagine about [name of second child] while you were pregnant with him/her?

What were some of your thoughts and fantasies about ____?

Do you think your thoughts and feelings during this time influenced the kind of person ____ turned out to be?

Why do you say that?

Did you try to influence your baby by the thoughts and feelings you had about him/her?

## PROBLEMS OR COMPLICATIONS WITH SECOND CHILD

Were there any problems or complications with this pregnancy? Either during the pregnancy or during the birth itself?

Who was the physician who gave you prenatal care and who helped deliver this baby? Did you smoke or drink while you were pregnant with [name]?

## THE TRIP TO THE HOSPITAL

Do you remember the circumstances of your trip to the hospital when you had [name]?

How did your husband act this time?

Was ____ on time, premature, or late?

What hospital was ____ born in?

Do you have any recollection of what it cost, and how long you were in the hospital?

Did you have any drugs or anesthesia when you gave birth to____?

## ANY IMMEDIATE SENSE OF DIFFERENCE

Was there any immediate difference—in temperament or behavior or just in your feeling about who this person was and was going to be—between your second baby and your first? I mean in the first moments, or hours, or days that you began to know him/her?

Can you say a little more about that? [wait]

Was there more crying? Or less?

More activity, or less?

How about sleeping and eating?

More or less irritable? Or more or less a content baby?

## NAMING SECOND BABY

Who was [name] named after?

How did you arrive at that name?

Do you remember vetoing any names that your husband chose, or vice versa?

What would ____ have been named if he/she had been the opposite sex?

## DESCRIPTION AND MEMORIES OF SECOND CHILD

Tell me something about [name of second] during his/her early months and years. [wait]

What kind of baby was he/she? [wait]

Strong or sickly?

Irritable or good-natured?

Active or more quiet?

In what ways would you say he/she was different from [name of first]?

Do any funny or special memories come easily to mind right now as you think about [name of second] as an infant?

Do you remember any "scares," like accidents or near-accidents, or illnesses when ____ was an infant?

Anything else distinctive that you can remember about ____ as an infant?

Do you think you could tell, even from that early age, something about the kind of a person ____ was going to turn out to be?

What kind of a person was that?


## FIRST CHILD'S FEELINGS WHEN SECOND CAME HOME; FUNNY STORIES

How did [name of first] react when [name of second] came home? Was he/she jealous?

   How did you deal with that?

Did [name of first] help you out in taking care of [name of second] and your later children?

   How important do you think [name of first] was in the upbringing of your later children?

     Why do you say that?

Do you remember any funny or humorous stories about things [name of first] did in looking after [name of second] when they were little?

Tell me one of your funny memories of when they were little.


## NURSING OR BOTTLE FEEDING: SECOND CHILD

Did you nurse [name of second] or feed him/her with a bottle?

   Why?

   For how long? Do you remember?


## ANYTHING DIFFERENT IN RAISING YOUR SECOND CHILD

What did you learn from raising your first child that you applied in taking care of your second? [wait]

For example, did you do anything differently with regard to your philosophy of crying and feeding, or in toilet training?

## THIRD PREGNANCY AND BIRTH, AND SUBSEQUENT CHILDREN

[Return to the questions beginning with "Second Pregnancy and Birth," and ask the sequence of questions developed for the second child about the third child, and do the same for subsequent children. The point is to have the parent talk individually about each of his or her children in some detail about things only a parent could know.]

## DISCIPLINE

When your children were little, how did you discipline them? [wait]

Did they sometimes need a spanking? Or did you try more to talk to them to get them to behave themselves?

Do you think most children need a spanking now and then?

Why do you say that?

## BEST AND WORST CHARACTER TRAIT: ALL CHILDREN

What would you say was the best thing about [name of first] as a child? What was his/her best character trait as a child?

And what would you say was the worst thing, the worst personality trait, about ____ as a child?

[Repeat the above two questions for each child in turn.]

## ANYTHING UNUSUAL ABOUT ANY OF YOUR CHILDREN

Would you say there was anything really unusual or extraordinary about any of your children when they were little? [wait]

What was that, and could you say a little more about it?

## *Questions for Fathers*

## FIRST CHILD

What is your firstborn's name?

About how old were you when ____ was born? And about how old was your wife?

## FEELINGS WHEN YOUR WIFE BECAME PREGNANT

Do you remember what you thought and felt when your wife first told you that she was going to have a baby? [wait]

Can you say a little more about that? What did you feel and what did you think about when you realized that you were going to be a father?

Had the two of you planned to start your family, or was it a surprise or an accident that your wife became pregnant?

Do you remember if you wanted a boy or a girl?

Why did you want a [boy/girl]?

## CONCERNS ABOUT FATHERHOOD AND RESPONSIBILITIES

What do you remember being most concerned about at that time? For example, do you remember being anxious about whether you were ready for such a responsibility? Or about finances? Or whatever?

What did you think then was the most important thing to do or to be in being a good father? [wait]

## FINANCIAL CONCERNS

Were you concerned about whether or not you would be able to support a family on your income? Or were you financially secure by the time [name] came along?

What were you doing for a living at that time?

Do you remember about how much money you were making then?

Did it seem like enough to you?

Where were you living at the time _____ was born?

## FUNNY OR MEMORABLE OCCURRENCES DURING WIFE'S PREGNANCY

Do you remember any especially funny incidents during your wife's pregnancy? Is there anything memorable about that time that sticks in your mind? [wait]

I'm thinking perhaps of those stories we hear about husbands having to get up in the middle of the night to get their wives a dish of ice cream or a jar of pickles, and so on. Do you remember anything like that?

## THE TRIP TO THE HOSPITAL

Can you remember the day that your wife's labor pains started and you got her to the hospital? Tell me that story—what were you doing, what time of the day was it, how did you get there, and so on? [wait]

What hospital did you go to?

Who was the doctor who helped deliver your first child?

Do you remember yourself as calm and collected and under control on the trip to the hospital? Or were you pretty nervous?

Would your wife agree with your recollection of how you behaved?

## WAITING FOR THE BABY

Tell me the story of what it was like for you waiting for the baby to be born. [wait]

Did you do any of the typical things expectant fathers are supposed to do in the waiting room? Like pacing the floor, chain smoking, and so on?

## FIRST THOUGHTS AND IMPRESSIONS OF FIRSTBORN

Can you recall now, so many years later, what your first thoughts and impressions were of [name] when you first laid eyes on him/her? What did you think and feel, and what did you see, when the nurse first held him/her up, or when you first held him/her? [wait]

What did he/she look like?

## YOUR FEELINGS ON FIRST BECOMING A FATHER

How would you describe your feelings on first becoming a father?

What did you do?

Who was the first person you called? Do you remember?

Did you hand out cigars or other things that new fathers are traditionally supposed to do?

## NAMING FIRST CHILD

Who was [name] named after?

How did you pick that name?

Was it more your choice, or more your wife's?

Do you remember any of the names that you rejected? Any names that ____ might have been called?

Why did you reject them, or why did your wife reject them?

What would you have named ____ if he/she had been the opposite sex?

## COST

Just for the record, do you remember what the hospital bill was?

## CHILD'S EARLY DAYS, MONTHS, AND YEARS

Tell me something you remember about [name] during his/her early days, months, and years—something about him/her as an infant. [wait]

What kind of a child was ____?

Do any special memories or stories come to mind now about ____ as a young child?

## TEMPERAMENT/DISPOSITION

Do you remember [name] as a happy and content baby? Or did he/she seem irritable?

Did he/she cry a lot? Or about what you'd expect?

Was he/she strong or sickly?

Was he/she active, or more the type to sit quietly and just take things in?

Could you tell, even from an early age, what kind of person ____ would be?

Could you see the basic personality characteristics that have remained the same as ____ has grown up?

How would you describe that person? What kind of a child was ____?

## SCARES, ACCIDENTS, OR ILLNESSES

Do you recall any "scares," like accidents or illnesses, during [name's] infancy or childhood? Was ____ ever seriously sick or injured during his/her early childhood?

What happened?

## YOUR RESPONSIBILITIES, CARETAKING

Did you get involved with the actual physical caretaking of your baby? Did you change diapers, feed him/her, get up in the middle of the night, and so on? Or was that primarily your wife's job?

In terms of you and your wife's "roles" as parents, did you see yourself as primarily the provider and your wife as the caretaker? Or was the responsibility more equal and shared for making money and for taking care of the children?

What is your opinion of the modern way of raising families? Both husband and wife might be working and child care is more of a shared responsibility between the two of them. Is that a good idea, or not?

Why do you say that?

## EARLY SIGNS OF LATER PERSONALITY TRAITS

Do you think you could see any of the characteristics of [name's] later personality in him/her from very early on? Something special or unique about ____?

What was that? What did you see in him/her from very early on?

## CHANGE IN YOUR LIFE AFTER CHILD WAS BORN

How big a change in your life did having the baby make? [wait]

Some people, when they answer this question, say, "Totally!" They say that the baby became the central focus of their home life and that they didn't have time for anything else, and so on. Would you agree with that?

## PHILOSOPHY OF CHILD-REARING

Could you talk a bit about your philosophy of child-rearing? How did you think children should be raised? [wait]

For example, when the baby cried, did you think that it was all right for him/her to cry for a while? Or did you think he/she should be looked after right away?

What about feeding? Did you feel that the baby should be fed on schedule, no matter what? Or did you feed him/her whenever it seemed that he/she was hungry?

Why did you think that?

Did you think about "spoiling" your child if you fed him/her right away, instead of waiting until feeding time?

What about toilet training? How soon did you feel that a child should be started on toilet training?

Why did you feel that way?

Do you remember any book that you read about how to raise children the best way?

What book was that, and what were some of the things it said to do?

Do you remember hearing any of the child-rearing philosophy that your mother followed when she raised you? For example, how you were fed, or toilet trained, and so on.

## NURSING OR BOTTLE FEEDING

Did your wife nurse your children, or did she use a bottle and a formula?

What was your opinion about that?

Do you think in general that children should be nursed or bottle fed?

Why?

## YOUR SECOND CHILD

Let's go on and talk about your second child. What is your second child's name?

How big of a difference in age is there between [name of first] and [name of second]?

## DIFFERENT FEELINGS THE SECOND TIME

Do you remember feeling any differently the "second time around," when you were waiting for [name] to arrive?

Had you planned to have another baby?

Do you remember whether you wanted a boy or a girl this time?
Why?

## STORIES ABOUT WHERE BABIES COME FROM

How did you explain to [name of first] about the upcoming birth of a new brother or sister? Did you use "fairy tale" explanations like "the stork" or "the cabbage patch"? Or did you try to talk about sex and love between men and women—that is, "the facts of life"?

How do you think [name of first] understood it?

Did you think it was important to talk about God in trying to explain to your child pregnancy and birth and where babies come from?

What do you think is the best approach to follow in telling children about where babies come from?

## THE TRIP TO THE HOSPITAL: SECOND CHILD

Tell me the story of the trip to the hospital when [name] was born. Where were you when your wife told you labor pains had started, what time of the day was it, how did you get there, and so on?

Was [name] on time, premature, or late?

Do you remember yourself as being in control, calm, and collected this time? Or were you still pretty nervous, even though this was the second time for you?

## FIRST THOUGHTS AND IMPRESSIONS OF SECOND CHILD

Can you remember now what you first thought and felt when you saw [name]? What were your first thoughts and impressions when you first saw or held him/her?

What did he/she look like?

## NAMING SECOND BABY

Who was [name of second] named after?

How did you arrive at that name?

Do you remember any of the other names you thought of and discarded before deciding on ____?

Why did you reject those names?

What would ____ have been called if he/she had been of the opposite sex?

Was ____ more your choice, or more your wife's?

## COST

What was the hospital bill this time? Do you remember?

## TRADITIONAL FATHER BEHAVIOR

Do you remember whether you went around handing out cigars, or anything like that when ____ was born?

Who was the first person you called to tell the news?

## DESCRIPTION AND MEMORIES OF SECOND CHILD

Tell me some of your memories and impressions of [name] during his/her early months and years. [wait]

Do any particularly funny or special memories come right away to your mind when you think about ____ when he/she was very young? [wait]

What kind of a baby was he/she?

   Was he/she strong or sickly?

   Did he/she sleep well? Or did he/she wake up a lot and cry a lot?

   Was he/she irritable? Or was he/she good-natured and content most of the time?

   Was ____ more the quiet type, or more active and energetic?

In what ways would you say [name of second] was different from [name of first]?

Do you think you could get a sense, even from an early age, of what kind of a person ____ was going to turn out to be?

   What kind of a person was that?

## EARLY SIGNS OF LATER PERSONALITY TRAITS

What characteristics of [name]'s personality traits and later life attitudes could you see in him/her from very early on?

Was there anything special or unique about ____'s personality that you could see right away?

## RELATIONSHIP BETWEEN THE TWO CHILDREN

Do you think that [name of first] had much trouble adjusting to the idea of a new baby in the house?

What do you remember about that?

Do you remember any funny stories about things that [name of first] said or did in relation to his/her little sister/brother?

## ACCIDENTS OR SCARES

Do you remember any "scares," accidents, near-accidents, or serious illnesses that happened to [name of second]?

## RESPONSIBILITY FOR CHILDREN, CARETAKING

Who was mostly responsible for taking care of your second child? Did you get up in the middle of the night to feed and change diapers, and so on? Or was that done mostly by your wife?

## THIRD AND SUBSEQUENT CHILDREN

[Return to the beginning of the questions on "Your Second Child" and ask them for the third, and for subsequent children, changing the wording where appropriate. Again, the idea is to spend some time and get personal recollections from a parent on each of his or her children when they were born and when they were little.]

## EXTENDED FAMILY

Were your parents or your wife's parents around to help out raising your children—for babysitting and the like?

How important a role did they play, as you remember?

What about your brothers and sisters, or your wife's? Were there uncles and aunts of the children around when they were little to babysit and help raise them?

## DOMESTIC HELPERS

Was there a maid, a domestic, or a nanny who helped out with the children when they were little?

What was her name?

What was she like? What kind of person was she?

How important do you think she was to the children?

Was she from a different country or a different ethnic group from yours?

## BEST AND WORST CHARACTER TRAIT WHEN LITTLE: ALL CHILDREN

What would you say was the best thing about [name of first] as a child? What was his/her best character trait as a child?

And what would you say was the worst personality trait about _____ as a child?

[Repeat the above two questions for each child in turn.]

## ANYTHING UNUSUAL ABOUT ANY OF YOUR CHILDREN

Would you say there was anything really unusual or extraordinary about any of your children when they were little?

What was that? Could you say a little more about that?

## Children As They Were Growing Up

### GENERAL IMPRESSIONS AND MEMORIES OF CHILDREN AS THEY WERE GROWING UP

Let's take some time now to concentrate on each of your children as he or she was growing up and going through adolescence. Can you try to give a brief sketch of your impressions and memories of each of them as he or she was then, in the teenage years? [wait]

Let's take [name of first] first.

What was the most individual or distinctive thing about _____ that made him/her different from your other children.

In what ways do you remember _____'s special personality expressing itself? What interests and talents did _____ have that were different from your other children?

Was _____ athletic or interested in sports?

Was _____ artistic or musically inclined?

Were there any severe illnesses or injuries that happened to _____ when he/she was growing up?

How did that happen, and how did it turn out?

Did ____ have lots of friends or was he/she more of a person with just a few close friends, more of a "loner"?

How did ____ seem to get along in school? Was he/she a good student, an average student, or something of a cut-up and more on the lazy side?

Do you remember any funny stories about trouble that ____ got into during these years? Any stories about funny or crazy things he/she did then that you still remember?

Anything else important about ____ as a young person that we haven't talked about?

Now, give me your impressions in the same way about [name of second]. Tell me something about ____ as he/she was growing up. [wait] [Repeat above questions for second child and subsequent children.]

## WHICH CHILD MOST LIKE YOU/MOST LIKE SPOUSE

Of all your children, which one do you think was the most like you, and which was most like your husband/wife?

Why do you say that? Which things are you thinking of when you say that?

## PRACTICAL MINDED VERSUS DREAMERS

Of all your children, which was more of a dreamer, artist, or a "poet," and which was more practical minded?

Why do you say that?

Which is more important—the practical side, or the artistic?

Why do you say that?

## ADOLESCENCE AS A TIME OF CONFLICT, STRESS, AND STRAIN

Many people say that adolescence is a difficult time for young people, a time of conflict and confusion where a lot of guidance is needed. Do you agree or disagree with that idea?

Why?

How do you think each of your children handled the stresses and conflicts of his/her adolescence when he/she was growing up and becoming physically adult? [wait]

Which of your children seemed to have a smooth time of it, and which seemed to have the most troubles as an adolescent?

Why do you think that was?

## ARE THE TEENAGE YEARS THE HARDEST?

Many people say that the teenage years are the hardest years in a person's life. Do you agree or disagree with that?

Why?

If you disagree, which years are the hardest in your opinion? Which stage of life do you think is the most difficult to live through?

Why do you say that?

## A GENERATION GAP IN YOUR FAMILY

Was there anything like what they nowadays call a generation gap between you and your children when they were growing up?

Did you ever feel like it was hard to communicate with your teenage children?

Did it seem like your ideas and experiences as a teenager were very different from your children's ideas, values, and experiences?

What do you mean? What were some of the main differences between your generation and your children's generation?

## Typical Rules and Conflicts

### DATING

What rules did you impose when your children began dating?

Did they have a time that they had to be home when they went out at night?

What time was that?

Was dating for your children very different from what dating was like for you when you were a teenager?

What were some of the differences?

What were you allowed to do and not allowed to do? What was the expected behavior on dates?

Did you ever forbid any of your children to date someone because you didn't approve of him or her?

What was that all about? Do you remember an example?

Did you always expect to meet the person your child was out with first, before they went out?

## MUSIC

What about music? Can you remember what you thought of the music that your children listened to?

What kind of music did your teenagers listen to when they were growing up?

What do you think of the modern rock and roll that young people listen to today?

Why do you say that?

Someone once said that "the differences between generations can be most dramatically expressed by the differences in their taste in music." Do you think there's any truth to that?

## CLOTHES AND HAIR

What did you think of your children's way of dressing or of wearing their hair when they were teenagers? Do you remember?

How did they dress and wear their hair then? What clothes and styles did they just absolutely have to have to be "in style"?

Do you remember any funny stories about some of your kids' styles of hair or clothing?

## SLANG

What do you remember about some of your teenagers' expressions? Do you remember slang words that you thought sounded ridiculous?

What were some of the slang expressions from their, and from your, teenage years? Do you still remember any of them?

## CURSING, DIRTY WORDS

Do you remember any of your children cursing when they got angry?

What was your attitude toward dirty words in the house?

If someone said a dirty word, what would be the punishment?

Was there anyone in the family who could really cuss? I mean, who could "cuss a blue streak" sometimes?

## DRINKING AND DRUGS

Do you remember any concerns you had over your children drinking or taking drugs?

Did any of your children experiment with drinking or with drugs when they were growing up, that you know of?

How did you deal with the subject of drinking when your children asked about it? What did you say about it to them?

> In your opinion, should young people know something about drinking, if only to know when to stop? Or are you against alcohol altogether?

What would your parents have done to you if they had discovered you drinking alcohol when you were a teenager? Or taking illegal drugs?

Was there liquor around when you were raising your family? Or did you not allow it around?

> Why?

Have you ever known anybody whose life was ruined by alcohol?

> Who was that? What happened?

## SMOKING

What about smoking? Were your children permitted to smoke cigarettes after they reached a certain age if they wanted to?

Did anyone in your family smoke? Such as you or your spouse?

What would the punishment have been if you had found that one of your children was smoking?

## SCHOOL GRADES AND HOMEWORK

What did you expect from your children in the way of academic performance?

Which of your children seemed to have an easier time of it in school, and which were less successful or less interested in school performance?

Was there a strong academic tradition in your family? Were the children expected to excel in school?

Considering the whole family—uncles, aunts, brothers, sisters, and so on—was there anyone who really accomplished a lot through schooling? Such as any lawyers, or Ph.D.'s, or doctors? Who were the people who were more inclined toward the more intellectual professions?

## AMBITIONS FOR CHILDREN

Did you have any special ambitions for any of your children?

What did each of them want to be when they grew up? Do you remember some of the things they used to say?

Based on your sense of the special talents and abilities that each of your children had, do you think that what they finally chose to do for a living turned out to be a wise choice for them?

## ADOLESCENT REBELLION

Do you think your children were pretty well adjusted when they were in their teenage years? Or did any of them seem headstrong and not too content?

Which of your children was more of a "rebel" than the others?

Why was he/she more that way?

Tell me some of the other times when your teenage sons or daughters seemed to be going through what we would call now "adolescent rebellion"—when they refused to go along with anything you said, and in fact seemed to do the opposite of what they thought you wanted them to do.

What happened as a result? Do you have any good stories to tell about any of your children as "teenage rebels"?

Do you think a little adolescent rebellion is normal for teenagers to go through?

Why do you say that?

Do you remember going through anything like that when you were a teenager?

Can you give me an example?

## WORST TROUBLE ANY OF YOUR KIDS GOT INTO

What would you say was the worst trouble that any of your children got into when they were teenagers? [wait]

Tell me about how that happened.

Do you remember how you felt at the time, and what you did to help set them straight and get them out of the trouble they were in?

Do you think they learned something from it?

What do you think they learned?

## DIFFERENCES BETWEEN YOU AS A TEENAGER AND YOUR CHILDREN

Were you different when you were a teenager from the way your children were when they were teenagers? [wait]

In what ways do you think you were different from the way they were?

What was the biggest single difference between your world as a teenager and the world of your children as teenagers?

## DIFFERENCES BETWEEN YOU AS A TEENAGER AND YOUR GRANDCHILDREN AS TEENAGERS

What about your grandchildren [if narrator has adolescent or teenage grandchildren]? How different do they seem to be from what you were like when you were a teenager?

Why are they different, if you think they are?

In what ways do you think teenagers are the same the world over and in every historical time? What's universal about being a teenager? [wait]

Do you think your grandchildren are being raised very differently from the way you were raised?

How? In what ways are they being raised differently?

Is it a change for the worse or for the better, in your opinion?

Can you see differences between the way your grandchildren are being raised by your children, and the ways you tried to raise your children?

## WERE YOU A STRICT OR LENIENT PARENT?

Would you say you were a strict parent during your children's teenage years? Or do you think of yourself as having been more lenient or easygoing?

Why do you say that?

Do you think your children would agree with you? Would they agree with your opinion about yourself as a parent?

What can you think of as an example of something that you required of your children when they were teenagers that you would call "strict"?

## STRICT OR LENIENT—GIRLS VERSUS BOYS

Do girls need more supervision than boys need, in your opinion? Or are the sexes pretty much equal in their need for supervision or freedom today?

Why do you say that?

## DID YOU BRING UP YOUR CHILDREN BETTER THAN CHILDREN ARE BEING RAISED TODAY?

Do you think your children were raised better than children are being raised today?

Why do you say that?

## DID YOUR KIDS HAVE IT EASIER THAN YOU DID?

Do you think your kids had it easier than you did when they were growing up?

In what ways?

Did they have things and opportunities that you did not have?

Like what, for example?

What about the other way around? Did you have things and opportunities or values and experiences that they didn't have?

Like what, for example?

## DO YOUR GRANDCHILDREN HAVE IT STILL EASIER?

Do your grandchildren seem to have it still easier, in your opinion?

Or do you think that in some ways it is harder to grow up now-adays than it was when you were a teenager?

Can you say a little more about that?

## MONEY FRUSTRATIONS

Did you ever feel frustrated in not having enough money to give your children everything that you wanted them to have? Or do you feel that, overall, your family didn't really want for anything?

If you had had more money or time for them, what more would you have liked to have done for your family?

How important do you think money is in raising children right?

## WERE YOU A PRETTY GOOD PARENT?

All in all, do you think you were a pretty good parent to your children when they were growing up?

What, if anything, would you have done differently if you could have the benefit of hindsight? [wait]

What do you think were some of the pressures on you that may have made it difficult to be the kind of parent that you wanted to be?

Do you think there were any lasting bad feelings between you and any of your children over some of the things that went on between you while you were trying to raise them?

## Children's Marriages

### CHILDREN'S MARRIAGES

Are any or all of your children married?

Which ones are married, and whom did they marry?

### CHILDREN'S COURTSHIPS

It is often funny to tell your memories of your children's court-ships—how they acted, your reactions to their spouses, and so on. Take each one in turn and tell me what you remember about them and their spouses at that time in their lives. [wait]

Tell me the story of [name]'s courtship and marriage as you remember it.

## FIRST IMPRESSIONS OF CHILDREN'S SPOUSES

Can you remember the first time [name] brought [name of spouse] around to meet you?

What were your first impressions of your son/daughter's future spouse? Do you remember?

Do you remember being immediately in favor of your son/daughter's choice? Or did you have reservations about the match at the beginning?

Why did you feel that way at the time?

Did you come to change your mind later, and if so, why?

## FUNNY STORIES ABOUT THEIR COURTSHIP

Can you remember any funny stories that you can tell about their courtship?

Maybe a story about their car breaking down and their getting in late?

What did you think of your [name of son/daughter-in-law]'s looks? What did he/she look like when you first met him/her?

What kind of clothes did he/she wear? And what about his/her hair style? What was the general overall impression he/she gave you?

## IN FAVOR OF OR OPPOSED TO THE RELATIONSHIP/ MARRIAGE

When you realized that they were serious, did you oppose the marriage, or did you wholeheartedly support it?

Did you have any reservations about the match?

What were they?

Do you think a reaction like that is typical for parents when one of their children is about to get married?

## CONCERNS ABOUT CHILDREN'S MARRIAGES

What were some of your concerns about [name]'s marriage?

Financial? Did it look to you like they could make it financially?

Stability? Did you have any thoughts about what might happen to the marriage in the long run?

On what did you base your opinions? Do you remember now?

## CHARACTERISTICS OF CHILDREN'S SPOUSES

Describe the person [name] married. What kind of a person is he/she?

Tell me something about [name of son/daughter-in-law] that comes to mind now about the kind of a person he/she is.

There's an old saying: "Birds of a feather flock together." And another old saying is: "Opposites attract." Looking at your son/daughter and his/her spouse, which of these sayings do you think most applies to them? Are they very similar to each other, or are they very different?

Why do you say that? Can you give me an example of what you mean?

[Repeat above "Children's Marriages" questions for each married child.]

## CHILDREN WHO DIDN'T MARRY

Did any of your children never marry?

Why do you think [name] never got married?

Do you think it was that he/she just never met the "right person"? Or do you think it was more something about ____ that just wasn't compatible with married life?

Why do you say that? Why do you think that?

Do you think there is such a thing as the "right person" for someone? Or is it more a matter of being ready for marriage, getting to know someone, and going through a lot of things together?

From your point of view, is it possible for a person to lead a full and happy life without having a family of his or her own?

Do you think ____ has a full and happy life?

It seems like many younger people now are not marrying and having children, and are devoting themselves to their careers and to self-fulfillment outside of marriage and family life. What do you think of this trend in our society?

Why do you say that?

[Repeat above questions for each unmarried child.]

## HOW CHILDREN'S MARRIAGES TURNED OUT

How did your children's marriages turn out?

Do you think that because of changing times your children's marriages were different from your marriage?

Why do you say that?

What are the differences between the institution of marriage in your time and marriage in your children's time?

## THE MAIN PROBLEMS OF MARRIAGE

What do you think are some of the main problems that every young married couple has to face? [wait]

How did you face these problems in your marriage, and how, in your opinion, did your children face them in their marriages?

Do you think that your grandchildren, if they get married, will have to deal with the same kinds of problems? Or have times changed so much that marriage itself is different nowadays, and therefore the problems are different?

Why do you say that?

## CHILDREN'S DIVORCES

Did any of your children's marriages end in divorce?

In your opinion, what led to the divorce? What were the causes?

Was your attitude toward divorce that it represented a "failure," or did you see it as a positive move under the circumstances, an attempt to move on in life in a positive direction?

How much support were you able to offer to your son/daughter during the time of the breakup of his/her marriage?

Were the problems and pressures faced by your son/daughter in his/her marriage different from the problems that you faced in your marriage?

Did you ever have a time of a lot of conflicts and problems in your marriage?

How did you handle your problems in your marriage, and do

you think your methods would have worked for your son/daughter?

## EASIER DIVORCES NOWADAYS

It is certainly true that both legally and in terms of people's values, divorces are easier to obtain nowadays than they were when you were younger. What do you think of this trend in our society?

Do you think the ease of divorce is a good thing or a bad thing?

Why do you say that?

What are some of the advantages that you see of divorces being easier to obtain, and what are some of the disadvantages?

Do you think that if divorces had been as easy to get years ago as they are now, you might have gotten a divorce rather than working through some of your problems?

Can you say a little more about that?

## EFFECT OF DIVORCE ON YOUR GRANDCHILDREN

If there were any children involved, what happened to them?

From your point of view, how do you think the divorce affected your grandchildren? [wait]

Did you see more or less of your grandchildren after the divorce?

How did you feel about that?

## EFFECT OF DIVORCE ON YOUR SON/DAUGHTER

Overall, how do you think your son/daughter came out of his/her experience?

How long did it seem to take before he/she returned to normal and began to have a positive outlook on life again?

## REMARRIAGE

Did he/she remarry?

Do you think that the second marriage was better than the first? Did he/she make a better choice this time?

Why do you say that?

What can you say about some of the characteristics of your son/daughter's second wife/husband? What kind of a person is he/she?

[Repeat for other children if appropriate. Include questions on courtship, spouse characteristics, and so on.]

## Your Children Now

Let's talk briefly about each of your children as they are now. What kind of a person is [name of eldest child]?

Has ____ turned out to be pretty much what you expected when he/she was little? Or have you been surprised by what he/she has done as an adult?

Why do you say that?

[Repeat for each child.]

### DO YOU STILL FEEL LIKE GIVING ADVICE?

Do you still sometimes feel like you'd like to give your children advice and make suggestions about how to avoid mistakes and be happy in life? Even though they are adults now with their own lives to live?

If you could—and if you think they'd listen—what advice would you like to give to them now? [wait]

Let's take [name of first]. From your perspective, what do you think of the life he/she is living, and what would make it better?

[Repeat for each child.]

### A MESSAGE TO EACH CHILD

If you can imagine your children listening to these tapes, say, in twenty-five years or more from now, long after you are gone, what would you like to say to each of them? [wait]

Let's take each one, and imagine him or her listening to this tape in twenty-five years. Say "Hello," and say something especially for him or her in turn.

Start with [name of eldest child]. What do you think he/she would like to hear you say in twenty-five years?

[Repeat for each child.]

Is there anything else that comes to mind that you'd like to say about any of your children now?

# Grandchildren

This is the section of the book where you can ask your narrator to take some time and talk about each of his or her grandchildren. As you might expect, this is usually a very easy section to do—what grandparent doesn't have something to say about his or her grandchildren?

There are specific questions developed for each grandchild, and more general questions about being a grandparent and about the differences between the generations. You can spend fifteen minutes or more on each grandchild, asking your narrator for impressions, advice, and personal messages. There are also additional general questions about how the modern world compares to the world of sixty or seventy years ago.

This is an important interview because in one sense the failure of communication between the grandparents' and grandchildren's generations is the whole point of this book. Because high mobility, urbanization, and cultural forces that encourage segregation of the generations have destroyed opportunities for daily interaction between grandparents and grandchildren, there is a lack of meaningful communication between them. As a result, young people today lack a personal historical perspective. They live in "peer cultures" with a "present-time-bound" mentality. Most of them have not acquired the personal feel for history that comes from absorbing a sense of the past from daily or frequent contact with older relatives. Contact with grandparents, in the words of Margaret Mead, allows children to "measure time in meaningful biological terms—when Grandmother was young, when Mother was young, when I was young."

Another crucial role that grandparents can play in the psychological and emotional development of their grandchildren comes from their ability to show how human beings can adapt to the tremendous social changes that have transformed the world in our time. As Margaret Mead observed, today's grandparent generation has lived through more change in its lifetime than any other generation in history. Because of that, "Grandparents . . . have now become the living repositories of change, living evidence that human beings can adjust, can take in the enormous changes which separate the pre-1945 generations from those raised after the War."*

When grandparents communicate their experiences to grandchildren, they make it possible for their grandchildren to be less fearful of change, and to cling less fiercely to the peer-group, present-bound mentality in which they have grown up.

This is an enjoyable and interesting session. It usually doesn't take a full two hours, probably about an hour or less to cover the topics here. As before, check the questions you want to ask, and get started.

## GENERAL QUESTION

Let's turn now to one of the most important parts of these interviews. I am referring to your thoughts, feelings, impressions, and hopes about your grandchildren. [Wait a few moments to allow your narrator time to make a spontaneous response to the general subject of grandchildren.]

## NAMES, AGES, AND WHICH CHILD'S CHILDREN

How many grandchilden do you have?
What are their names, which of your children do they belong to, and about how old are they now?

## IMPRESSIONS OF EACH GRANDCHILD (GENERAL)

I'd like to ask you to take some time and talk a little about each one of them, and to give me some of your thoughts and impressions about each of them. [wait]

*Mead, Margaret. "Grandparents as Educators," pp 66–75. *The Family as Educator*, Hope Jensen Leachter (Ed). Teachers College Press, Columbia University, New York, 1974.

Why don't we start with your first grandchild? Who was your first grandchild?

## FEELINGS ON FIRST BECOMING A GRANDPARENT

Since [name] was your first grandchild, there are probably some special memories associated with him/her. Can you remember and describe some of your feelings when you first became a grand-mother/grandfather? [wait]

Did your becoming a grandmother/grandfather change the way you thought about yourself at all?

In what ways? How did it change the way you thought about yourself?

What did you actually do when you first heard the news that ____ had been born? Do you remember?

How did you think about your role as a grandparent? What did you think you might be able to do for your grandchildren?

## IMPRESSIONS OF EACH GRANDCHILD (SPECIFIC)

Let's go back now to your impressions of [name of first].
About how old is ____ now?

## TYPE OF PERSONALITY

How would you describe [name]'s personality, in your own words? [wait]

What kind of a person is he/she?

## TEMPERAMENT

What kind of a temperament would you say [name] has?
Would you say he/she is more outgoing or more the quiet type?
Is he/she more of an excitable person or more calm and easygoing?
Is he/she happy and optimistic? Or more on the melancholy side?
Any other characteristics of mood that you notice?

## LOOKS, AND WHO HE/SHE TAKES AFTER

What does he/she look like?
Does [name] "take after" in looks someone else in the family? Do

you see a family resemblance with, perhaps, someone from a different generation of the family?

Which of his/her parents do you think ____ takes after the most?

## A SPECIAL MEMORY OR A FUNNY STORY

Can you tell me a special memory about [name] that sticks in your mind? Something that you two did together perhaps that you remember, or something funny that you saw him/her do?

## WHAT KIND OF AN ADULT HE/SHE WILL BE

From your impression of what kind of a young person [name] is now, what kind of an adult do you think he/she will turn out to be?

Why do you say that?

## ANYTHING OF YOURSELF IN HIM/HER

Do you see anything of yourself in [name]? Either personality traits, or looks, or special skills and talents?

What things in him/her do you see that remind you a bit of yourself?

## SPECIAL CHARACTERISTICS, STRONGEST PERSONALITY TRAITS

Could you identify something especially characteristic about [name] that you see? Something that distinguishes him/her from your other grandchildren?

What would you say are his/her strongest personality traits?

## WHAT FUTURE YOU SEE FOR HIM/HER

What kind of a future do you see ahead for him/her? Do you think you can foresee any of the things he/she will have to go through, based on your experience of the world and your knowledge of the kind of a person [name] is?

What will be the most difficult lesson ____ will have to learn, in your opinion?

What do you think of the world he/she is growing up in?

Could you say a little more about that?

## THINGS YOU ARE PROUD OF AND THINGS THAT WORRY YOU

What are the things about [name] that you are the most proud of? [wait]

And what are the things that disappoint you, or that worry you the most about the way ____'s life seems to be going?

What do you think he/she has to do to change?

## WHAT HE/SHE STILL HAS TO LEARN ABOUT LIFE

What do you think [name] still has to learn about life?

Why do you say that?

## A SPECIAL MESSAGE FOR [NAME]

Imagine [name] listening to this tape, say twenty-five years from now. If you could leave a bit of advice for him/her, or some of your knowledge especially for him/her, what would you say? [wait]

## NEXT GRANDCHILD

Okay, let's go on now and talk about your next grandchild. About how old is [name of next grandchild] now?

[Repeat the questions developed for the first grandchild for each child. Take your time and allow impressions to be expressed. Usually it is easier to discuss the children of one child's family in order, and then go on to the children of your narrator's other children.]

## POET/ARTIST AND PRAGMATIST/REALIST

Of all your grandchildren, which would you say is most like a dreamer, a poetic/artistic type, and which is most like a realist or practical type?

Why do you say that?

Which ones seem to have their heads in the clouds, and which ones are more practical, with their feet on the ground?

Is there anybody from your generation of the family that they take after in this sense? I mean, which of the family members were dreamers, and which were more practical people?

Which of your grandchildren do you think will probably make the most money?

Why do you say that?

Which side of life is more important—the artistic, visionary side, or the practical side?

Why do you say that?

## INTELLECTUAL/ACADEMIC GRANDCHILD, AND MOST SENSITIVE GRANDCHILD

Which of your grandchildren seems to you to be most oriented toward academic success and intellectual achievements? Which one seems to you to be more of a "thinker"?

And which seems to you to feel things most deeply? Which grandchild would you say is the most "sensitive"?

## WHICH WILL HAVE A DIFFICULT TIME IN LIFE, AND WHICH AN EASIER TIME?

Which of your grandchildren do you think will have a more difficult time of it in life, and which seems to you to be more apt to have it easier?

Why do you say that?

## WHAT WILL BE THE MOST DIFFICULT THING FOR YOUR GRANDCHILDREN TO FACE?

Based on your knowledge of what is happening today in the world, and based on your knowledge of your grandchildren, what do you think will be the most difficult thing for them to face in the future?

What do you think will be the greatest problems that your grandchildren's generation will have to overcome?

## YOU AS A GRANDPARENT

What kind of a grandparent are you? How would you describe yourself as a grandparent?

Do you babysit much? Or did you when the kids were young?
Were you able to teach any of your grandchildren any of your
values and outlooks on life when they were growing up?

Were you able to help them out financially?

Were you pretty distant, or were you pretty close to your grandchildren when they were growing up?

Did you have a tendency to spoil them when they were around?

Why do you say that?

Why do you think it seems pretty natural for a grandparent to
spoil a grandchild?


## YOUR EFFECT ON YOUR GRANDCHILDREN

Do you think you had much of an effect on your grandchildren
and on their values when they were growing up?

What things do you think they learned from you?

Which of your values do you wish you'd been better able to pass
on to your grandchildren?

Why do you say that?

What are some of the things that you think are important that
don't seem to be so important to your grandchildren?


## YOUR GRANDCHILDREN'S EFFECT ON YOU

What about your grandchildren's effect on you? Have they been
able to teach you anything about yourself or about the modern
world?

As a result of contact with your grandchildren, have any of your
values changed?

Give me an example. How have you changed some of your ideas
as a result of knowing and talking to your grandchildren?


## DO GRANDCHILDREN EVER ASK ABOUT THE PAST AND
## ABOUT FAMILY HISTORY?

Do your grandchildren ever come to you to find out about the
family's history and about how things were when you were their
age?

What do they seem to want to talk about most?

Do they seem very interested in the history of their family?

How important do you think it is for people to know about their family's traditions and history?

Why do you think that?

## WHAT THEY WANT TO KNOW AND WHAT YOU WANT THEM TO KNOW ABOUT YOU

What do your grandchildren seem to want most to know about you when they come to visit and talk?

What do you most want them to know about you? What do you want them to know about you as a person, and to remember about you?

## CONTACT WITH GRANDCHILDREN

About how often do you see or talk to your grandchildren?

Do you wish you could see them more often?

Do you feel you have a pretty full relationship with your grandchildren? Or do you feel that you are not as involved in their lives as you would like to be?

What would you like to communicate to them or do for them if you did have more contact with them?

## ROLE AS A GRANDPARENT, AND MISTAKES OF GRANDCHILDREN

Do you play a very important role in the lives of your grandchildren now?

Looking back, did your grandparents play a bigger role in your life than you are playing in the lives of your grandchildren?

Why do you think that is?

Do you sometimes wish that you could keep your grandchildren from making mistakes in their lives?

What kinds of mistakes do you think some of them might be making?

Do you think it is ever possible to protect younger people from making mistakes in their lives? Or do you think it's probably better to leave people alone to learn about life in their own way?

Why do you say that?

## IMPORTANCE OF THE GRANDPARENT/GRANDCHILD RELATIONSHIP

How important do you think the relationship is between a grandparent and a grandchild?

Why do you say that?

How important was your relationship with your grandparents when you were growing up?

Do you still think about your own grandparents even now? Do you ever think about some of the things they taught you and about the kind of people they were? Or have they faded in your memory?

## CHILD-REARING TODAY

What is your opinion of the way children are being raised today? [wait]

Why do you say that? Could you talk some more about it?

What would you say is the biggest difference between the way you were raised and the way children are being raised today?

What about the difference between how you raised your children and the way they are raising their children?

If you see differences, what are some of them? How are your grandchildren being raised differently from the way you raised your children?

Suppose you had been the one to raise your grandchildren for some reason. What do you think you might have done differently, or what would you have tried to emphasize more in raising them?

## YOUR CHILDHOOD COMPARED TO YOUR GRANDCHILDREN'S

Do you think your childhood was better than your grandchildren's?

Why do you say that? What was better or worse about it?

## DO CHILDREN HAVE IT EASIER TODAY?

Do children today have it easier than you did when you were young?

Why do you say that?

In what ways do you think they have it easier?

In what ways do you think they have it tougher than you?

Have you ever been angered by the attitude of some young people who seem not to appreciate what they have?

What don't they seem to appreciate enough, in your opinon?

Do you think that in some respects children today might have a harder time growing up than children of your generation did?

Why?

What do you think of the idea that although young people today have more material things, they might be lacking in some spiritual values, or guidance, or something in the realm of feeling?

Can you say a little more about that?

What about the idea that because the world today is so complex and fast moving, children may have a harder time trying to decide on their values than children of an earlier time?

Do you agree with that, or disagree?

## YOUNG PEOPLE'S VALUES

Do you feel that some of the values of younger people are wrong or mistaken? [wait]

Which of their values do you feel this way about?

Why do you feel they are wrong?

Can you think of any examples of young people you know whose values and ideas you disagree with?

## VALUES THAT NEED TO BE PRESERVED

You are an elder of our society, and it is important that you express your opinion about what things are important and should be preserved. From your point of view, what values and ways of behaving are most important and need to be reemphasized?

Do you feel that some of your values and ways of living are in danger of dying out forever in the modern world after your generation is gone?

What values and lessons are those?

Why do you think they might be in danger of dying out in the modern world?

## BEST AND WORST EFFECTS OF MODERN WORLD ON GRANDCHILDREN

What's the worst thing about the way children are being raised today—the worst effect that the modern world has had on your grandchildren?

   Can you say more about that?
And what is the best thing? What's the greatest advantage that young people have who are growing up in the world today?

   Can you think of any other advantages?


## THE FOOD KIDS EAT TODAY

What do you think of the food kids eat today? [wait]


## GREAT-GRANDCHILDREN

Do you have any great-grandchildren?
[If "No"]: Do you think you will live to see any of them?
[If "Yes]: What are their names?

   About how old are they now?
   Whose children are they?
   What are they like? Can you describe them for me?
   How often do you see them?


## WHAT YOU WOULD LIKE THEM TO KNOW ABOUT YOU

If they don't get a chance to get to know you very well, what would you like them to know about you?


## IDEA OF THIS TAPE BEING LISTENED TO IN 50 TO 100 YEARS

What do you think of the idea of sending a message to your great-grandchildren or great-great-grandchildren 50, or 100, or even more years from now?
Do you feel that you have anything to say to people who might be listening, say, 75 years from now?
Does the idea of talking across time to somebody 100 years in the future seem strange or funny to you?
What do you think the world is going to be like then?

## THE WORLD OF YOUR GREAT-GRANDCHILDREN

What kind of a world do you think your great-grandchildren are going to have to grow up in?

Can you say a little more about that?

## A SPECIAL MESSAGE FOR EACH GREAT-GRANDCHILD

Is there anything special you would like to say to or about your great-grandchildren? Something that they might listen to years from now on this tape.

Let's address each of them by name now, and you can say something especially for each of them from you.

# Historical Events

❧❧❧❧❧❧

During the interviews, whenever you are discussing personal or family topics that fit into some kind of chronological framework in your narrator's life, you may want to begin to introduce Historical Events questions. These are general questions that both stimulate your narrator's memory about the time period in question, and provide valuable opportunities to bring "history" down to a personal level, the level at which these events were felt by your narrator. Asking questions like those which follow helps to establish a sense of time perspective in the listener, and helps younger people feel connected to the great historical and mass events of the past.

This historical feeling is one of the important dimensions of personal identity that has been lost or diminished in the modern world. It is one of the consequences of the break-up of close contact across the generations of a family. Asking Historical Events questions is easy and fun for the interviewer, and usually stimulates the narrator to tell stories that are important, both for an understanding of the personality of your narrator, and for the historical sense of perspective of your younger listeners.

Each generation is shaped by the times, and this chapter helps you to direct your narrator's memory to observations about a wide range of historical events and personalities. For example, if you want to understand someone who is now fifty-five to sixty years old, you must attempt to understand what World War II meant

177

to that generation. Similarly, for someone sixty to seventy years old, you must talk about the Great Depression. For someone seventy to eighty years old, it's World War I and the Roaring Twenties, and for someone eighty-five or older, it's World War I and prewar society and culture.

Most of what you record will be of great value to the feelings of the younger members of the family. Older people who have lived through times of war and dislocation, or through periods of expansive prosperity followed by unemployment, are in a unique position to pass on their knowledge and sense of perspective about such events. The reflections of older people on wars or hard times or financial insecurity are crucial to helping younger people cope with their own times of personal and cultural stress. Communicating this experience is a truly important, immediately useful, and deeply needed function that only the older generations can perform for the younger generations.

You can devote a whole session or more to a Historical Events interview, talking your way through the various topics presented here. You can ask a question at random from practically anywhere in this chapter and get an interesting response. Questions about presidents, wars, medical advances, the impact of TV, the atomic bomb, the sexual revolution, and many others are all presented here.

Or you can weave historical events questions into the other interviews. Suppose during your discussion of your narrator's youth and young adulthood you reach a point where you want to ask something more general or historical. You may be bored with the direction of the narrative and just want to introduce a different topic, or your narrator may naturally begin a discussion of what was going on in the world then. It's not very difficult to introduce into the framework of the narrative the subject of historical events. You might phrase something like this:

"Let's take a little different turn now and talk about some historical events. I'd like to ask you about some of your memories of the world events that were going on during the period of your life that we are talking about now. We were discussing your teenage years and early twenties, which would have been from about 1920 to about 1930. What do you remember about what was going on in the world then? [wait] For example, do you remember Prohibition and the Roaring Twenties?"

## THE TURN OF THE CENTURY

Do you remember the turn of the century—New Year's 1900?

Do you remember any big celebrations for the beginning of the twentieth century?

Did you go to one? Or do you remember your parents or family members going to a big turn-of-the-century celebration?

What do you remember?

Where were you living, how old were you, and what were you doing in 1900?


## AUTOMOBILES

How about automobiles? Do you remember when the first automobiles started appearing?

What did people think of them?

What did you think of them?

Can you remember what you felt and thought the first time you saw one?

Who had the first one in your family or neighborhood?

What did the first ones look like?

Did you ever think at that time that they would end up practically taking over the world of transportation?

I suppose at the time that people didn't think much about oil or gasoline, or worry about an energy crisis.


## TRANSPORTATION BEFORE AUTOMOBILES

Before cars came along, did you have a horse to get around on?

What did the horse look like? What was its name?

People just walked most of the places they wanted to go, didn't they?

How did people get around?

Did you ever see a runaway horse? I've heard that a runaway horse was exciting, and something to watch out for.

What did people do when there was a runaway horse?

## LOCOMOTIVES

What about trains? Do you remember the first time you traveled on a railroad train?

Where did you go, and what was it like?

## TELEPHONES

Did you always have a telephone, even when you were young? Or can you remember a time without them?

What did the first phones look like? Did you have a party line? Did you have to go through an operator to place a call?

How did people communicate? By letters? Or did they just live closer together so they could communicate face-to-face more easily?

## ELECTRICITY

Did you always have electricity in your house? Or can you remember a time when it was not available?

What did people use for light and heat without electricity?

Do you remember when electricity first came into your house, and what it was first used for?

Did you have an electric refrigerator? Or did you use an icebox?

What was an icebox like? How long did things stay cold, where did the ice come from, and so on?

What did people think of electricity at first? Did they think it was dangerous, and were they against it, like people today think about nuclear power?

## FIRST AIRPLANE

How about the first airplane? Do you remember that? The first time you ever saw one?

Tell me what you did, and what the other people did, the first time you heard an airplane coming and saw one fly over?

What about the first time you ever rode in one? Do you remember that?

What was the occasion, and where did you go?

What did you think of it?

Would you have believed it then if someone had told you that within your lifetime people would make a trip to the moon and back? If they had told you that when you first heard about airplanes, would you have believed they could progress that far?

What do you think they will accomplish next?

## FIRST PRESIDENT REMEMBERED

Who was the first President of the United States you remember?

1900—McKinley [Ask about any memory of McKinley's assassination in 1901.]

1901—Teddy Roosevelt
1904—Teddy Roosevelt
1908—Taft
1912—Wilson
1916—Wilson
1920—Harding
1924—Coolidge
1928—Hoover
1932—Franklin Roosevelt
1936—Franklin Roosevelt
1940—Franklin Roosevelt
1944—Franklin Roosevelt

What do you remember? Did you ever see him, or did you just hear people talking about him, and read about him in the papers?

## FIRST ELECTION VOTED IN

Do you remember the first election you voted in?
    Do you remember whom you voted for, and why?
Were you very interested in national politics at that time?
    What were some of the issues of the day that people all talked about? Do you remember?
    Did people seem to be as interested in the day-to-day goings-on of the President then as they seem to be today?
What political party did you belong to?
    Why? Why did you support one party and its candidates over the other?

## VAUDEVILLE

What was vaudeville?

   When was its heyday?

   Did you ever go to vaudeville shows?

   Who were some of the stars of it? Do you remember?

   What happened to bring about vaudeville's decline, in your opinion?

      Was it the movies?

## THE *TITANIC*

Do you remember when the *Titanic* sunk?

   What do you remember?

   What did you think and feel, and what was the reaction of other people?

   Did you know of anybody who was killed on the *Titanic*?

   What is it about the sinking of the *Titanic* that still fascinates people even now, seventy years later?

## WORLD WAR I

What do you remember about World War I? [wait]

   How did World War I affect you? [wait]

   Where were you living, and what were you doing around that time—from about 1914–15 through 1919?

Do you remember people talking a lot about the issues of peace and war, and whether the Americans should or should not get involved in the war in Europe?

   Do you remember some of the arguments for and against getting involved in the war?

      What did you think, and why did you think that?

   Wasn't there a lot of argument, not only about whether or not to get involved, but even about what side to go in on?

      Whom do you remember as the people who were "isolationists," that is, against getting into the war, and the people who supported the Americans entering the war?

## THE *LUSITANIA*

Do you remember the sinking of the *Lusitania*?

   What happened as you remember it?

What did it mean to you?

What was its significance? What did it mean to the people of the United States?

## WOODROW WILSON

Do you remember President Woodrow Wilson?

What did you think of him?

What did most people think of him? What was he like as a leader?

Did you vote in any of the elections when he was running for president?

Do you remember anything else important about President Wilson that has stayed in your memory?

## WAS ANYONE YOU KNEW IN THE WAR?

Did you know anybody who had to go to war in World War I?

What happened to them? What branch of the service did they go in, and what experiences did they have?

Was anyone you knew killed in the war?

Who was that? Tell me something about him.

## JOB IN WORLD WAR I

Did you have a job during World War I?

What job was that, and was it related in any way to the war effort?

## SOCIAL CHANGES DURING WORLD WAR I

I've heard that during World War I great social changes took place. People left the farms and moved to town, jobs changed, pay got better, and so on. Do you remember those years as a time of change?

What are some of the changes you remember?

Do you remember a lot of new people coming into your town or neighborhood to live or work during those years? Or did a lot of people leave your area and go elsewhere for work?

What about women going to work in the war effort? Do you remember changes taking place, with women getting good jobs and working outside the home, and so forth?

What did you think of that? In those days, which people were considered "foreigners" or "outsiders"? For example, nowadays Spanish-speaking people and black people are trying to make it in American society. They are trying to climb the economic and social ladders. But back during the years of World War I, what immigrant groups were moving in? The Italians? Germans? Irish?

What did people think of these new groups of people and their ways?

What did you think of them?

[For whites]: Do you remember whether there were many black people around in those days?

Did you have much social contact with black people then?

If you had to summarize those years—the years of World War I— what would you say was the biggest change that took place during that time?

## THE RUSSIAN REVOLUTION

Do you remember reading much or hearing much about the Russian Revolution in 1917? About Lenin, the Bolsheviks, and the Communists?

Were you interested in that?

Why, or why not?

Did people talk about it a lot?

Were people afraid of bolshevism and communism then?

Anything else you remember about people's reactions to the revolution in Russia?

## ARMISTICE DAY

Do you remember Armistice Day when the war finally ended? [wait]

What was that like? I've heard that people went out and danced in the streets and celebrated like never before or since. Is that the way it was?

People have said that the end of World War I saw the greatest outpouring of public emotion that they'd ever seen. The greatest, most joyous public celebration of their lifetimes. Would you agree with that?

Why was it such a happy occasion?
Did you go out and celebrate? What did you do?


## THE FLU EPIDEMIC OF 1918

Do you remember the flu epidemic of 1918?
What was it like?
Did anybody you knew die in that epidemic?
What did people do to try and protect themselves?
Do you think that the more recent strains of flu are comparable
to the 1918 epidemic that you witnessed?
Why, or why not?
Do you think that anything like the flu epidemic of 1918 could
happen again?


## WOMEN'S VOTING RIGHTS

Do you remember when women got the vote? [wait]
Tell me about that.
Do you remember anything about the "women's movement"
or the "suffragette" movement back then? During and after
World War I?
What do you remember about the women's movement during
and after World War I?
[If female]: Did you register and vote?
What did your husband, father, and brothers think about
the movement for women's suffrage? Do you remember?
Do you see any similarities between the women's movement back
then for the vote, and the women's liberation movement we hear
about today, fifty years later?
Why do you say that?
What are the differences, and what are the similarities?


## THE INCOME TAX

Do you remember when the federal income tax first came in?
What did you think of it?
Do you remember any of the debates that went on about it?
At the time, did you have any idea that the income tax, and the

growth of the federal government, would go as far as they have today?

What do you think of this change?

Why do you say that?

## RADIO

Do you remember when radio first came in?

Was it a big thing around your town?

Do you remember when you first got one?

What were some of the first things people listened to on the radio? Do you remember?

What was the situation like when you listened to the radio? Was it more or less like television? Would people come over and sit around the radio to listen to their favorite programs?

What did your first radio look like?

Did people think that radio was "dangerous" and that too much listening to it would help to destroy the morals of the young people, and so on—the way people talk today about television?

## THE TWENTIES

What can you say about the twenties, the Roaring Twenties? We hear so much about what a wild and fun time that was supposed to have been. Can you remember what it felt like to be alive in the twenties? [wait]

Do you agree that it was a wild and exciting time in history?

Why do you say that?

If you agree that the twenties was a wild time, why do you think it was? What caused it to be so wild?

## DANCES IN THE TWENTIES

Did you ever do any of those dances we have heard about, like the Charleston and the Black Bottom?

What were those dances like? Do you remember? Can you describe them?

Where did people go to do them?

Do you remember whether people thought that they were scandalous?

## HAIR BOBBING, WOMEN SMOKING

What was it like when women first began to bob their hair?

[For women]:

Did you bob your hair?

Did you think of it as a new thing to do, and did you consider it to be a bit rebellious?

Was everybody doing it, or just a few women?

Why did women bob their hair?

[For men]:

What did you think when women first began to bob their hair?

Do you remember when your wife or sister(s) or any women you knew first bobbed their hair, and what you thought of it at the time?

How about smoking? Did you, or any women you knew, begin smoking in public about this time?

What was the general attitude toward women smoking then?

What was your attitude toward women smoking back then?


## MUSIC IN THE TWENTIES

How about music in the twenties? What kind of popular music did people listen to then?

I've heard the twenties called the "Golden Age of Jazz." Did you like jazz, or listen to jazz performers?

What else could you say about the music of the twenties? Could you characterize it—its mood, or the kinds of feelings it expressed and communicated?

Do you think the music of the twenties reflected the mood of the times?

What was that mood, according to your recollections?

How did the music of the twenties make you feel?


## MOVIES AND MOVIE STARS

What about movies in the twenties? Did you go to the movies much then?

Do you remember any movie stars that you especially liked or admired?

What roles do you remember them in?

What qualities in them did you especially admire?

## LINDBERGH'S FLIGHT ACROSS THE ATLANTIC

Do you remember when Lindbergh first flew across the Atlantic? Was that exciting or inspirational to you?

Do you remember how you felt about it then, and can you describe what happened and how people felt about it?

How can you communicate how people felt about it to a young person today who has seen men walk on the moon? Do you think it is comparable in terms of human achievement and courage?

## PROHIBITION

What about Prohibition? What was Prohibition all about? What do you remember about it? [wait]

Did you support the movement for Prohibition, or were you against it?

Why?

What exactly was a speakeasy?

Did you ever go to one?

Describe a speakeasy for me. What did you do to get in, and once you were in, what was it like?

Do you think that drinking beer and whiskey during Prohibition was something like young people today smoking marijuana? In the sense that because it was illegal, it was more fun?

What about all the stories of gangsters and violence during Prohibition—stories about Al Capone and other gangsters who controlled the beer and liquor business? What do you remember about that?

Were these activities really very much in the public eye then? Did people hear about it and talk about it a lot?

Did you ever actually see any violence associated with Prohibition or with illegal beer and whiskey?

Did you ever make any "bathtub gin"? Or did you ever make any homemade beer yourself?

How did you make it, and what did it taste like?

## SPORTS FIGURES IN THE TWENTIES

Do you remember some of the great athletes or great teams or great moments in sports during the twenties?

Do you remember Babe Ruth?

Who were some of the great athletes of that era besides Babe Ruth?

Who were they? What did they do?

Did you ever actually see them in person?


## THE STOCK MARKET CRASH OF 1929

I guess everyone your age remembers the stock market crash of 1929. [wait]

What were you doing then?

Where were you living?

Do you remember the events of that week, when the bottom fell out of the market?

What was that like? Can you describe what you felt and what you remember about it?

Did you have any money invested in the stock market?

Did you lose anything in the crash?

Did you know or know of anyone who lost everything in the crash?

What do you think was the cause or causes of the crash, and of the Great Depression that followed?


## THE DEPRESSION

We hear so much about the Great Depression of the 1930s and how it affected people. What can you tell me about your experiences during the Depression? What was it like for you living through the Depression? [wait]

Did you have a job?

Did your husband/wife have a job?

Did anyone in your family really suffer during the Depression? I mean, have a hard time finding work and making ends meet, lose his home, and so on?

Was it hard for you personally to get by during the Depression, or were its effects felt mainly by other people, people not particularly close to you?

## HARD TIMES, FORECLOSURES, POOR PEOPLE, BREAD LINES

Did you personally know of or have much contact with people who were really suffering in the Depression? I mean, people who were on the bread lines or unable to find work.

What was a bread line? Did you ever actually see one?

How about foreclosures on loans, and people losing their property? Did any of these things personally affect you or someone you knew?

What were people's attitudes toward such things?

Did people generally feel that the banks had the right to call in their loans, or did they feel that the banks were wrong and that people had the right to stay in their homes even though they could not pay on time, because there were no jobs and their poverty was not completely their fault?

Can you say a little more about that? What did you think about these issues?


## BANK PANICS

What about bank panics? Do you remember those?

What was a bank panic?

Did you ever actually see or participate in a run on a bank where people all went at once and tried to draw out their money?

What happened? What was it like?

Were you, or was anyone you knew, affected by the bank failures during the Depression? I mean, did you or they actually lose money in a bank failure?

Do you remember when Roosevelt closed all the banks in 1932?

What was that like? What did you think, and what did you do?


## EFFECT OF THE DEPRESSION

How did the Depression affect the ordinary person? [wait]

What did people do to get by? [wait]

Can you say a little more about what kinds of things people did to help each other out during the hard times of the thirties?

## WERE PEOPLE HAPPY, DID THEY STILL BELIEVE IN THE SYSTEM?

I've heard it said that in spite of everything, people still helped one another and still had faith in the system and in their country. Would you agree with that?

Why do you think that was?

Were people able to be happy even during the depths of the Depression? Or was it a pretty bad time to live through, with not much reason or capacity to be happy?

Why do you say that?


## WHY THE UNITED STATES DIDN'T HAVE A REVOLUTION

Why do you think there wasn't a revolution in the United States during the Depression? In other countries, dictatorships took over, but here the main social institutions remained intact. Why was that?

Did you ever hear any revolutionary talk in the thirties?

What about Communists in the thirties? I've heard that their ideas were widely talked about as the Depression got worse. What did you think of their ideas? [wait]


## FRANKLIN ROOSEVELT, ELEANOR ROOSEVELT

What did you think of President Roosevelt? [wait]

What are some of your memories and impressions of him as a person, and as a leader?

Did you ever see him, or hear him talk?

What did you think of his wife, Eleanor Roosevelt? What was she like as a person?

Did you admire her?

Why, or why not?

Did you follow Roosevelt's policies—the various New Deal programs—very closely?

What did you think of them?

Did these programs really help much to get us out of the Depression?

Were the New Deal programs successful, in your opinion?

Why, or why not?

Did you generally support Roosevelt, or were you opposed to him politically and to his policies?

Why, or why not?

Do you remember the election of 1932, the Bank Holiday, and the first 100 days of Roosevelt's administration?

What was that like? Can you describe the feelings of the people and the mood of the country then?

What did Roosevelt do for the people at the depths of the Depression? How important was he in keeping the country together?

## THE LABOR MOVEMENT

You must remember the beginnings of the labor movement, when working people were trying to organize labor unions. [wait]

What can you tell me about that?

Can you tell me anything about your personal experiences, if any, with labor unions or the labor movement?

Did you ever see any demonstrations or picket lines?

Did you ever see any violence, like civil disturbances or riots, associated with the labor movement?

Tell me about that. What did you see, and what happened?

In general, would you say you were in favor of the labor movement, or were you generally opposed to it?

Why did you feel that way?

## THE RADICAL THIRTIES

People talk about the thirties as being politically a radical time. Do you remember any of your impressions of the political activity or the revolutionary talk of those times?

Did you get involved in any of those ideas or activities in any way?

What were the main political and social issues of the day in the thirties?

What did you think of communism at that time?

Did you actually know any Communists who were trying to promote their ideas about the government and the society?

## THE WOBBLIES

Who were the Wobblies, the International Workers of the World? Did you ever hear of them?

I've read they were anarchists or Communists or something like that. Did you know anything about them?

Did ordinary people talk about these kinds of things and follow them in the news?

What did you think of the Wobblies?

Why?

## OTHER POLITICAL FIGURES OF THE THIRTIES

Who were the politicians Huey Long and Father Coughlin, and what do you remember about their programs?

Do you remember hearing about them or listening to them at all?

What did you think of them and their ideas?

## LONG-TERM EFFECT OF THE DEPRESSION ON YOUR VALUES AND PERSONALITY

How do you think living through the Depression affected you? [wait]

Why do you say that?

What would you say was the long-term effect of the Depression on you? How do you think your experience of it colored your values and feelings for the rest of your life? [wait]

Do you think it made you more security conscious?

What about your attitude toward banks? Did the Depression cause you to be reluctant to put your money in banks?

Why?

What about your attitudes toward certain forms of investments, like the stock market or real estate?

What do you think of investing in the stock market today?

What about real estate investments? Did living through the Depression teach you anything about real estate as a good or a bad investment?

What do you think of real estate investments today? Do you think real estate is generally a good investment?

Did living through the Depression make you more conservative or more radical in your political thinking?

Why?

Have you yourself directly benefited from some of the changes that came about as a result of government programs that started during the Depression? I am thinking of things like Social Security, or federally insured deposits in banks, for example.

## DO YOU THINK THERE COULD BE ANOTHER GREAT DEPRESSION?

Do you think we could ever have another Depression like the one in the thirties?

Why?

Do you believe government officials and professors when they say there are enough differences in the laws and in the economy to make another severe Depression like that one impossible?

Why?

## ADVICE ABOUT LIVING THROUGH HARD TIMES

Since you lived through it, and you have learned a lot about economic ups and downs, what advice can you give to younger people about how best to protect themselves and their money? [wait]

If we do ever have another Depression, what should a person do to best survive?

What investments do you think are the best ones to make?

Do you agree that education is generally one of the best investments anyone can make?

## THE RISE OF FASCISM IN EUROPE: HITLER AND MUSSOLINI

Do you remember hearing much about Hitler or Mussolini before World War II broke out?

What did people think of them?

What did you think about them?

Did you feel during the thirties that another war was sure to break out? Did people follow the news in Europe and fear and worry about war breaking out again?

In other words, what was the mood of the times when you heard about the tensions in Europe? Did people really expect war to break out again, or did they more or less hope for the best and try not to think about it too much?

What about Hitler and his persecution of the Jews? Did people hear a lot about it during the thirties, or was it not so much in the public eye?

What about Mussolini and Italian fascism? Did you think about that much? Or did the people you associated with just not think about foreign affairs all that much?

## WHAT IT WAS ABOUT THE TIMES THAT MADE PEOPLE FOLLOW SUCH LEADERS

What was it about the times that made the Germans and Italians follow such leaders? How could such people come to gain power? Have you been able to explain this to yourself?

Do you think that there is a potential in all countries to follow such leaders if things get bad enough? Or do you think that the world is a better place now and that people have learned things?

Why do you say that?

What advice can you give to younger people from your experience about politicians? What do you think people should look out for in a political leader?

Why do you say that? Can you give me an example of what you mean?

## THE RADIO SHOW "WAR OF THE WORLDS"

Do you remember when H. G. Wells's "War of the Worlds" played on the radio and scared everybody out of their wits? That was the radio play about men from Mars invading the earth. I've read that people believed it and panicked because they didn't know it was just a play.

What did you think when you heard about it?

There's a theory that many people were feeling fearful because of their intuition that war was about to break out in Europe. When they heard the play, it gave all their fears a concrete expression. Do you agree with that theory? Does it partly explain why people reacted as they did?

## WHAT YOU FELT WHEN WAR BROKE OUT IN EUROPE

When the Germans finally did invade Poland, and war actually broke out in Europe, what did you feel about it?

Did you think the United States should have gone in the war immediately, or were you more of an isolationist at the time, hoping that it was something that the Germans, French, Russians, British, and Italians could settle among themselves?

Why did you think the United States should, or should not, have immediately become involved in the war?

## PEARL HARBOR

Where were you on the day the Japanese attacked Pearl Harbor? [wait]

Tell me about what happened to you on that day. Tell me the story of that day. [wait]

What did you do?

What did people feel?

Did they feel fear, or confidence in Roosevelt and America, or what?

What did you feel on that day?

Where were you living when the Americans entered the war?

Where were you working?

## WHAT THE AMERICANS WERE FIGHTING FOR

When the time came and the United States entered the war, what did you understand the war to be about? I mean, what was it that the Americans felt they were fighting against, and what were they fighting for?

I don't mean only that America was fighting because a foreign power had attacked us. I mean, what principles did the ordinary person feel we were fighting for?

Do you think the underlying values and principles that we fought for in World War II are still with us today in the United States?

Why do you say that?

## WAS ANYONE IN THE FAMILY IN THE WAR?

Did anyone you knew of in your family have to go into the military?

What happened to them? What branch of the service were they in, and what experiences did they have?

## YOUR WAR EXPERIENCES

Were you directly involved in the war effort?
In what way?
What were some of the things ordinary people did to help out the war effort?
If you were in the service, can you take some time now to tell me about some of your experiences? Where were you, what did you do, and so on? [See section in Youth chapter on military experiences.]

## WAS ANYONE YOU KNEW KILLED IN THE WAR?

Did anyone you knew die in the war?
Who was that?
What was he/she like as a person?
Do you know how he/she died?
Do you think he/she died in vain?
Why, or why not?

## CHANGES IN YOUR LIFE AS A RESULT OF THE WAR

Were there a lot of changes in your life as a result of the war?
In your opinion, what was the biggest change in your life as a result of the war?
Can you say a little more about that?

## TREATMENT OF JAPANESE-AMERICANS

Did you know any Japanese people, or know of any, who were living in this country who were treated badly because their native country was at war with the United States?
What happened to them?
I've read that in California, Japanese people were made to go into concentration camps and that they lost their homes and property and freedom. Do you remember hearing about that, and what did you think of it at the time?

Looking back now, do you still think it was a good or fair policy to take toward Japanese-Americans?

Recently, groups of Japanese-Americans have gone to court to ask the government to pay damages to them for the property they lost and the suffering they experienced during their imprisonment during World War II. Do you think they deserve some money for this?

Why, or why not?

## FOOD AND GAS RATIONING IN WORLD WAR II

Do you remember food and gas rationing?

How did that work?

Do you think we'll see rationing again, considering all the talk about the energy crisis, potential gas shortages, and so on?

Do you have any pointers about how to get along and survive under a rationing system? How did you economize and stretch your supplies?

## BLACKOUTS

Do you remember blackouts during World War II? What was a blackout?

What were blackout curtains? Did you have them in your house?

What was a blackout supposed to accomplish?

## VICTORY GARDENS

What were victory gardens?

Did you have one?

## SOCIAL CHANGES DURING THE WAR

Historians say that during the war years, many more rural people moved into the cities, and that black people and women began to take jobs they could never get before and began to be paid more. Do you remember being aware of these trends where you were living?

What did you think of more and more women working outside of the home, in factories and offices?

[For nonblack narrators]: What about blacks? Do you remember more black people coming to your area to work?

What did you think of that?

Did you have much social contact with black people in those days?

[For black narrators]: Did you move from where you were living to take advantage of new job opportunities during the war?

Where did you move from, and where did you move to?

Did you have much social contact with whites in those days?

Who was Rosie the Riveter?

What were some of the jobs that women started to perform during the war years that they couldn't have gotten at any other time?

## WHAT ORDINARY PEOPLE DID TO SUPPORT THE WAR EFFORT

What were some of the things ordinary people did to support the war effort, if they weren't actually in the service?

What were some of the things you and your family did, that you remember?

Did you buy war bonds?

Did you have to forgo pay raises and promotions during the war?

How about food? Did you have meatless days, and so on?

What was a meatless day?

What else did people do to support the war against fascism?

## MORE MEMORIES OF THE WAR YEARS: 1939–45

What other important things do you remember about the years of World War II? [wait]

What can you say about the mood or the feeling of those times to a younger person who wants to understand what living through World War II was like?

Did you ever doubt that the United States and its allies would win the war? Was there ever a time when it looked bleak for the future of democracy in the world?

## ROOSEVELT AS A LEADER

What was Roosevelt like as a leader during the war? [wait]
  Did he inspire confidence in the people?
    How did he do that?
  I've heard that he had a unique quality in his voice, a quality that made people feel he could be trusted. Is this true, or just the memories of people who loved Roosevelt?
  What about his handicap? What did people think about his being in a wheelchair?
  Do you think that in some ways Roosevelt was too powerful? That he might have become a dictator himself in some ways?
    Why, or why not?

## ELEANOR ROOSEVELT

Why was Eleanor Roosevelt admired so much?
  What did you think of her?

## ROOSEVELT'S DEATH, TRUMAN

What did you feel when you heard Roosevelt had died? [wait]
Do you remember what you were doing on the day you heard the news?
Describe what you remember of how people behaved, and how they felt when Roosevelt died.
What did you think of Truman at the time?

## THE ATOMIC BOMB

Do you remember when they dropped the atomic bomb on Japan? [wait]
  What do you remember about that day?
  What did you think of it? Do you remember how you felt?
  How did other people react to it?
  Did you think about what it meant for the future? Or were you just thankful that the war was finally over?
  Did people understand what had happened? Did they understand then what the atomic bomb was, and what it meant for the future of mankind?

People have criticized the United States for dropping the bomb. They say that the military could have selected a deserted island and dropped it there, to demonstrate to the Japanese that they had no chance except to surrender. Instead they chose to drop the bomb on two cities and killed thousands and thousands of people. What do you think of this criticism?

Why do you say that?

## YOUR FEELINGS WHEN THE WAR ENDED

How did you feel when the war finally ended?

What did you do on that day?

[If narrator is old enough]: How would you compare the end of World War I to the end of World War II?

How would you compare the mood of the people?

## NAZI ATROCITIES

How did you feel when people began to realize what evils the Nazis had done in World War II? [wait]

How do you think such things could happen—the systematic, bureaucratic murder of millions of innocent people, Jews, Gypsies, and others? Have you ever tried to explain to yourself how human beings could do such things?

What have you concluded?

Do you think that the German people and culture were basically different from other people in their capacity for evil? Or do you think that something like Nazism could happen anywhere, given the same circumstances and the same type of leaders?

Could you say a little more about that?

## IMPORTANCE OF WORLD WAR II TO YOUR GENERATION

So far, World War II has been the greatest mobilization of human effort of the twentieth century. It shaped the people who lived through those years, and its outcome has shaped all of the events of the second half of this century. Do you agree that if someone younger than you wants to understand your generation, he or she has to understand what World War II meant to people your age, and to other people old enough to have lived through it? [wait]

Why do you say that?

What was the meaning of World War II? What did it mean to you and your generation to defeat fascism in Europe and Japan? [wait]

Can you describe what it felt like to live through those years, to follow the war, to participate in the war effort, and finally to see peace?

Do you find it strange that now the United States regards communism as its great enemy, and Russia as its adversary, but that during World War II the Russians and Americans were allies against the Germans?

How do you explain that?

Do you agree that World War II is the most important "historical event" to understand if a younger person wants to understand your generation? Or do you think other historical events are of equal importance in understanding your generation?

What events were those?

Why do you say that?

## WONDER DRUGS AND MODERN MEDICINE

Do you remember when the wonder drugs of modern medicine first started to come out? Like penicillin or sulfa drugs?

Do you know anybody who was saved by these drugs?

Do you know of anybody who died before we had these drugs who probably would have been saved if they had been invented earlier?

Who was that?

## MODERN APPLIANCES

How about the beginnings of modern appliances around the house, like washing machines, dryers, vacuum cleaners, food disposals, and so on? Did these make much of a difference in your life? Did they seem to give you and your family more leisure time?

Do you remember your first washing machine?

What make was it?

What about your first refrigerator/freezer?

If you remember iceboxes, how did they work? Where did the ice come from, how long did things stay cold, and so on?

## THE SUBURBS

When did people start to move to the suburbs? When did the suburbs start to be built up?

Did you move to the suburbs yourself?

Do you think the suburbs are a good place to raise kids, and a good place to live?

Why, or why not?

Why did so many people start moving out to the suburbs following World War II? What was the attraction?

What do you think of the idea that the suburbs are too boring, that there is too much sameness and lack of diversity, so people who grow up there don't really learn much about how to get along in a world with many, many different kinds of people and different values?

Do you remember any vacant land that you could have bought years ago that is now completely developed into houses and shopping malls?

Where was the edge of the city that you remember from after the war?

## THE CHINESE COMMUNIST REVOLUTION

Do you remember reading about or hearing much about the Communist revolution in China? About Mao Tse-tung and the defeat of the Nationalist Chinese?

What did people think about that?

Did people follow what was happening very closely?

What did you think of it?

## TELEVISION: FIRST EXPERIENCES AND IMPACT ON SOCIETY

Tell me about your first experiences with television. What did you think of it at first?

Do you remember any of the first programs you used to watch?

When did your family first buy a TV? Did you get one when they first came out? Or did you wait a while?

At that time, did people criticize TV and the values it promoted? Or was it thought of more as an exciting invention and as entertainment?

What did you think of it?

Did you have any idea then that it would become so important in the lives and daily routine of most people in our society?

Some people say that TV is the most important day-to-day change that has taken place in people's lives in the postwar period. Do you agree with that?

Do you think that too much TV is bad for children?

Why?

What do you think can be done about it?

## POLIO AND THE POLIO VACCINE

What kind of a disease was polio?

Did you know anybody who had it, or who died of it?

When the vaccine for polio first came out, what did people feel about it? Was it thought of as a great miracle of modern medicine?

Do you think that someday cancer, which is the most frightening disease of our time, will also be conquered by modern medical science?

## THE KOREAN WAR

Did the Korean War of the early 1950s have much of an effect on you or on any of the people you knew?

What kind of a war was the Korean War? Did people think of it in the same way as they thought of World War II?

Why were the Americans fighting in Korea? Did it seem clear to you and to the ordinary person just what the Americans were doing in a war halfway around the world?

Did people think it was a war to stop communism?

Did anyone you knew have to go over there and serve in the army?

Did anyone you knew get killed in the Korean War?

What happened to him?

What kind of a person was he?

Do you think he died in vain?

Why, or why not?

## McCARTHY AND McCARTHYISM

I've heard a lot about Joseph McCarthy and the McCarthy Era when everybody was so frightened about the "Communist Menace" and so on. What do you remember about those times? What was that all about?

Do you remember Senator McCarthy as a public figure?

What did you think of him?

Do you think he exaggerated the influence of Communists in the American government, or was he pretty much on the right track?

Why do you think people characterized McCarthy's practices as "witch-hunting"? Do you agree that he was a destructive figure in American politics?

Why do you say that?

## COMMUNISM

What do you think of communism? [wait]

What do you think communism is? Could you describe your understanding of communism in a few words?

Have you ever actually known someone who was a Communist?

What kind of people do you think become Communists?

Do you think communism is evil?

Why, or why not?

Do you think that communism is a real danger to the things you feel are most important, or do you think that some people are paranoid about it and exaggerate things?

Why do you say that?

## AIRPLANES

Have you ever flown in an airplane?

When was the first time you ever flew? In what kind of a plane, and where did you go?

What was the flight like?

What do you think about airplane travel?

In your life, you've seen a lot of changes in people's ways of traveling. Is it still amazing to you that you can travel by airplane in a couple of hours to places where it would have taken you days and days before?

When you first saw an airplane, did you ever think air travel would progress the way it has—halfway around the world in hours, and to the moon and back?

What do you think of that?

What's the farthest you've ever flown on an airplane? The longest distance you've traveled?

Do you remember the first airplane you ever saw? What did people do, and what did they think of it?


## PRESIDENT EISENHOWER

What did you think of Eisenhower as president?

Does anything stand out now from your impressions of Eisenhower as a man and as a leader?

Did you ever see him, or hear him talk?


## THE CIVIL RIGHTS MOVEMENT OF THE 1960S, AND RACISM

What were your impressions of the civil rights movement of the 1960s when black people in the United States started demonstrating, sitting down in bus stations, and so on, to get equal rights?

What do you think were the causes of their protests and demonstrations?

Did you understand what they were trying to do? Were you on their side?

Do you think there is still a lot of prejudice against black people?

In your opinion, what is the cause, or causes, of prejudice against black people?

Do you think that black people are themselves prejudiced against white people and other people in the same way? Or have they reacted to prejudice against them that was there in the first place?

[If nonblack]: If you look into your heart, do you find that you have any bad feelings or prejudices against black people?

Why, or why not?

Do you think that eventually the prejudice against black people will gradually just go away, in the same way that prejudices against

Italians or Irish people has diminished? Or do you think the case of black people is different?

Why?

Do you think that the different races are basically different, or do you think that they are all basically equal, and that the differences between them are just the result of different customs, values, and opportunities?

Why do you think that?

Do you think that World War II, especially against Hitler and his philosophy, was a war against racism and ideas of racial superiority, because of all the Nazi talk about the "master race" and so on?

If so, do you see any similarities between the racial prejudices that some people feel against black people, and the discredited racial philosophies of the Nazis?

What do you think about that?

Do you think that racial prejudice is a serious danger to the peace of the world?

If so, what do you think people can do to overcome it in themselves and in others?

## PRESIDENT KENNEDY'S ASSASSINATION

Do you remember President Kennedy's assassination? [wait]

What were you doing when you heard the news?

Can you describe what you felt and thought, and what you did?

Do you believe that there was a plot to kill Kennedy that has been covered up, or do you think that Oswald acted alone?

Why do you think that?

Do you think we'll ever really know the truth?

Do you think the course of world history would have been very different if he had not been killed?

Why? What would have been different?

If you think Kennedy was murdered as part of a plot, why do you think somebody wanted him dead? Why was he killed?

A few years ago, newspapers published evidence of how certain secret agencies of our government had plotted to have foreign leaders killed—for example, people in the CIA tried to have Castro killed, and so on. If this is true, do you think these goings-on might have had something to do with Kennedy being assassinated?

## THE VIETNAM WAR

What did you think about the Vietnam War? [wait]

Many people were opposed to the Vietnam War because they thought that the war was immoral and did not believe in fighting it. From your greater age and experience of other wars, would you say that the war in Vietnam was any different from, or less necessary than, the other wars of your lifetime?

Why do you say that?

In your opinion, what were the Americans fighting for in Vietnam? If it was so clear what World War II was all about, and it was so clear then that we should be fighting against fascism and totalitarianism, why was it so unclear and controversial what we were doing in Vietnam? Do you have any ideas about that?

What was your opinion of the peace demonstrations that went on all over the country as people began to try to get the government to end the war?

Do you think the demonstrators were sincere?

Did you agree with them?

Why, or why not?

Did you personally ever go on a demonstration against the Vietnam War?

Why, or why not?

Do you think, all in all, that the demonstrations did any good, or do you think that they were harmful?

Why?

Were you personally affected by the Vietnam War? For example, were any of your relatives in the war, or was anyone you knew?

Was anyone you knew killed in the Vietnam War?

What kind of a person was he?

Do you think he died in vain?

Why, or why not?


## MARTIN LUTHER KING'S ASSASSINATION

How did the murder of Dr. Martin Luther King affect you? [wait]

What kind of a man do you think he was?

Could you say a little more about your impressions of him?

Did you ever hear him speak? If so, where was that?

Do you think they got the truth about who shot him, and why? Or do you think there was a cover-up?

Why do you think that?

Were you affected by any of the riots that exploded all over the country in 1968 after he was killed?

In what way were you affected?

## PRESIDENT NIXON

What did you think of President Nixon? [wait]

What did you think of Watergate? [wait]

Were you glad when he finally resigned from the presidency, or did you feel sorry for him, or both?

Why?

What was the mood of those times? How do you remember people feeling about Nixon and Watergate? [wait]

Do you think he was guilty of the crimes he was accused of committing—obstructing justice, covering up, and so on?

Do you think it was right that he should have resigned from office?

Do you think he should have stood trial and possibly gone to jail?

Why, or why not?

## PRESIDENT FORD

What did you think of President Ford?

Do you think he was right to pardon Nixon?

Why, or why not?

## PRESIDENT CARTER

What kind of a President was Jimmy Carter? How would you rate him compared to the other presidents you have seen?

Why do you say that?

What do you remember about the hostages in Iran? What should the United States have done about that that it didn't do?

## PRESIDENT REAGAN

How would you rate President Reagan compared to the other presidents you have seen?

Why do you say that?

What do you think of President Reagan's age? He is the oldest president the United States has ever had.

Do you think his energy and obvious ability is doing something to change people's attitudes about the capabilities of older people?

## RATE THE PRESIDENTS YOU HAVE SEEN

Of all the presidents you have seen in your lifetime, which was the best, in your opinion?

Why do you say that? What characteristics make you choose him?

And which was the worst, in your opinion?

Why? Why was he the worst?

## WOMEN'S LIBERATION

Have you been affected in any way by the women's liberation movement of recent years?

In what way have you been affected?

What do you think of women's liberation? [wait]

What do you think it's all about? What do you think these women are trying to accomplish?

Do you think they are right? Are you on their side?

Are you in favor of the Equal Rights Amendment to the Constitution that has been the focus of so much political activity by the women's movement?

Why, or why not?

Do you see many differences between the women's suffrage movement for the vote in 1915–20 and the modern women's movement?

What are the main differences, in your opinion?

Would your life have been any different if there had been a women's liberation movement like the one today when you were younger?

In what ways do you think your life might have been different

if there had been equal job opportunity for women, equal pay,
and so on for women when you were younger?

Do you think we will ever have a woman as President of the United
States?

Why, or why not?

What do you think of the idea of a woman president?

What do you think of the idea of a woman vice president? Do
you think it's an idea whose time has come?

What did you think of the nomination of Geraldine Ferraro as the
vice presidential candidate by the Democrats in 1984? [wait]

What was your impression of her as a person and as a possible
president?

How important do you think her nomination and campaign
were to young women and to the image of what women can
accomplish?

Why do you say that?


## OVERPOPULATION

What do you think of there being so many people around these
days? Do you think overpopulation is a serious problem?

Was it different in your youth? Does it seem to you that things
are more crowded now than they were then?

Some people say that overpopulation is the most serious problem
that the world faces today. Do you agree with that?

Why, or why not?


## THE ENERGY PROBLEM AND NUCLEAR POWER

What about the energy crisis? What are your thoughts about that?
[wait]

Has the price of gasoline and oil directly affected you very much?

In what ways?

What kind of a car do you drive now, and how much mileage
does it get?

Do you think it's a good idea to have all of these nuclear power
plants all over the place? [wait]

Do you agree or disagree with the idea that nuclear plants should
be shut down and people should try to conserve more and rely

more on safe sources of energy, such as solar or wind power?

Why, or why not?

Do you think nuclear power plants are dangerous?

What did you think of the nuclear reactor meltdown accident at Three Mile Island a few years ago? That's where they had to shut down the reactor and a lot of radiation almost leaked out.

What are your thoughts about the first nuclear meltdown in history—the accident in the Soviet Union at Chernobyl in May of 1986?

Do you think something like a meltdown could happen again?

Would you ever live next to or near a nuclear power plant?

Why, or why not?

Do you think there is or was really an energy crisis, or do you think it has just been made up by the oil companies and the newspapers and TV?

## NUCLEAR WEAPONS AND THE THREAT OF NUCLEAR WAR

What are your thoughts and feelings about nuclear weapons and the threat of nuclear war in the world today? [wait]

Do you think this is the greatest danger that the human species has ever faced?

Could you talk about this a little more?

Do you think that a nuclear war would mean the end of all life on this planet, or do you think that some humans might survive?

When the atomic bomb was dropped in Japan to end World War II, did you then realize that a completely new era in human history had begun? Did people realize what had happened then?

What do you think should be done about this danger? Do you think the average person can do anything?

What advice could you give to a younger person, from your perspective, about coping with the threat of nuclear warfare in the world today?

## THE MASS MEDIA

How do you feel about the influence of the mass media—radio, TV, newspapers, and so on—in our society today?

Do you think the newspeople, for example, have too much power and influence in our society, or do you think they do a pretty good job of keeping people informed?

Compared to news coverage before TV, when people mostly read newspapers and later listened to the radio, how much more or less informed are you now?

What's the big difference now? Is it just the speed with which people find out about things?

Is it better to read an article about something, or watch a TV show about it?

Why do you say that?

## OUTER SPACE, ASTRONAUTS, SPACE TRAVEL

What are some of your thoughts on mankind exploring outer space? [wait]

What did you think of the astronauts traveling to the moon and back? [wait]

Do you think that someday people will travel to other planets and stars, and maybe live on them?

What do you think of that?

Would you like to take a trip into outer space?

Do you think it is mankind's destiny to travel to other stars and planets someday? Is it mankind's destiny to colonize the galaxy?

## A WORLD GOVERNMENT

Do you think that someday there will be just one government for the whole world? National states will cease to exist, and all the people of the world will live together and be united under one government, like the United Nations, but more effective.

If you think there might one day be a world government, do you think then that maybe mankind will evolve to the point where war will no longer be necessary?

How far away are we from such a state of affairs, in your opinion?

## THE SEXUAL REVOLUTION, ABORTION, HOMOSEXUALITY

What is your opinion of the so-called "sexual revolution" of today, where young people are having sexual relations at younger and younger ages, teenage pregnancy rates are up, and marriage is no longer thought to be important as a context for sexual relations? [wait]

Why do you think that?

What are some of the positive things, and some of the negative things, that you see about the new sexual freedom?

Do you think birth control techniques and the medical conquest of most forms of venereal disease have contributed to modern sexual values?

What about herpes? Do you think herpes is a kind of deserved punishment for those who are sexually promiscuous?

Can you say a little more about that?

What about legalized abortion? Is this part of the modern sexual revolution, and what do you think of it?

What about the idea that sex is for pleasure, and need not be a part of either marriage or the desire to have children? Do you agree or disagree with this attitude, and why or why not?

What about homosexuality? What do you think of gay people, or of people who prefer their own sex?

Do you think there is something wrong with them?

Why, or why not?

Have you ever known a homosexual?

Do you think homosexuality was just as common when you were younger, but now people just talk about it more openly?

What about sex on television? Do you think that there is too much sex shown on TV? Or doesn't it matter all that much?

If you think so, why do you think so? What damage does watching sex on TV do to the viewers?

What do you think of magazines like *Playboy*, *Penthouse*, *Hustler*, and other sexually oriented magazines?

Do you think they should be sold publicly to whoever wants them?

Why, or why not?

In general, what do you think of the trend in modern society that allows people to look at more nudity and sexually explicit photographs, films, and stories?

Why do you say that?

## TECHNOLOGY AND TECHNOLOGICAL CHANGE

What do you think about all the technology that surrounds us today—computers, chemicals of all kinds, nuclear power, and all of the gadgets to do everything you can think of? Do you think there's too much technology around today, and that people might be better off getting closer to nature?

Why do you say that?

What about the speed of change? Things change so fast nowadays. New inventions appear, and within a few years they have changed our lives. I'm thinking of TV, or of medical treatments like organ transplants, or computers. How can a person keep up with what's new?

How do you keep up with all the new things coming out?

Do you think that these changes are for the better, or for the worse? [wait]

Why, or why not?

## BIGGEST DIFFERENCE BETWEEN LIFE TODAY AND LIFE WHEN YOU WERE YOUNG

If you thought about, and picked out one aspect of the modern world that strikes you as the biggest change from when you were growing up, what would you say? What's the biggest difference between life today and life when you were young? [wait]

If you can't think of just one thing, mention a few things that come to mind that you think are the biggest changes or differences.

## WHAT THINGS STAY THE SAME?

What things are always the same, even though the world seems to have changed so much? [wait]

I mean, what things do you think every person has to face no matter what period in history he is born into? [wait]

I'm thinking of things like the fact that all people have to make a living, find meaning in their lives, cope with sadness and loss of loved ones, come to terms with growing old, and come to terms with death. Do you agree that these things and others are universal for everyone, and that in that sense history doesn't matter?

Can you say anything more about this subject?

## ADVICE TO YOUNGER PEOPLE ON COPING WITH CHANGE

Could you give any advice, based on your experience, to younger people today on how to get along and cope with all the new ideas and things that are likely to come along during the course of their lives? We are sure to witness more wars, inventions, social changes, economic problems, and so on. How can a younger person prepare himself or herself for that?

Can you say a little more about that?

Your generation has lived through such tremendous changes in this century that just by living through it you are something of an expert on coping with change and new ideas. How did you do it? [wait]

Are you still interested in new inventions and new ideas?

What new inventions are interesting to you now?

How do you keep an open mind about these things?

## ANYTHING I FORGOT TO ASK ABOUT YOUR LIFE IN THE TWENTIETH CENTURY

Is there anything else that I forgot to ask about, or that you would like to say about your life in the twentieth century?

## THANK YOU

Thank you very much for talking with me.

# *General Questions, Unusual Life Experiences, and Personal Philosophy and Values*

To many people, the questions developed in this chapter are the most interesting of all. This chapter is not meant to be the first one you consult in your Life History Interview. These are more the kinds of questions you will begin asking after you have established some rapport with your speaker, and after he or she has become more sure of what is involved in the interview sessions.

Many of these questions are matter-of-fact, light, or humorous; many others are about serious topics. As in the previous sections, you should go through this chapter and mark those topics which you find interesting and which you think others might like to hear your speaker talk about. There is a wide range of topics covered here. In general, these questions are somewhat more introspective, their purpose partly to try to provide a way to approach some of the wisdom and life philosophy that many people have achieved, and partly to elicit responses on the unique events of your narrator's life.

Some of these questions are about "issues," such as abortion, the sexual revolution, or civil or political disorders. Important

217

basic values and emotions underlie your speaker's answers to questions like these, which help to reveal what kind of a person your narrator is. Other questions are more subjective and less "issue oriented." For example, the question on "Anything Strange or Unusual" that has happened to your narrator opens the door to a discussion of occult or psychic beliefs. Such beliefs and feelings are often passed on in families, and it is interesting to hear people talk about their ideas on these subjects. Stories about natural disasters are interesting and exciting. I've heard many tales about escapes from fires, tornadoes, and great storms. One man I interviewed was in the San Francisco earthquake as a young boy. The "Closest Brush with Death" question opens up the way to a general discussion about death and dying and mortality. These questions, along with the ones about sex and the sexual revolution, can be most difficult to ask, especially if you are interviewing one of your own parents. But if you can ask some of these questions (use your intuition and the rapport you have to know whether it's best to ask these questions or skip over them) you can get some extraordinarily valuable responses and reach a level of communication with an older relative that you may never have reached before.

This chapter is usually not meant to be gone through in a single session. Rather, you can come back to different questions developed here when you feel like changing the direction or tone of another interview session. Or, you might want to spend fifteen minutes or so of each session after the first few on questions from this chapter. Included are questions about ESP, death and dying, friendship, sports, dreams, fashions, religion, TV values, outer space, the sexual revolution, anxieties in the modern world, old age, marriage, art, changes in the modern world, and many others. Each one will help your narrator to reveal a part of himself or herself to you and to future listeners and viewers. Asking these questions can prove to be highly rewarding to your goal of stimulating your narrator to express his or her personality and life story in the most characteristic and personal way.

## Superstitions, ESP, Psychic Experiences

### ANYTHING STRANGE OR UNUSUAL

Has anything strange or unusual ever happened to you? [wait]

Something that you couldn't explain? [wait]
Tell me about it.

## ESP

Do you believe in ESP?
Why, or why not?
Have you ever experienced ESP, or known of anybody who did?
Tell me about that.
If ESP exists, how do you think it might work? What is your theory about what causes ESP experiences?
Did you ever have a premonition—a feeling or a hunch that something was going to happen before it happened?
Tell me that story. What happened?
Did you ever have a premonition that somebody was going to die before he or she died? Or that there was going to be or had been an accident? Or do you know of such a story?
Tell me that story. What happened?

## GHOSTS, SOULS, SEANCES

Do you know any stories about ghosts, or about haunted houses?
Did you ever see a ghost? Or something that you think might have been a ghost?
Tell me that story. What did you see?
Do you believe that the soul of the dead stays around for a while after a person dies?
Do you believe that human beings have souls?
What is a soul?
Have you ever attended a seance, or known anybody who did?
What happened?
What do you think of those kinds of things?
Have you ever felt the presence of a dead person, even though he or she was unmistakably gone, dead, and buried?
If so, what do you think explains that?
When you were a child, was there a "haunted house" in your neighborhood?
Can you describe it, and tell of any funny or scary things that you did there?

## UFO'S

Do you believe in UFO's? That is, unidentified flying objects, or flying saucers?

> Why, or why not?
>
> Have you ever seen something in the sky that might have been a flying saucer, possibly of extraterrestrial origin—from outer space or from another planet?
>
>> Tell me what you saw, and what you think it was.
>
> Do you think UFO's are spaceships from other planets or solar systems, or do you think they just exist in the imaginations of the people who think they see them?
>
>> Why do you say that?

## PSYCHIC EXPERIENCES, FORTUNE-TELLERS

Have you, or anyone you know of in your family, ever had or claimed to have had psychic experiences of any kind?

> Like visions, or being able to heal certain illnesses, telling what another person is thinking, foretelling the future, and so on? [wait]
>
>> Who has had any of these experiences that you know of?

Do you believe that psychic experiences really exist and have something to do with a supernatural world, or do you think that psychic experiences are really just the workings of people's imaginations and aren't true?

> Why do you say that?

Have you ever visited a fortune-teller?

> What did she say? Can you tell me what happened?

## SUPERSTITIONS/GAMBLING

Are you superstitious?

> What are some of the superstitions that you believe in? For example, will you walk under a ladder, or open an umbrella inside the house?
>
>> Any others?
>
> Was your mother or father superstitious?

Do you believe in good luck?

> What's the luckiest thing that ever happened to you?

Do you believe in bad luck?

What's the unluckiest thing that ever happened to you?

Were you ever lucky at gambling, or did you ever win anything at a drawing, or something like that?

Do you or did you ever like to gamble?

What kind of gambling? Sports? Cards? Casino?

Which sports, card games, and casino games are or were your favorites?

What's the most money you ever won gambling?

Tell me the story. How did you win?

What's the most money you ever lost gambling?

Tell me that story. What happened?

Based on your experience, do you have any tips for anyone who might want to gamble?

Under what circumstances should one never gamble?

Is there anyone in the family, or in the history of the family that you know of, who had unusually good luck? Or bad luck?

Who was that, and what are some of the stories about him/her?


## Natural Disasters, Fires, Weather

### FIRES, EARTHQUAKES, TORNADOES, OR OTHER NATURAL DISASTERS

Have you even been in or seen a forest fire?

Where? What happened? Can you tell me about it?

What about other natural disasters? Have you ever seen or been in a tornado, flood, hurricane, or earthquake?

Where and when?

What happened? Can you describe it, and tell the story?


### FIRE IN A HOUSE OR BUILDING

Have you ever been in a fire in a house or a building?

Where and when was this, and what happened?


### DROUGHTS AND DUST STORMS

Have you ever been in an area where there was a really bad drought?

When was that? What happened? Can you describe it?

Did you ever see a dust storm?
  When was that? What was it like? Can you describe it?

## FLOODS

Have you ever been in or seen a flood?
  Where and when?
  What happened? Can you describe it and tell the story?

## COLDER WINTERS AND HOTTER SUMMERS

Do you think winters were rougher in the old days?
  What's the coldest and hardest winter you remember?
    What happened that winter? What did the people do?
What kind of heat did your house have when you were growing up?
  What did the family do to keep warm?
What's the biggest snowstorm or blizzard you remember?
  What was it like? What happened, and what did you do?
How about summers? Were they hotter and drier in the old days?
  What's the hottest summer you remember?
  What happened then? What did the people do?

# Death and Dying

## MAJOR ILLNESSES AND CLOSENESS TO DEATH

Have you ever had any major, serious illnesses in your life?
  What happened? When was that, and how did it come about?
  What kind of treatment did you undergo?
  Were you close to death at that time?
    Did your closeness to death bring about any changes in you or in your values afterward?
    What effect do you think this had on you?

## CLOSEST BRUSH WITH DEATH

What's the closest you've ever been to your own death? Did you ever have a "brush with death" through an accident or an illness?
  Tell me the story. What happened?

Do you remember what went through your head at that time?
At that very moment, or at the time of greatest crisis? [wait]
> Some people say that a drowning man's life flashes before his eyes at that moment. Did anything like that happen to you in your brush with death?

How did this experience with death change your life afterward? [wait]
> Can you say anything more about that?

## THOUGHTS ABOUT DEATH

Do you think much about death now? [wait]
> What do you think about it?
>
> Have you evolved your own philosophy about death and what it means to you?

Do you fear death?
> Why, or why not?

What do you think one's attitude toward death should be? [wait]
> Do you think a philosophical or religious attitude is most meaningful? Or would you say fortitude and courage in the face of death are virtues?

Are you ready to die? I don't mean right now, but would you say that you have accepted the fact that you will die?

## AFTERLIFE

What do you think happens to people when they die? [wait]
> Do you believe in an afterlife?
>
> If so, what do you think it might be like?

Do you think you'll see your mother and father, or your spouse and all those you have lost when you die? [wait]

## A CRUCIAL PERIOD IN YOUR LIFE WHEN YOU CONFRONTED YOUR OWN MORTALITY

Was there ever a period of time in your life when you were terribly afraid of dying? Or when you were seized with dread at the idea of death, and realized deep down your own mortality?
> When was that?
>
> What was going on in your life at that time?

How did you deal with those feelings? How did you come to resolve them?
Did you ever have a dream about your own death?
What was the dream?

## THOUGHTS FOR THE YOUNG ABOUT DEATH AND DYING

Could you say anything to your grandchildren or great-grandchildren or other younger people about their fears and concerns about death and dying, and their desire to live a full life in spite of the fact that we are mortal? [wait]
Do you think that young people are more afraid of dying than old people?
Why do you say that?

## MOURNING, THE DEATH OF A LOVED ONE

From your experience with the death of a loved one, about how long does it take to pass through a period of mourning after you lose somebody?
What should a person expect? Several months? A year or more? From your experience, how long before you start to feel good about things again?
What could you say to a young person who might be going through a period of mourning for a loved one? What should he or she expect during a period of mourning or loss?

## YOUR FUNERAL

Have you made plans to be buried in any particular place? Are your affairs in order in that respect?
Do you have any special wishes for your funeral or burial?
Do you want to be cremated?
If you were cremated, what would you want done with your ashes?
What do you think of the cost of funerals these days?
Would you favor a simple ceremony, and burial or cremation at low cost, or would you like a gala affair with an expensive casket, a marble marker, and a big wake or send-off?
How would you like people to remember you at your funeral or after it? What do you want them to think of?

Is there any special piece of music or poem or prayer that you would like played or read at your funeral for the people who will be gathered there?

Why do you choose that?

Do you have a favorite charity or special place that you would want your friends and relatives to donate to in memory of you?

What charity or place is that?

Why do you choose them?

## YOUR EPITAPH

What words do you want written on your tombstone? [wait]

Have you ever thought of writing your own epitaph?

## HOW IT MAKES YOU FEEL TO TALK ABOUT DEATH AND DYING

How does it make you feel to talk about death and dying?

Do you think people should talk about it and talk about their feelings about it? Or do you think it's better not to talk about it too much?

Why?

## HOW YOU WOULD MOST LIKE TO BE REMEMBERED 100 YEARS FROM NOW

How would you most like to be remembered in 100 years?

What would you most like people to know about you in 100 years?

Do you think you will be remembered at all in 100 years?

Do you care if you are or aren't?

Why, or why not?

# Dreams

## DREAMS

Do you think dreams are important?

Do you think they mean anything?

What do you think they mean?

Did you ever have a dream that was very important to you?

Tell me about it. Why was it important?

Did you ever have a dream that prophesied the future, or seemed to foretell the future?

Tell me about that.

Do you believe that dreams sometimes can foretell the future?

In what way? How could they do that, in your opinion?

Do you remember ever having a dream that caused you to change your mind about something? Or a dream that caused you to do something that you might not have done otherwise?

What dream was that? What did it cause you to do?

What's the very first dream or the earliest dream you remember having in your life?

Did you ever have any childhood dreams that you remember?

Did you ever have a recurring dream?

What happens in that dream?

What do you think it means?

What's the most memorable dream you ever had?

What was going on in your life at that time?

Did you dream about anything last night?

Tell me what you remember of that dream.

What's the most recent dream you remember?

Tell it to me.

# Jokes

## MEMORABLE PRACTICAL JOKES

Did you ever like to play tricks, like practical jokes, on people?

Tell me about one you played on somebody that was funny.

What's the most memorable practical joke you remember that someone else played on you?

Who played it? And why did he/she do it?

## YOUR FAVORITE JOKES

Do you like jokes? Do you like to tell jokes?

What are a couple of jokes that you like to tell? Can you tell me some?

Tell me another one.

What's the most recent joke you remember hearing?

Why do you think people often have trouble remembering jokes?

What do you think of ethnic jokes—like jokes about blacks, Jews, the Irish, Poles, and so on?

Do you generally like them and think they are funny? Or do you think they offend people and shouldn't be told?

Why do you think that?

## Fashions, Tastes, and Styles

### FASHIONS AND STYLES IN CLOTHES AND HAIR WHEN YOU WERE YOUNG

What were the fashions and styles in clothing when you were young? Can you describe what people wore when they dressed up?

What about when they were dressed casually? What did you wear when you were just relaxing around home?

What did you wear when you went to work?

What about bathing suits? Can you describe the bathing suits people wore when you were young?

What kinds of shoes did people wear? Can you describe them?

What about hair styles and hair lengths?

How long was the men's and women's hair, and how did they comb it?

### YOUR TASTES IN FOOD, YOUR "SPECIALTY"

What are your tastes in food? Are you something of a gourmet? Or would you say your taste runs more to just plain, good food?

What are some of your favorite things to eat?

If you could have your absolute favorite meal, without regard to cost, what would it be? You know, if this were your last meal and you could have anything on earth, what would you have?

Are you especially good at preparing some specific dish or meal, one that is considered your specialty?

What is that, and who taught you to make it?

Can you describe in detail how you make it? What's the recipe, and are there any "secret" ingredients or procedures?

## YOUR TASTES IN ALCOHOL/DRINKING

How about your tastes in liquor, wine, or beer? What do you most prefer to drink when you drink?

What is your favorite drink?

Do you have a favorite brand of beer, wine, or spirits?

Do you know much about wine and the differences between vineyards and the different years the wine was bottled?

If you know something about wines, how did you come to develop this knowledge?

Do you remember the first time you ever drank an alcoholic beverage?

Tell me that story. What happened?

What was the attitude in your family when you were growing up toward liquor?

Did you have that same attitude about drinking when you were raising your family?

What was different, if anything?

Did you ever get really drunk in your life?

What happened? Tell me a story about once when you got really drunk.

What did you do? Anything stupid?

Do you still like to take a drink now and then?

Was there anyone in the family that you knew of who was good at making homemade liquor, wine, or beer?

Who was that, and do you know how he/she made it, or any stories about it?

Did you ever drink any of it?

During Prohibition, did you obey the law and give up drinking, or did you drink in private?

Why?

What did you think of Prohibition?

Do you remember anything about the women's temperance movement that led in part to the Prohibition amendment?

What do you remember about it?

Do you think it's important to teach children something about alcohol and how to handle it? Or do you think it's best just to tell them not to drink at all?

What's the best way to educate children about what alcohol is and what it does?

## YOUR TASTE IN CLOTHES

What about your taste in clothes? Would you say you are a pretty conservative dresser, or a more flashy dresser, or don't you care very much?

Why do you think you are that way? Where did your values in clothes come from?

What's your favorite color in clothes?

How important do you think it is to dress well in life?

Why do you say that?

Do you think you can judge another person on the basis of how he or she dresses?

What do you mean by that?

What do you think of the way young people dress nowadays?

## DOGS AND CATS

Are you a "dog person" or a "cat person"? Which pet do you prefer?

Why?

What's your favorite type of dog or cat?

Tell me about one of the memorable dogs or cats you've owned.

Did any dog or cat you had ever save your life or protect you? For example, by warning you of a fire or scaring away a burglar?

Tell me that story.

## Religion

### THE BIBLE

Do you read the Bible much?

Did you ever read the Bible much?

What are some of your favorite passages or chapters?

Why are they your favorites?

Do you think everything in the Bible is true?

What do you mean by that?

Do you think the Bible is a book directly inspired by God? Or do you think of it as more of an historical account of the teachings of certain wise men and peoples of the Middle East a few thousand years ago?

## PRAYER

Do you ever pray?

Who taught you to pray?

Were you ever in a crisis in your life where you prayed?

When was that? Can you tell me what happened and why you prayed?

Do you think that prayer actually works in the sense that it can influence the course of events? Or do you think it is more psychological and makes people feel better and perhaps more honest with themselves?

## BELIEF IN GOD

Do you believe in God?

[If yes]: How do you know God exists? [wait]

At what time in your life did you most feel God's presence? [wait]

Tell me about that.

[If no]: How do you know God does not exist?

At what time in your life did you most feel that God did not exist? [wait]

Tell me about that.

## DID YOU EVER ACTUALLY SEE ANYBODY DIE, IMMORTAL SOULS

Did you ever actually see anybody die? I mean, actually be present at the moment of his or her death?

Who was that, and what happened?

What was that experience like for you? Can you remember?

Do you believe that something special happens at the moment of death when life leaves the body?

What happens? At the exact moment of death, what happens?

Do you believe that human beings have souls?

What is a soul? Can you explain your concept of a soul, and what you understand a soul to be?

Do you believe that human souls are immortal?

## MIRACLES

Have you ever witnessed a miracle? [wait]

What happened? What did you see?

Do you believe in miracles?

Why do you say that?

What do you think causes miracles to happen?

## A RELIGIOUS EXPERIENCE

Did you ever have a religious experience or conversion experience at any time in your life? I am talking about some kind of intense emotional and spiritual awareness that had a strong effect on you and your beliefs and values.

What happened? Can you tell me about it, and tell me what it meant to you?

What was going on in your life then, and how did your religious experience affect you afterward?

## ARE YOU A RELIGIOUS PERSON?

Would you call yourself a religious person?

What do you mean by that?

What about church? Have you been active in your church in your life?

What times were you most active, and what times least active, and why at those times in your life?

What have been some of your church-related activities, and which of these has been most rewarding to you?

## A TYPICAL SUNDAY IN YOUR HOME WHEN YOU WERE A CHILD

Think back on a typical Sunday [Saturday for Jewish narrators] in your family when you were growing up. Can you just reminisce a bit and tell me what an average Sunday was like? For example, when did you get up, what did you do, when and what did you eat, did you go to church, when was the big meal of the day, who would be there, what did you do for entertainment, what went on in the afternoon and evening, and so on until you went to bed. Can you just take your time and describe that to me?

## CHANGES IN RELIGION AND RELIGIOUS VALUES

Do you think there has been a decline in religion and religious values in the modern world?

Why, or why not?

Do you think this is a change for the better, or for the worse?

Why do you say that?

Do you think that organized religion can still offer ideas that are valuable to young people in the modern world?

What do you think organized religion can offer?

Do you think that all people undergo spiritual quests in their lives, in the sense of trying to create or find personal meaning for their lives?

Is organized religion important for this kind of spiritual development, or do you think it can and often is done by oneself?

## MODERN CHANGES IN THE CATHOLIC CHURCH (FOR CATHOLICS)

What do you think about the changes in the Mass that came in after Vatican II? [wait]

What did you think when the Mass began to be said in English?

Do you think something was lost? Or gained? Or both?

What was lost, and gained, in your opinion?

What about making the eating of meat on Fridays optional?

What about the saints? Were any of your favorite saints no longer considered saints after Vatican II?

Do you think, in general, that the changes in the Church were for the better or for the worse?

Why do you say that?

Could you say a little more about it?

## CULTS AND DIFFERENT NEW RELIGIOUS MOVEMENTS

What do you think of all these cults and different religions that so many people seem to be following now?

Was there much of that around when you were young?

What is your opinion of things like meditation and chanting? Or of the Hari Krishnas, Yogis, Buddhists, and the like?

What do you think it means when young people are joining with these new and different religions?

Do you know anything about the other great religions of the world? Such as Islam, Buddhism, Hinduism, or Confucianism?

Do you think all religions are equally true? Or is one more true than the others?

Which one is the true one?

Do you think that all religions are essentially saying the same thing? Or do you think there are great and important differences between the religions?

Would you agree that there is really one God, and all the religions are different interpretations of this same God's nature? Or are the different religions worshiping different Gods?

What about astrology, the signs of the Zodiac, and so on. Do you think there is anything to it?

Did you ever follow astrology yourself? Do you read your horoscope in the paper or check up on your sign?

What is your sign? Do you know?

Do you think there is anything to astrology? Or do you think it is just superstition and basically nonsense?

Did horoscopes or astrology ever predict anything for you that seemed to be more than just coincidence?

When and what was that?

## SPIRITUAL TURNING POINTS OF YOUR LIFE

If you had to pick a spiritual turning point in your life, would you be able to do so? [wait]

I'm thinking about an intense or important time in your life when you were questioning the meaning of your life or beliefs up to that point, and deciding what you wanted to be and do in the future. [wait]

That includes either rejecting old beliefs or accepting new ones. [wait]

Can you talk about any stages like this in your personal spiritual growth and development? Did you ever experience a period in your life like this?

Have you experienced periods of change and questioning like this more than once in your life? Is it something to be expected throughout life, in your opinion?

Can you say a little more about that?

When you meditate privately on the meaning of your life—on the most important things that you did or thought or felt—what do you think about?

Could you say anything more about that?

### IMPORTANCE OF A GREAT CAUSE IN LIFE

Do you think it is important for a person at some time in his or her life to identify with some great cause? Is it important to work for something greater than yourself, or to work for the greater interests of all?

What do you mean by that?

Do you feel that you ever worked for or had such a great cause in your life?

I am thinking, perhaps, of the feelings you may have had during World War II, or some religious purpose you feel you may have had. Or some injustice you felt people had suffered that had to be righted.

Could you say anything more about feelings like that?

## Love and Sex

### FIRST LOVE

Tell me the story of your first love. [wait]

What happened? How did it end up?

## LOVE AT FIRST SIGHT

Do you believe in love at first sight? [wait]

Why, or why not?

Has it ever happened to you?

Tell me about it.

Has it ever happened to anybody you know?

How did he or she describe it?

If you do believe that love at first sight can happen, how could you explain it?

## IMPORTANCE OF BEAUTY—"GOOD LOOKS"—IN LIFE

How important would you say beauty or attractiveness is in life? I mean, physical beauty, as when a person is "good-looking"?

Young people and teenagers often seem to be especially concerned with their and others' looks. Do you think that younger people exaggerate its importance, or not?

Why do you say that?

In your experience, does the importance of physical attractiveness stay relatively the same, regardless of how old a person is?

How do you think being good-looking or beautiful stands up to other characteristics of a person, such as creativity, honesty, artistic talent, making a lot of money, sincerity, or being a hard worker?

Do you think beautiful people are happier, on the average, than plain-looking people?

Why do you say that?

What advice would you give to a younger person who might think that he or she is not attractive enough to find the happiness and love he or she seeks in life?

When you first saw or met your spouse, were you attracted to him/her by the way he/she looked?

What was it about the way he/she looked that you were attracted to? Can you remember it and define it?

Describe him/her now as you see him/her in your mind's eye. What did he/she look like when you first saw him/her?

## ROMANTIC LOVE AND SEX

Romantic love and sex are very important to people. Have you learned anything about love and sex in your life that you could pass on to your grandchildren that might be of help to them in achieving a full and happy love life? [wait]

How important do you think sex is to a happy life?

Why do you say that? Can you say a little more about that?

Of the different forms of love, how important is romantic or sexual love, in your opinion?

Why do you say that?

Do you think sex and love should always go together? Or do you think sometimes they have little or nothing to do with each other?

Can you say a little more about that?

Do you think there are basic differences between men's and women's attitudes toward sex, and if so, what are those differences?

Can you say anything more about that?

## SEX EDUCATION

Did you ever get any sex education when you were young? Or was sex not talked about very much?

What do you think about that now?

What is your opinion on sex education in the schools? Do you think sex education should be taught in the schools? Or at home? Or not at all?

Why?

What is the best way for a young person to learn about love and sex, in your opinion?

Can you say a little more about that?

Do you think spending time on or around a farm is a good way to learn something about sex?

Many people seem to find it difficult and uncomfortable to talk or communicate about sex and sexual feelings. Why do you think that is, and what do you think can be done about it?

## THE SEXUAL REVOLUTION

Do you think that sexual attitudes and behavior have changed a lot—the so-called sexual revolution—since you were young?

In what ways have they changed, in your opinion?

Are these changes for the better or for the worse?

Why?

Do you think things have really changed a lot, or do you think people just talk more about it now?

Why do you think that?

Nowadays V.D. is a big problem, but it is not usually a life-threatening problem. When you were young, was V.D. one of the diseases that people were afraid of?

Do you remember hearing much about venereal diseases when you were growing up? Or was it something that people hardly ever talked about?

## BIRTH CONTROL, THE "DOUBLE STANDARD," FAMILY PLANNING

Some observers say that the pill and other effective birth control techniques are the underlying causes of the sexual revolution. Do you think that is true?

Do you think that the fear of getting pregnant was the main reason that young women were taught and expected not to have premarital sex in earlier times?

What about the "double standard," where young men were expected to experiment with sex, but young women were not supposed to? Now that women have the pill and other effective birth control techniques, is the double standard no longer in existence?

What do you think about that?

What about family planning, planned parenthood? Do you advocate family planning?

Do you remember the planned parenthood movement, with Dr. Margaret Sanger and others, when you were thinking about raising a family?

Did you plan the spacing of your children?

In your opinion, what is the ideal spacing between children? How many years should parents wait between one child and the next?

What are your reasons for saying that?

## ABORTION

What do you think of the abortion issue? [wait]

Do you think that abortion is morally wrong?

Why do you say that? Can you say something more about that?

Do you think that it is morally wrong to make a woman bear a child if she really doesn't want it, or can't take care of a child?

Why do you say that?

Do you think it is morally wrong to bring a child into the world if the child is not really wanted by its parents?

Can you say anything more about that?

What about fathers in abortion cases? Should fathers have something to say about whether or not their child should be aborted?

Should the abortion issue be a spiritual and religious question? Or should it be more of a common-sense decision about what is in the best interests of the mother, the father, and the rest of society?

Why do you say that?

Do you think that abortion should be allowed in cases where tests show that the baby will be born with genetic defects, or retarded, or deformed?

Who should make the decision?

It's known that women often feel depressed after having an abortion. Do you think that maybe a woman should go on and have the baby even if she has some doubts about it, or even if she is not married, and then count on her natural feelings for the child to give her satisfaction? Instead of taking the "easy way out" and having an abortion?

Why do you say that?

It's likely that your granddaughters and grandsons will have to face a decision about abortion some time in their lives. What advice do you think you could give them about this question, based upon what you know now?


## HOMOSEXUALITY

What do you think about the homosexuals, the so-called gay people who are around today? [wait]

Do you think there is something wrong with them? Or do you think there is nothing wrong with them at all? [wait]

Do you think homosexuals are dangerous to society, or that they are really not doing anybody any harm?

Do you think homosexuals should be able to have any jobs they want, or should they be kept out of certain jobs, such as teaching or the armed forces?

Why do you say that?

Why do you think some people feel so strongly about the issue of homosexuality? [wait]

Have you ever known a homosexual man or woman?

What were they like?

Other than their sexual preferences, what kind of people were they?

What would you think if one of your children announced that he or she was homosexual? Or if one of your grandchildren said that?

Would you try to talk him or her out of it?

Do you think homosexuals are mentally ill?

Why do you think that?

## PROSTITUTION

What do you think of prostitution? Do you think it should be legalized?

Why, or why not?

Have you ever known a prostitute?

What kind of a person was she?

Do you think prostitutes are mentally ill and criminals? Or do you think it's a free country, they are making a free choice, and people should be allowed to do what they want?

## NUDISM

What do you think of nudist camps?

Have you ever been to one, or have you ever wondered what it would be like to visit one?

What about a nude beach? That's where people (friends and strangers) go swimming without any clothes on. What do you think of that?

Do you think things like that should be illegal? Or do you feel "live and let live" in this area?

Why?

Have you ever gone skinny dipping?

Tell me about it.

# Work

## A JOB THAT YOU HATED

Did you ever have a job that you absolutely hated?

What job was that?

What was it about the job that you hated so much?

What did you do about it?

## A BOSS YOU COULD NOT GET ALONG WITH

Did you ever have a boss on a job whom you just could not get along with?

What made him so hard to get along with? What was he like?

What do you think makes people act that way?

What finally happened between you, that boss, and that job?

## THE JOB YOU MOST LIKED

Of all the jobs you have held in your life, which one did you most like? In which one were you the happiest?

Why were you happiest on that job? What did it do for you?

## THE HARDEST WORK YOU EVER DID IN YOUR LIFE

What's the hardest work you ever did in your life—the hardest job you ever had?

Why? What made it so difficult?

Do you think that physical or manual labor is harder than mental labor?

Why, or why not? Can you give me an example?

## UNEMPLOYMENT

Have you ever been unemployed?

How did you feel when you were unemployed? How did you feel about it?

Did you think it was your fault? In the sense that you were just lazy, or didn't want to work?

Why were you unemployed? What caused it?

What did you do about it?

Did anyone help you out at that time?

Who was that, and why did they help you?

What kind of help did they give? Loans? Or just emotional support and good advice?

Did you find yourself feeling obsolete or worthless, or bitter and angry about not being able to find a job?

Do you remember any incidents of people not treating you with respect, or looking down on you because you couldn't find a job?

What happened, and how did it make you feel?

Did you ever get fired from a job?

What happened? Can you tell me the story?

Why were you fired?

What was your point of view, and what was your boss's?

How did it make you feel?

Did you ever quit a job before you had another one lined up?

What were the circumstances, and how did it work out?

Do you think quitting a job without having another one can be a good idea?

What could you say to younger people who might find themselves unemployed? What should they do, and how should they keep their spirits up when they can't find a job?

What kind of an attitude do you think is the best to have if you are unemployed?

## THE WORK ACHIEVEMENT OF WHICH YOU ARE MOST PROUD

Of all the things you accomplished during your working life, which is the achievement of which you are most proud?

Why does that accomplishment stand out in your mind? Can you say a little more about it? Why does that strike you as your most satisfying achievement?

## *Money*

## SMARTEST BUSINESS DEAL OR INVESTMENT EVER MADE

What's the smartest business or financial deal you ever made in your life?

Was it mostly luck? Or do you think you had the foresight and good sense to plan your investment wisely?

What things did you consider when making your decision to invest?

How much did you end up making? If you don't want to give the exact figure, how about an approximate percentage? Did you double your money, or quadruple it, for example?

## DUMBEST BUSINESS DEAL OR INVESTMENT EVER MADE

What's the dumbest financial deal you ever made? The investment or purchase on which you lost the most money?

How did it come about that you made such a dumb move?

How did it affect you?

What did you learn from it?

## DID YOU EVER MISS A CHANCE TO GET REALLY RICH?

Did you ever miss a chance to get really rich, if you had done something or other at a certain time? I mean, if you had bought land you were thinking of buying, but didn't, many years ago, or something like that.

What was the investment you are thinking of, and what would it be worth today if you had bought it?

## LAND OWNERSHIP, STOCK MARKET INVESTMENTS

How important is it to own a piece of land, in your opinion?

Do you own any land?

How did you come to own the land you now own?

Describe the property you own. What kind of a property is it?

In your experience, do you think other investments are smarter than investments in land?

What about the stock market? Have you successfully invested in the stock market? Or do you think it is not wise to get involved?

Why do you say that?

What investment strategies have you followed in the stock market?

Would you advise a young person to become involved in real estate or stock market investments if he or she wants to have a financially secure future?

Why do you say that?

## RICH PEOPLE/POOR PEOPLE, MONEY

Do you think rich people have just as many problems as poor people?

Why do you say that?

How important do you think money is to being happy?

Do you think money is the most important factor for happiness?

If not money, then what?

Who is the richest person you've known in your life?

How did he or she acquire the money, and did he or she seem to be happy with it?

Do you think some people have a talent for making money, just as others have a talent for music or singing or athletics?

If you believe this is true, then what does it mean for someone who doesn't have that talent? Should he or she stop trying to do something he or she isn't suited for, and focus on his or her own talents instead?

## POVERTY

Have you ever been really poor? [wait]

What did you do about it?

Have you ever been absolutely dead broke?

What were the circumstances, and what did you do?

Have you ever been hungry? I mean, really hungry, and not knowing where your next meal was coming from?

If you have, how did that come about, and what did you do?

Have your feelings about money changed a lot in your life? What were your feelings about acquiring money when you were young, and how have these feelings changed as you've grown older? [wait]

Why do you think that has happened?

How did you learn about money and how to handle, manage, and acquire it?

If you've never been really poor yourself, have you ever known any really poor people?

What do you think are some of the causes of poverty?

What do you think of voluntary poverty, such as that chosen by monks or some nuns, or the poverty of some artists who sacrifice material comforts for their vision and their work?

A famous religious leader once commented on the "spiritual poverty" of the industrial nations, where material wealth and the conquest of nature have become the highest values. Do you think it's true that spiritual poverty is worse than material poverty?

Why do you say that?

## Crime and the Law

### STEALING

Did you ever steal anything? Even as a kid? [wait]

How did you feel afterward?

What did you learn about yourself from the experience? [wait]

If a person was hungry, couldn't find a job, or couldn't support his or her family, do you think he or she would be justified in stealing? Or would it still be morally wrong?

Why do you think that?

### HAVE YOU EVER BEEN ARRESTED?

Have you ever been arrested?

What were you arrested for? Can you tell me the story?

What happened? How did it turn out?

What did you learn from the experience?

### YOUR ATTITUDE TOWARD POLICE

What is your basic attitude toward the police? Do you think of them as being on your side? Or do you regard them more with mistrust?

Why do you think you feel that way?

Give me an example of an experience you had with the police that justifies or explains your basic attitude toward them.

Have the police ever saved you or helped you out?

What happened?

Have you ever been abused or treated with disrespect by a police officer?

## HAVE YOU EVER BEEN ROBBED OR MUGGED?

Have you ever been burglarized or robbed or mugged? Or have you ever seen a robbery?

What happened? Tell me the story.

What did it feel like for you?

Who helped you out the most afterward?

About how long did it take you to return to normal?

Do you think it had any lasting effect on you?

What did you learn from it?

## CRIME AND DRUGS

Was there much violent crime—crime in the streets—when you were young, as far as you remember? [wait]

What do you think of that?

If there is more of it in the modern world, what do you think explains it? What are its causes?

What was different about the world you grew up in that made violent crime less common?

Is crime in the streets another example of deteriorating morals in today's society? Or can it be explained by poverty? Drugs? Or what?

What should be done about crime in the streets, in your opinion?

What do you think one person can do?

What about drugs? Was there anything like the drugs and drug abuse we see today when you were young?

What do you think it's all about? And what can you say to young people about the use of drugs and their possible dangers?

What about the temperance movement and Prohibition? Wasn't alcohol abuse similar to the drug abuse of today?

I've heard that alcohol was destroying the moral fabric of our nation in the teens and twenties, and that's why women began a crusade to close the bars and prohibit alcohol. Do you remember that?

## THE DEATH PENALTY

Do you favor the death penalty for certain crimes?

Why, or why not?

What crimes do you think deserve the death penalty?

In general, do you think the law and judges are too soft on criminals?

Why do you say that?

What do you think should be done about it?

## LAWSUITS AND LAWYERS

Have you ever been involved in a lawsuit, either as the plaintiff or the defendant?

What was it all about?

What happened?

What do you think of lawyers? [wait]

What kind of people do you think tend to become lawyers?

Do or did you have a trusted lawyer who helped you and advised you on legal matters throughout your life?

Who is or was that?

What kind of a person is or was he/she?

Would you advise a young person to study the law as a profession? Or do you think there are too many lawyers around now?

Why do you say that?

## Fights, Enemies, Violence

### FIGHTS YOU'VE BEEN IN

Have you ever been in a fight as an adult? Or as a young adult?

Tell me about a memorable fight you had in your life.

What happened?

Who won?

Tell me about a fight that you lost. What happened, and how did you feel about it?

How important do you think it is for people to know how to physically defend themselves, and to physically fight back if necessary?

Do you think that sometimes a person has to fight? Or are you more nonviolently oriented, and believe that a person should turn the other cheek if possible?

Why do you say that?

## HAS ANYBODY EVER PULLED A GUN OR A KNIFE ON YOU?

Has anybody ever pulled a gun or a knife on you? Have you ever been confronted with a weapon?

What happened? What were the circumstances?

What did you do?

How did you feel about it afterward?

## HAVE YOU EVER PULLED A GUN OR A KNIFE ON ANYBODY?

Have you ever pulled a gun or a knife on anybody? Or confronted anybody with a weapon?

What happened? What was going on?

How did it turn out in the end?

How did you feel about it afterward?

## A MEMORABLE FIGHT YOU WERE IN AS A YOUTH

Tell me about a memorable fight you were in as a youth. Does anything stand out in your mind?

Do you have a classic story you can tell about standing up to a bully and fighting back?

What happened? Tell me that story.

Did you get in a lot of fights when you were a kid? I mean in grade school or junior high and high school? Were you a scrappy kid, in your recollection?

What about fights between you and your brothers and/or sisters? Did you fight a lot between yourselves?

Who used to beat up whom? And when did you stop, as you remember it?

Did you used to have to defend your younger brothers and/or sisters in fights with other neighborhood kids? Or vice versa?

Do you remember any good stories about other kids tangling with your family, and what happened?

What was the attitude of your parents toward fighting?

Did they punish you for fighting? Or did they allow or encourage you to defend yourself?

## YOUR GREATEST ENEMY

Who was your greatest enemy in your life? Did you ever have a real enemy?

Who was that, and what was the origin of your conflict? Why were you enemies?

What kinds of things went on between you two during your feud?

Was the feud ever resolved? Was there ever a reconciliation?

Someone once said that only people with strong characters have enemies. Do you agree with that, and what do you think he meant by that?

## ANYBODY YOU WISH YOU HAD PUNCHED BUT DIDN'T

Thinking back, if you had to do it over again, is there anybody you'd have liked to have punched in the nose, but didn't?

Who was that, and why do you wish you'd punched him or her?

What did he/she do to you to make you wish you had punched him/her out?

Why did you hold back from hitting him/her?

Why now, years later, do you still sort of wish you'd slugged him/her—just one good punch in the nose?

## ANYBODY YOU DID PUNCH OUT

Is there anybody you remember whom you did punch out?

What happened? Tell me about one time that you punched somebody in the nose who really deserved it.

How did you feel about it then, and how do you feel about it now?

## PERSONAL VIOLENCE, SELF-DEFENSE, NONVIOLENCE

Are personal violence and fighting ever justified, in your opinion?

What circumstances make it justified, if it ever is?

Do you think of yourself as a pacifist? Or are you sympathetic to pacifist and nonviolent ideas?

What do you think of the teachings of men like Gandhi or Dr. Martin Luther King on nonviolence?

They believed that nonviolence would call forth the impulse for peace in the mind of the person acting in a violent manner. Do you agree with that philosophy?

Why, or why not?

How important do you think it is for kids to know how to fight or to defend themselves?

Did you ever try to teach your children to defend themselves?

What did you teach them, and why?

When you were a kid, did anybody in your family teach you how to fight and encourage you to defend yourself if necessary? Or did you just figure out how to take care of yourself on your own?

## THE POWER OF FORGIVENESS, AND AN EYE FOR AN EYE

Do you think that forgiving somebody for a wrong he or she did to you is something that a mature person should be able to do?

Why do you say that?

Do you think it is possible, really in your heart, to forgive someone who has wronged you? Do you think, in other words, that there is ever really true forgiveness?

Can you give me an example of a time in your life when you tried and succeeded in forgiving someone for a wrong he or she did you?

Whom do you think the forgiving is for? The one who is forgiven, or the one who gives up a desire for vengeance in his or her heart?

What do you mean by that?

What about an eye for an eye? Do you think it is also true that sometimes you should seek and deliver revenge in order to pay somebody back for a wrong done to you?

Can you say anything else about that?

Can you give me an example of a time in your life when you

paid somebody back in good measure for what he or she did to you?

How did you feel about it afterward?

## Heroism, Saving Lives

### WERE YOU EVER A HERO?

Did you ever have a chance to be a hero? For example, did you ever save somebody's life or protect somebody who needed help?

Tell me that story. What happened?

### DID ANYBODY EVER SAVE YOUR LIFE?

Did anybody ever save your life?

Tell me that story. What happened?

## Differences Between the Generations

### HOW YOUNG PEOPLE SHOCKED THE ESTABLISHMENT IN YOUR YOUTH

What were the things young people did in your youth to shock the establishment? Like today, young people grow long hair or shave their heads, take drugs, walk around half naked, smoke, do wild dances, and so on. What did they do when you were young?

I know that in the early 1920s, women first bobbed their hair, smoked cigarettes, and wore short skirts, and young people drank liquor. Can you think of anything else young people did that shocked their elders?

How about dress styles or hair styles?

Do you think that every generation has to express some of those tendencies—to do something to shock the older people?

Why do you think that?

### DOES EVERY GENERATION REVOLT AGAINST THE PREVIOUS ONE?

Do you think that every generation has to revolt in some way against the previous generation?

Why? Or why not?

If they do, do you think there is ever anything really new in these revolts?

Why do you say that?

Does it seem to you that your generation also revolted against some of the ideas and values of your parents' generation?

What do you remember about that?

Looking at young people today, what does it seem to you that they are doing to revolt against the older generations?

Why do you say that?

## MUSICAL PREFERENCES AND THE DIFFERENCES BETWEEN THE GENERATIONS

What do you think of the idea that one of the most important reasons for and examples of the communications gap between older people and youth is the difference in their tastes in music? [wait]

Do you think this idea has some merit, or do you disagree with it?

What do you think of the music young people listen to today?

Why do you say that?

What do you think of rock and roll?

Why do you say that?

## "YOUTH IS WASTED ON THE YOUNG"

Do you agree with the saying "Youth is wasted on the young"?

Why do you say that?

In what ways is youth wasted on the young? What is it that they don't appreciate when they are young?

If you had your youth back, knowing what you do now, what would you do differently, if anything?

Why?

# Friendship

## YOUR BEST FRIEND AS AN ADULT

Who is, or was, your best friend in your adult years?

Describe him/her. What is/was he/she like?

What were some of the things about him/her that made you best friends?

What other qualities did/does he/she have that you especially admired?

Can you tell me some of the most enjoyable things you do or have done together?

What happened to him/her?

Who is your best friend now?

Can you describe him/her?

What qualities in him/her and in you do you think make you best friends?

What kinds of things do you do together?

## THE MEANING OF FRIENDSHIP, FRIENDS NOW

What would you say is the meaning of a friend, of friendship? [wait]

What makes a real friend?

Would you say that you are a true friend to others? Do you have the qualities that you feel are important in a friendship?

Are you the kind of person who makes friends easily, or does it take some time for you to become friends with someone?

Can you say anything more about this trait of yours?

Who are the people in your friendship circle now? And what are some of the things you do together?

# Sports

## YOU AS A SPORTS FAN, GREAT MOMENTS IN SPORTS

Are you, or were you, much of a sports fan?

What sports did you like most, and which teams did you root for?

In general, do you think athletes are better today than they were years ago? Or do you think they were better in the past?

Why do you say that?

Think of some examples of great athletes today, and compare

them to great athletes from your generation. Who were some of the greats that would stand out in any era?

Which baseball team do you think was the greatest ever to play the game?

Why do you say that? Who was on that team?

What great games of theirs do you remember seeing?

What was your favorite baseball team? Whom did you root for?

Who was the greatest baseball player ever to play the game, in your opinion?

Why him? Why was he the greatest?

What about football? Which football team was the greatest ever, in your opinion?

Why were they so great?

Do you remember seeing any of their memorable games?

Who was the greatest football player ever to play the game, in your opinion?

Why him?

Who was the greatest boxer of all time, in your opinion?

Did you ever see him fight?

Why do you think he was the greatest?

How do you think the boxers of today would stand up to him?

Of all the sports, boxing seems to be the most violent, and people always talk about making it illegal, especially after someone dies after a boxing match. Do you think boxing should be banned? Or changed?

Why, or why not?

How do you think it should be changed?

How about basketball? Which was the greatest team, and who was the greatest player, in your opinion?

Why?

What about tennis? Who was the greatest tennis player, in your opinion?

Why?

Any other sports heroes that you especially admired?

Who were they, and what did they accomplish that made them so great?

Did you ever witness a really memorable sports event? Like Babe Ruth signaling his famous World Series home run? Or Bobby Jones winning the grand slam in golf? Or something like that?

Can you describe it?

## WHY SPORTS RECORDS ARE ALWAYS FALLING

How do you explain the fact that records keep falling and falling, and that athletes seem, at least by the clock, to be getting better and better?

Do you think it is explained by better training methods, equipment, and nutrition, for example? Or are people being born with more capabilities of speed and strength?

## IMPORTANCE OF SPORTS

Do you think that sports are important for people? Or do you think that sports are a low priority compared to other things?

Why do you say that?

What things are more important?

Do you think sports are important for building character, as well as for physical fitness?

Why? What character traits do you think they build?

What about physical fitness? How important is it in life, and how important are sports to maintaining it?

What do you think it says about sports in our country that an athlete can make ten times as much money in a year as the President of the United States?

Can you say a little more about that?

## YOU AS AN ATHLETE

As an adult, were you much of an athlete yourself?

What kinds of sports did you play?

What were you the best at?

How good were you?

Did you ever try a sport that you just could not get the hang of, no matter how hard you practiced?

What was the hardest sport for you?

Was you husband/wife much of an athlete?

What was his/her sport?

Was your husband/wife much of a sports fan?

How important do you think exercise and physical fitness are to good health and to staying happy?

> Have you been interested in physical fitness in your life? Or has it been a low priority for you?

> Why?

## Food, Weight Problems, Health Habits

### FOOD, DIETS, AND WEIGHT PROBLEMS

Have you ever been very overweight, or very underweight in your life?

> What caused you to get that way?

> What did you try to do about it, if anything?

Did you ever have to go on diets, or did you ever study nutrition to determine what to eat and what not to eat?

> What have you concluded about how to control your weight?

> What works best for you?

Does your "body type" tend to run in the family? I mean, is there a tendency toward being overweight or underweight in the family?

> Who in the family do you look like in body type?

Did you pay a lot of attention to the kinds of food your kids ate?

> What was your attitude toward sweets?

> Did they have all these junk foods that kids eat today, like sugar cereals and candy and soda pop, when you were young, or when your kids were growing up?

> > What is your opinion of that type of food?

What foods should people eat if they want to live a long life?

> Why do you say that? How do you know?

Have you ever been a vegetarian?

> What do you think of vegetarianism?

> If you like the idea of being a vegetarian, is it because you think it is healthier? Or is it for ethical reasons about not killing animals?

### SMOKING

Do you now, or did you ever, smoke?

What did you smoke? And why did you start smoking?

Who in your family smoked?

Did you quit smoking?

    Why did you quit?

    How did you manage to quit? Was it difficult for you?

Do you think it is really as bad for your health as they say it is? Or do you think the warnings are exaggerated?

Do any of your children smoke?

    What was your attitude toward smoking when you were raising your children?

    What would have been the punishment if you had caught one of your children smoking when he or she was a teenager?

Do you have a classic story from your childhood about smoking and getting sick?

## SLEEP HABITS, INSOMNIA CURES

Are you a light sleeper? Or are you one of those people who drop off and sleep soundly throughout the night?

    About how much sleep on the average do you need at night?

    They say that as a person gets older, he or she needs less sleep. Have you found that to be true for you?

    Were you or are you an early riser, or do you like to lie in bed and sleep late if you don't have to get up?

    Do you wake up at the same time each morning no matter when you go to bed? Or do you wake up at a certain time each night, and then go back to sleep?

        Why do you think you do that?

    What about naps? Do you take naps, and do you think naps are a good idea?

Have you ever had insomnia or had trouble getting to sleep or staying asleep during your life?

    In general, what do you think causes sleep problems in people?

    What do you do when you can't fall asleep? Do you have any techniques that work for you?

    Do you know of any good cures for people who have trouble sleeping?

    Do you think that people's sleep problems are caused by psychological stress and worries that are bothering them so much that they can't get to sleep?

When you were little and had trouble sleeping or had a nightmare, what did your parents do to help you fall asleep?

Did you do the same with your children when they woke up afraid?

## Parents and Children Growing Up

### DIFFERENCES AND SIMILARITIES, YOU AND YOUR PARENTS

In what ways are you different from the way your mother was? And in what ways are you similar to her? [wait]

How about your father? In what ways are you different from him? And in what ways are you similar to the way he was? [wait]

Which parent do you look the most like?

### DIFFERENCES FROM WHAT YOUR PARENTS WANTED YOU TO BE

Do you think you ended up to be the kind of person your parents wanted you to be?

In what ways did you, and in what ways didn't you fulfill your parents' plans and expectations for you?

### YOUR CHILDREN: PRIDE AND DISAPPOINTMENTS

What about your children? In what ways were you disappointed with the way things turned out for them, and in what ways were you the most proud of them?

Can you say a little more about that?

### IS THE MODERN WORLD HARDER TO GROW UP IN?

Do you think it is harder for a kid to grow up in the modern world than it was in the world you grew up in?

Why? Or why not?

Could you say a little more about that?

## GOING AGAINST PEOPLE'S ADVICE AND OPINIONS

In your life, did you ever go against everybody's advice and do something despite their opposition and disapproval? [wait]

> What was that?
>
> How did it turn out?
>
> Did you end up wishing you'd heeded their advice, or do you think it was something you had to find out for yourself?

# Intuition, Rational Planning

## SHOULD YOU TRUST INTUITION OR PLAN THINGS RATIONALLY?

In important decisions, should a person go with his or her feelings and intuition? Or do you think it's better to analyze things carefully, seek advice, figure out options, and be very deliberate about what you do?

> Which approach has worked out best for you?
>
>> Can you give me an example?

What about in matters of love? Should a person go with his or her feelings and intuition? Or should he or she try to keep a level head, and coolly figure out what is best?

> Can you give me an example from your life of what you mean?

# Vacations, Travel, Places Lived

## FAVORITE VACATIONS

Are there any favorite places that you always liked to go for vacations?

> Describe that place, or those places.
>
>> What did you like so much about going there?

Tell me about your most memorable vacation.

> Where did you go, what did you do, and what made it so memorable?

What's the most exciting thing that ever happened to you on a vacation?

> I'm thinking of things like getting chased by a bear, falling in

love, getting lost in the woods, getting caught in a storm, or something like that. Did anything like that ever happen to you on a vacation?

Tell me what happened.

Did you have a place that you could go to in the summer or on the weekends?

Where was it?

Can you describe what it looked like?

What was it like when you first started going there, and what is it like now?

Can you remember and tell me about some of the good times you had there?

Is the place still in the family?

What happened to it?


## YOUR FAVORITE SPOT IN THE WORLD

What's your favorite spot in the world—your favorite place to visit or to be?

Why there?

Can you describe it for me and how you feel there?

What's the most beautiful place you've ever seen? I mean, from the point of view of physical, scenic beauty?


## YOUR TRAVELS

Do you, or did you, ever like to do a lot of traveling?

What do you like most about traveling?

What countries in the world have you visited?

What country is your favorite to visit?

Why?

Have you ever had any memorable adventures on any of your travels?

Tell me one of them. What's the most memorable thing that ever happened to you on one of your travels?


## THE DIFFERENT PLACES YOU'VE LIVED

Tell me about all of the different places you've lived in your life.

What were the reasons you moved?

Which place did you like the best?

Why?

Which place did you like the least?

Why?

Which of the places you've lived do you call "home" now?

How important do you think it is for a person to have some roots in a community in order to be happy?

Why do you say that?

Is it more important to be able to move and adapt to new situations and places? Or is it more important to be able to stay in one place and put down roots?

It seems like people move around a lot more these days than they used to. Do you think that is true, and if so, why is it that people move so much?

When you moved to the different places in your life, did you ever have trouble adjusting to the new place, making friends, leaving your old friends behind, and so on?

In your opinion, about how long should a person give him or herself in a new place to get adjusted? Does it take a year? Two years? More? Less?

Did you ever move to a new place, try it for a while, and decide it wasn't worth it and pack up and go back home?

What happened, and how did you decide to do that?

Did you regard your going back as a defeat of some kind, or did you look on it as a smart move on your part to go back to what you knew best?

A famous writer once wrote a book called *You Can't Go Home Again*. Do you agree or disagree with that saying?

Why, or why not?

I wonder what he meant by that?


## Schooling, Education

### YOUR FAVORITE SUBJECT IN SCHOOL

What was your favorite subject when you were in school?

Why was that your favorite subject?

What was it about you and your personality that attracted you to that subject?

Did you have a teacher in that subject who was especially good and who showed a special interest in you?

    Who was he/she, and what were some of his/her qualities that you admired?

Did you ever have a chance actually to apply your favorite subject to make money later in life? Or was it more of a hobby or an interest instead of something you used in your work?

## THE VALUE OF EDUCATION

How important do you think formal schooling and formal education are to a person's personal development in life?

    Why do you think that?

Do you think kids these days take school as seriously as kids did when you were young? Or do they seem less serious about it?

    Why do you say that?

How important is education to kids these days?

How important is educational achievement compared to personal qualities like common sense, the capacity to love, self-respect, and knowing the right way to treat people?

What about life experience? Do you think life experience is more important or less important than formal education?

    What do you mean? Could you say a little more about that?

Sometimes people with a lot of formal education and degrees seem to be socially clumsy and obnoxious. Do you think this is true at all, and if so, what do you think accounts for it?

    Can you think of an example of this type of person from your experience?

    What was he/she like?

## Mental Problems, Emotions, Psychiatrists

### INSANE PEOPLE

Have you ever known anybody who was crazy? Who was insane? A nut?

    What happened to him/her? How did he/she act?

What do you think causes people to go crazy?

Who's the craziest person you ever knew? I mean, the mentally sickest?

What did he/she act like, and what happened to him/her?

Do you think that a lot of people who are walking around, holding jobs, and more or less carrying on in society, are really pretty crazy if you got to know their minds on the inside?

Why do you say that?

Do you know, or did you know, anybody who you think was nuts, but didn't really show it that much?

Well, if he/she didn't show it that much, what was it about him/her that makes you say he/she was crazy?

Do you think that sometimes a whole society can go "crazy"? Like, for example, Hitler's Germany during World War II?

How could a sane person survive in a society that had gone crazy?

## NERVOUS BREAKDOWNS

Did anyone you know ever have a nervous breakdown?

What happened?

What do you think was the cause or causes of it?

In general, what do you think might lead up to people feeling that they were about to have a nervous breakdown? What causes mental symptoms like these? [wait]

What is a nervous breakdown, in your opinion?

Do you think a nervous breakdown has a lot to do with stress and pressures in daily life?

What do you think people should do if they feel such pressure and stress that they think they might have a nervous breakdown?

## FEELINGS OF HAVING A NERVOUS BREAKDOWN

Did you ever feel like you were going to have a nervous breakdown? [wait]

When was that? What happened? Can you tell me about it?

What was going on in your life then that led up to your feeling so bad?

What finally happened? How did you finally manage to get through that period in your life?

Who helped you the most?

What did you learn from it?

Can you say a little more about what you learned from that time in your life?

## PHOBIAS, FEARS

Have you ever had a phobia, something that you were really afraid of, or afraid to do, or something you just couldn't stand the sight of?

I'm thinking of things like being totally repelled or terrified by snakes, or spiders, or high places, or elevators, and the like.

Have you ever known anyone like that, someone who had a phobia?

What was he/she afraid of and how did he/she act?

What do you think causes such fears?

What do you think caused yours, now that you think about it?

What advice can you give to somebody else who might be terrified of some unknown or sudden fear like this?

## LIFE'S STRESSES AND PRESSURES

What have you learned in your life about how to handle stress and pressure when it starts to build up? [wait]

What do you do when you feel yourself under a lot of pressure or stress?

Do you try to find somebody to talk to about it? Or are you more the type to go off by yourself and think it through alone?

Whom do you talk to about personal problems or the stresses you are under? Friends? Relatives? A psychiatrist? A clergyman?

Do you think talking it over is generally a better way to handle problems than not talking about it?

Why do you say that?

What about blowing off steam? Is that a good way to handle stress?

When you blow off steam, how do you do it? Do you get really mad and yell? Do you get out and get some exercise? Get drunk? Do you sit quietly someplace and relax? What do you do?

## WHAT YOU ARE LIKE WHEN YOU ARE ANGRY

What are you like when you get really angry? [wait]

Are you the type who blows up and screams and yells and breaks things? Or are you more inclined to keep it inside and act very cold toward the person you are angry with, and plan revenge?

Which is the best way to handle anger, in your opinion? Should a person let it all out, or try to keep it inside?

Why do you say that?

Can you tell me of a memorable blowup or fight you had with somebody? A time when you decided that you just couldn't take it anymore and really told somebody off?

How did that feel?

How did it turn out? What happened?

What do you think of the approach of just trying to forget your anger and turn your mind toward something else? Do you think that is a smart way to handle anger?

Are angry and hateful feelings just as valid and important as loving feelings? Should a person give anger "equal rights" as an important emotion? Or should a person try to suppress it?

Why do you say that? Can you give me an example?

What do you think of the advice to turn the other cheek? Is that a good idea, in your opinion?


## MOST SEVERE SHOCK YOU EVER RECEIVED

What's the most severe shock or scare you ever received in your life? [wait]

How did you recover?

What about fear? What's the most frightened you've ever been in your whole life? [wait]

What happened? How did you recover from it?


## PSYCHIATRISTS AND PSYCHOLOGISTS

What do you think of psychiatrists and psychologists? [wait]

What is it that they do for people, in your opinion?

Do you think it is a good thing that people have psychiatrists and psychologists to go to and talk about their problems? Or is it not such a good thing, in your opinion?

Why do you say that?

When you were growing up, whom did people tend to go to if they wanted to talk over their problems? Their parents or family? Their clergyman? Friends?

Do you think that was a better system, or do you think sometimes going to an objective professional counselor might be a better idea?

Why?

Have you ever been to a psychiatrist or psychologist?

Why did you go?

Was it a useful experience for you?

Do you think that you might have benefited from going to a psychiatrist or psychologist during some of the harder times of your life?

Why do you say that?


## PSYCHOANALYSIS

What do you think of Sigmund Freud and psychoanalysis—where people go to a psychiatrist and lie on a couch and talk about their experiences as children, and so on?

Why do you say that?

Do you think it is true that a person's character and later happiness depend on what happens to him or her in early childhood? Or do you think other times in a person's life are just as important as childhood experiences?

Why do you say that?

Did you ever know anyone who was psychoanalyzed, and was he or she any different afterward, that you could see?


## IS THERE MORE ANXIETY IN THE WORLD NOW?

Some philosophers have said that the modern world can best be called "The Age of Anxiety." Do you agree with that? [wait]

Why, or why not?

What is it about the modern world that makes people so anxious all the time, in your opinion?

Do you think it might have something to do with the decline of religion, the break-up of the family, economic insecurities, nuclear weapons, the loss of small communities, and so on?

What else can you think of that contributes to people's anxieties?

Would you say that, in general, the average person today is more anxious more of the time than the average person fifty years ago?

Why do you say that?

Do you think that maybe people were just as anxious in the past as they are today, but they didn't talk about it as much? Or is there a definite difference in anxiety level?

What is your advice to younger people on the best way to face and handle anxiety and nervousness? [wait]

## DIARIES AND VALUE OF WRITING DOWN YOUR PERSONAL THOUGHTS

Did you ever keep a diary?

Do you think it's a good idea to keep a diary?

Why?

Where is the diary now? Would you ever feel comfortable allowing others to read your thoughts?

What do you think of the idea of writing down your private thoughts during an important, special time in your life, or maybe during a difficult, stressful period in your life?

Did you ever write down these kinds of private notes to yourself and then read them over later?

What did you think when you read them again?

What do you think of these tapes and interviews we are recording right now? Do you feel that they are something like a diary? And what do you hope happens to them in the future?

Would you advise young people to write down their private thoughts, mainly for themselves, during a time of special importance or a hard time in their lives?

What is its value, in your opinion?

## DEPRESSION AFTER ACHIEVEMENT

Did you ever feel depressed after achieving something you had struggled for for years? [wait]

Could you say more about that? What are you thinking of?

What do you think causes that reaction in people?

Do you think it is a normal reaction?
Why, or why not?

## SUICIDE

Every human being has thought about suicide at some time or another, even if only as an idea. Did you ever think about suicide during a low point in your life? [wait]
What made you reject suicide? [wait]
What made you renew your faith in life in spite of its pain and suffering, and go on?
Why is it, in your opinion, that sometimes when you feel really down, it is hard even to remember what it was like to feel good? Why is there this tendency to forget that time will pass, that things will get better, and that you will feel better again?
Do you think that time itself can heal all wounds?
Can you say a little more about that?
Have you ever known anybody who did commit suicide? [wait]
Why do you think he or she did it?
Did you ever feel guilty about it, and tell yourself that maybe if you'd tried more, you could have saved him/her?
How did you resolve those feelings?
What long-term effect did his/her suicide have on you?

## A SPECIAL MESSAGE TO YOUNGER PEOPLE ABOUT LIFE'S CRISES

Do you think you could say anything to your children, grand-children, and other younger people that might help them during the times of trial and crisis that are sure to come in their lives? [wait]
Could you say anything more about that?

# Life's Turning Points

## A TURNING POINT IN YOUR LIFE

Looking back, would you say there was ever a turning point in your life? [wait]

What was it?

Why do you remember this as the greatest turning point of your life?

How did your life become different from the way it was before?

Have there been other crucial points in your life when your future seemed to turn on an important decision you had to make, or on your reaction to something that happened to you?

What were those most important times, as you recall?

Did you ever second-guess yourself afterward and wonder what would have happened to you if you had done something differently during these crucial turning points of your life? Or were you the type, once you'd made a decision, to never look back?

Which is the best way to be, in your opinion?

Why?

What kinds of thoughts have you had about how things could have been different? How could things have turned out differently if you had made a different decision or reacted in a different way?

Do you feel that you are approaching such a time of change in your life now? Or do you think that you'll live out your life pretty much as you are?

Can you say a little more about that? I mean, do you sense in yourself a further spiritual transformation or mental development? Or do you think you will stand firm with your values and meditations until death? [wait]

## World Leaders, Memorable Characters

### WORLD LEADERS OF THE GREATEST STATURE (MEN)

Of all the male world leaders and political and religious figures that you have seen or heard about, which one was of the greatest stature and achievement, in your opinion? [wait]

Why?

Who else would you rank as the greatest world leaders of your lifetime?

Why do you pick them?

What did you think of the following world figures during your lifetime, and were you ever inspired by or interested in what they did and stood for?

Churchill
Einstein
Freud
Gandhi
Lenin
Mao Tse-tung
Martin Luther King
Franklin Roosevelt
Wilson
Are there any others I have left out?

## PROMINENT WOMEN OF THE TWENTIETH CENTURY

Of all the prominent political or religious women leaders of the twentieth century, which one stands out in your memory as the woman of the greatest influence, achievement, and stature?

Why do you pick her?

What was it about her that was so impressive to you?

Any other great women of your lifetime who made an impression on you?

What did or do you think of the following women world figures, and were you ever inspired by or interested in what they did and stood for?

Marie Curie
Dorothea Dix
Amelia Earhart
Indira Gandhi
Margaret Mead
Golda Meir
Eleanor Roosevelt
Margaret Sanger
Mother Teresa
Are there any others I have left out?

## MOST FAMOUS PERSON EVER KNOWN

Who is the most famous person you ever met or knew?

What were the circumstances of that meeting or relationship?

What was your impression of him/her?

What was he/she famous for?

Who is the most famous person you ever saw—not necessarily met, or knew, but saw?

What were the circumstances?

What were your impressions?

## THE MOST MEMORABLE CHARACTER OF YOUR HOMETOWN

Who's the most memorable character of your hometown that you remember?

What was he/she like? Why do you suppose you remember him/her now?

What was it about him/her that was so memorable?

## THE MOST MEMORABLE CHARACTER OF YOUR LIFE

If you had to pick one person out of all the memorable characters you have known in your life, whom would you pick? Who has been the most memorable character of your life?

Why do you pick him/her?

Can you describe his/her personality and some of the memorable things you and he/she did together?

What happened to him/her?

Any other really memorable characters you remember and can describe?

# Old Age

## BEING OLD

Did you ever think you'd live to be as old as you are now?

What does it feel like being your age?

What's the best part about being [age of narrator]?

What's the worst part?

Do you feel old? Do you think of yourself as being old?

At what age do you consider it appropriate for a person to be referred to as "old"? At what age is a person no longer "middle aged" and can appropriately be thought of as an older person?

Do you prefer some other term, such as "elderly" or "senior citizen," or is "old" good enough?

Why do you think some people are upset by the term "old"? What else should a person who has lived a lot of years be called?

Do you think of people who are older than you as "old"?

Do you know many people who are older than you are?

Are you a very different person now from the person you were when you were in, say, your twenties, thirties, or forties? [wait]

In what ways are you different, and in what ways have you stayed very much the same?

Would you say that the differences in you now from when you were in your twenties, thirties, and forties are mostly physical? Or is it more in personality and knowledge, that is, mental or psychological differences?

Why do you say that?

## TREATMENT BY YOUNGER PEOPLE

How do young people tend to treat you, generally?

Do you think that young people have the same respect for older people today that young people had when you were growing up?

Why do you think that is?

What do younger people lose, in your opinion, by not talking more and paying more attention to older people and what they know?

Could you say a little more about that?

And what about older people? What do they lose by not talking more and communicating better with younger people?

# Marriage

## WHAT IS IMPORTANT TO A GOOD MARRIAGE

What makes for a good marriage? [wait]

Do you think social class is important? Should the two partners be of more or less the same social class?

Why do you say that?

How important is physical appearance and sex appeal?

Why do you say that?

How about a good job and money in the bank? Do you think money is important for young people who are thinking about getting married?

Why do you say that?

How much money did you have in the bank when you got married?

Would you say, in general, that young people should put off marriage until they have good jobs and money in the bank?

Why, or why not?

Do you think being in love is more important than any of the above?

Why, or why not?

Do you think that love can overcome any obstacles to marriage?

Why, or why not?

What would you say being in love means, anyway? What does it mean to be in love?

Can you say a little more about that?

What are the best reasons, in your opinion, for getting married?

And what do you think are the worst reasons for getting married?

Or, what are some of the common mistakes people make? What are some of the bad reasons for getting married that you have seen?

Why did you get married?

Was that, or were those, good reasons for getting married, now that you look back on it?


## YOUR PERSONALITY AND YOUR SPOUSE'S

Did you and your spouse have similar personalities, or would you say you were very different in certain ways?

In what ways were you similar, and in what ways were you the most different?

What would you say was the single biggest difference between you?

And what was the thing that you shared the most in common?

You know the sayings, "Birds of a feather flock together" and "Opposites attract." Which saying would you apply to you and your spouse?

Why?

## AREAS OF DIFFERENCE OR DISAGREEMENT IN YOUR MARRIAGE

Without overemphasizing it, I'd like you to describe some of the differences between you and your spouse, and how you handled conflict and differences of opinion. What would you say were the biggest areas of difference or disagreement in your marriage? [wait]

For example, do you remember differences about work versus family, how to raise the kids, politics, sex, money, or anything else of importance?

If you had to pick out one single area where you always differed with your spouse, what would that be?

Do any great arguments about this stand out in your mind?

Tell me about one of the all-time biggest arguments between you and your spouse that you ever had. I'm talking about one where you punched a hole in the wall and drove off in a storm, or you packed up and left, or threatened divorce.

What happened, and how did it end up?

How important is it in a good marriage for both partners to be able to express their anger and fight it out?

Why do you say that?

About how long were you married before you really began to get to know your spouse and understand the basic differences and similarities between the two of you?


## COMPARING YOUR SPOUSE'S AND YOUR CHILD-REARING PHILOSOPHY

What is your impression of the philosophy of child-rearing that your husband/wife held and practiced?

In what areas did you disagree with your spouse about how to raise the children?

Which of you was the more strict parent?

Why do you say that?

Do you think your children would agree with you on this?


## YOUR MOTHER-IN-LAW

In general, how did you get along with your mother-in-law?

Was there ever an open conflict between the two of you?

What was it all about?

What kind of a person was your mother-in-law?

Why do you think there are so many mother-in-law jokes around?

Do you know any good mother-in-law jokes?

What do you think the explanation is for the tension and conflict that often exists between people and their mothers-in-law?

How did your spouse get along with your mother?


## EXTRAMARITAL AFFAIRS

One of the most difficult times in a marriage can come when one or the other spouse becomes involved in an extramarital love affair. Has anything like that ever happened to you, or to anyone you know? [wait]

How do you think such a thing ought to be handled in a marriage, if it does occur?

Do you think that an extramarital affair ought to be immediate grounds for divorce?

Why do you say that?

What do you think are some of the reasons that people become involved in extramarital affairs? [wait]

Do you think that being with one person, and one person only, for life is really sometimes asking too much of human beings?

Why do you say that?

What do you think of the idea that the extramarital affair is a symptom of a deeper problem in the marriage relationship? Do you subscribe to that theory?

Some people say that not only is an extramarital affair not necessarily damaging to a marriage, but that it can actually put new life into the relationship. What do you think of that theory?

Why do you say that?

Suppose, for whatever the reasons, one partner in a marriage becomes involved in an extramarital affair. Do you think he or she should keep it secret and be discreet, or do you think that the other person should be told about it?

Why do you say that?

What is your opinion of marriage counselors and other types of therapy for an ailing marriage?

Is there anything you can say that might be useful to some younger person who might find himself or herself in that position? Either as the one having the affair, or as the one who has found out that his or her spouse is having an affair. What would you suggest he/ she do?

How can he/she understand it and perhaps feel better about it?

Why do you say that?

Do you think that a marriage could ever come back and be stronger than before after an affair by one or both of the partners? Or is the hurt inevitably something that can forever damage a relationship between two people?

Why do you say that?

## ADVICE AND OBSERVATIONS ON THE EMOTIONS OF BREAKING UP OR DIVORCE

Breaking up a love affair is one of the most painful experiences in life. Do you remember any of your close relationships that came to an end? Young people sometimes feel that it's the end of the world, that they'll never get over it.

Can you say anything that you think might get through to a person who might be going through a painful separation, a person who has ended a close relationship and who feels that he or she will just never feel good again? [wait]

In your opinion, is it partly just a matter of time?

From your experience, about how much time does it take to get over it when you break up an important relationship? How long before you forget the pain and start over again?

What's a realistic amount of time to expect? A couple of months? A year? More than that?

## Racism, Prejudice

### RACISM, PREJUDICE

What would be your reaction if one of your grandchildren or one of your children married a black/white man/woman [opposite of narrator]?

Why? [wait]

What about marrying an Oriental—a Japanese or Chinese? How would you react to that? [Substitute white, if appropriate, whatever's different from your narrator.]

Why?

Do you think that interracial marriage is the same as marrying from different religions?

Why?

Do you think that people's attitudes will ever change to the point where racial characteristics will not be important at all in the way people treat each other?

Why, or why not?

When you were young and courting, who were the groups that you would have been forbidden or at least discouraged from marrying? For example, if you are a Protestant, would you have been discouraged from marrying a Catholic, or a Jew, and vice versa?

Why?

## ETHNIC PREJUDICE

Did you ever experience any incidents of prejudice against you because of your being [Irish, Polish, German, Japanese, English, African, or whatever; fill in the ethnic identity of your narrator] when you were younger?

Tell me about one of those incidents? What happened?

What did you do about it?

How did it make you feel?

What about prejudice against your parents or grandparents? Did you ever hear them talk, or hear stories, about prejudice against them and what they did about it?

What about calling them names? What was an ethnic insult that would provoke a fight from you or your ancestors if anyone called you or them that name?

Did you ever hear someone use that term, or hear stories about it?

What about jobs? Were people of your ethnicity discriminated against when they tried to get certain jobs?

Do you know any stories in the family about being denied a job because of where your people came from?

## Music, Dance, The Arts

### MUSIC IN YOUR LIFE

Did you or do you like to sing or play a musical instrument?

Which instrument do you play? Are you any good?

What about listening to music? How important would you say music is in your life?

What kind of music do you most like to listen to?

Did you try to teach your children an appreciation for music?

What do you think of the music young people listen to today?

Why do you say that?

What do you think of rock and roll music?

Do you think it is dangerous or in bad taste? Or do you like some of it?

What rock and roll musicians do you like? Do you know any?

Tell me the names of your favorite singers and performers.

What is so good about him/her/them, in your opinion?

What are some of your favorite songs by him/her/them?

Do these songs remind you of a feeling, or someone in particular, or a certain time in your life?

Who was that? And when? And what was his/her significance in your life?

Are there any songs of recording artists that you play over and over when you are in a particular mood?

Which songs? What do you feel when you play them and what do you like so much about them?

### WHAT PEOPLE DID FOR MUSIC BEFORE RADIO, TV, AND RECORDS

Before radio and phonographs and television, what did people do when they wanted to hear some music?

What did you do, or where did you and your family go to hear music?

Did families make their own music?

What kind of music did your family make?

What about church or in your religion? Was there a lot of emphasis on music there?

## DANCE IN YOUR LIFE

What about dancing? Are you much of a dancer?

Who taught you to dance?

What were some of the dances people did when you were young? Can you describe them and tell how they were done?

Can you remember whether some of the older people were scandalized by the dances the young people were doing then?

What do you think of dancing as an art form? I am thinking of ballet or of modern dance.

Have you ever been to a professional dance performance?

## IF YOU COULD BE AN ARTIST

If you could have been, or could be, an outstanding painter, writer, poet, musician, actor, sculptor, or dancer, which of these would you most like to be? Which most appeals to you? [wait]

Why do you think you chose that form of artistic expression?

Do you think your artistic preference tells a lot about the kind of a person you are?

Do you think that being an artist gives more to humanity than being a scientist or political figure?

Why do you say that?

Of all the artists you know of in the field you chose, which has had the most influence on you?

Which of his/her works are the most meaningful to you?

## AMUSEMENTS AND RECREATION AS A YOUNG PERSON AND NOW

What were some of the favorite amusements or things you did for recreation in your younger days?

What are some of your favorite amusements and recreational activities now?

Have you had any lifelong hobbies or interests? Things that you liked to do when you were a kid that you still do now?

What are those?

## THE MOVIES AND THEATER

What do you think of the movies? [wait]

Tell me who some of your favorite actors and actresses were and are.

What were some of the great roles you saw them in?

What was so great about the performance? Can you describe it?

What, in your opinion, are your favorite movies of all time? What do you think are some of the best movies you've ever seen?

Do you like to go to the movies now?

What's a recent movie that you saw that you liked?

What's better, live theater or a movie?

Why do you say that?

What are some of the great plays and great actors you have seen in live performances in your lifetime?

What's the last good play you saw?

Name your favorite stage play.

Have the movies and television, to your knowledge, affected theater negatively? Or do you think it's still possible to see good live drama?

Who's your favorite playwright?

## Medicine and Cures

### MEMORIES OF DOCTORS AND DENTISTS

Do you have any memories of doctors and the way they treated people when you were young?

Did you have a family doctor when you were growing up?

Who was he and what was he like?

Did they make home visits in those days?

Were there many women doctors around then?

What were people's attitudes toward women doctors?

Do you think doctors acted differently then than they do now?

In what ways? How did they act differently?

How about dentists? Do you remember any of your experiences with dentists when you were young?

How did dentists perform their services when you were younger?

Do you remember any memorable visits to the dentist's office?

I've heard that dentistry was a lot more painful in the old days. Is that true?

## CURES FOR WARTS

Do you know any good cures for warts?
What are they, and who told you about them?
Have these remedies ever worked for you?

## CURES FOR HICCUPS

Do you know any good cures for hiccups?
Who told you that cure?
Has it ever worked for you?

## WILL MODERN MEDICINE EVER CONQUER CANCER OR OLD AGE?

Do you think modern medicine will ever conquer cancer, just as it has conquered polio, TB, and so on?

What about aging? Do you think they will ever figure out how to stop the aging process so that people will live for hundreds of years, and in effect, "old age" will be conquered?
Would you like to live for 500 years or so?
Why, or why not?
What would you do with yourself for 500 years?

## Family Changes, The Environment, Inventions, Outer Space

### CHANGES IN THE FAMILY AND FAMILY VALUES

What changes have you seen in the family and in people's attitudes toward the family in your lifetime? [wait]
Does it seem to you that younger family members pay less attention to what the older family members have to say nowadays? Or has it always been the same—the younger people want to find out things for themselves, and don't listen to the older generation?
Have the older members of families lost authority?
Why do you say that?
Do you think that some of the changes in the family have con-

tributed to the widespread "age of anxiety" that seems to characterize the modern world?

Why? Do you think people were more secure in their families and about family values in earlier times?

What about working mothers, holding well-paying jobs outside the home? How common was this in earlier times, and do you think this is a change for the better or for the worse?

Why?

In earlier times, "father knew best." There wasn't as much questioning of family authority, but there wasn't as much freedom either. Is the trade-off worth it? More freedom, but less security? Or do you think things were better in the past?

Why do you say that?

## VALUE OF CONSERVATION, WILDLIFE, WILDERNESS

Do you belong to any conservation organizations, like the Sierra Club, the National Wildlife Federation, or something like that, which aim to preserve wilderness areas and restrict real estate development?

Are you generally in favor of or opposed to organizations that work to save the wilderness, preserve the environment, and so on?

Why?

In your opinion, what is the value of the wilderness? Why should we keep the wilderness untouched?

Are you much of an outdoors person?

Can you take care of yourself in the woods?

Who taught you an appreciation of the out-of-doors and how to take care of yourself in the woods?

What's your favorite wilderness spot to visit?

Can you describe it? What does it look like and how does it make you feel?

Would you rather go to the beach or to the mountains?

Why?

## POLLUTION AND A SIMPLER LIFE

Did people think much about pollution, chemicals, and industrial waste when you were growing up?

What do you think can be done about the pollution of our water and air by industrial processes and industrial production?

Is the government strong enough in this area? Should there be more regulation of industry to get the environment cleaned up, even if it means that things will cost more and industry will make less money?

Do you think it might ever be possible for the modern world to return to a simpler life, where so much technology and pollution might not be necessary?

If you could, would you like to turn back the clock, so to speak, and return to a simpler life?

Why?

## COMPUTERS

What do you think of computers?

They say we are living in an age of computers, the "information age," and so on. What do you think that means?

Do you know anything about how computers work?

Do you care how computers work?

Do you think computers make life easier for people? Or are they just one more new thing to get used to?

## ROBOTS

What do you think about robots? Do you think we'll ever have machines that walk around and talk to us, do our housework, take care of the kids, and so on?

Would you own a robot, if you could?

## LIFE IN OUTER SPACE AND ON OTHER PLANETS

What do you think about extraterrestrial beings? Do you think mankind will ever make contact with intelligent beings from another planet, solar system, or galaxy?

Do you think there is other intelligent life somewhere in the universe?

Why do you say that?

What do you think will be the result when this happens?

What will be the effect of contact with a nonhuman civilization on art, religion, philosophy, and other human endeavors?

## MANKIND TRAVELING TO OTHER PLANETS

Do you think people will ever travel in spaceships to other planets, solar systems, and galaxies?

Would you like to go on a spaceship, if you could?

Do you think mankind is destined one day to go out into the stars and colonize other planets?

Why or why not?

## OLDER PEOPLE IN SPACE

They say that older people are better suited for space travel than younger people, because they adapt better to weightlessness. The ideal age for an astronaut might be someone in his or her sixties or older. What do you think of that? [wait]

# Social Changes, Progress, Your Generation's Insights

## WOMEN AND THE DRAFT

Should women be drafted into the armed forces, in your opinion?

Why, or why not?

If women are in the armed forces, should they go into combat during wartime?

Why, or why not?

## RIOTS OR CIVIL DISTURBANCES

Have you ever seen or been in any riots, civil disturbances, or demonstrations?

Tell me about them. What have you seen or participated in?

If you were a participant, why were you there? What were your reasons for being there?

Have you ever been in a political demonstration, such as a labor picket line, or a demonstration against a war, nuclear power plant, government policy, or something like that?

Where, when, and why?

Did any of the demonstrations you've seen or been in turn violent?

What happened?

What did you do?

We hear so much talk about terrorism, hijackings, etc. these days. What is terrorism and what do you think causes it?

Do you think that you, personally, are in any danger from terrorism?

Do you think terrorists are just crazy people, or do you think they are trying to accomplish something in the real world?

What is it that you think terrorists are trying to do?

What do you think should be done about terrorism?


## IS MANKIND PROGRESSING?

Do you think mankind is progressing toward a better world? Or do you think that things seem to be getting worse? [wait]

[If better]: What is better now about the world compared to how things were in your youth?

Can you give me some examples?

[If worse]: What was better about the old days, in your opinion, before the modern world brought so many changes?

Can you give me some examples?

Is anything really better? For example, what do you think about the following things about the modern world:

Medical miracles like cures for polio, or organ transplants, open heart surgery, and so on? Are these advances really worth it?

All the inventions for consumers, like TV, videotape recorders, movies, radios, and so on? Is life better with these things?

Modern transportation. What do you think of airline travel nowadays, or the highways and new cars? Is life better because of these?

Communications. Long-distance telephone calls, computer information exchange, and so on?

And finally, what do you have to say about air conditioning?


## THE VALUE OF THE OLDER WAYS OF DOING THINGS

We are all so caught up now in the modern world with its technology and inventions and new ideas. What are we in danger of losing forever after your generation is gone?

What should be saved of the knowledge and insights of your generation that you feel is not fully understood by the younger generations?

In what ways were the older ways of doing things better?

Could you say a little more about that?

In what ways were the older ways of doing things worse?

What ways of doing things were worse?

## Best and Worst Year

### THE BEST YEAR OF YOUR LIFE

If you had to pick one year of your life out as the very best year, what year would you pick? When were you the happiest you've ever been in your life?

Why? What was so good about that time in your life?

### THE WORST YEAR OF YOUR LIFE

How about the bad times? If you had to pick the lowest year of your whole life, what year would you pick?

Why? What happened during that year?

How did you make it through that year?

Who helped you the most during that time?

In what ways did he/she help you?

## Overcoming Problems, Preventing Mistakes

### HOW TO OVERCOME PROBLEMS AND LIVE A GOOD LIFE

Could you say anything to younger people about how they might overcome their problems and live a good and happy life? [wait]

What's the most important thing to remember when faced with a difficult problem, an unhappy time, or something important? [wait]

### PREVENTING MISTAKES

It seems to be an almost universal desire of older people to try and prevent younger people from making the same mistakes that they made. With this in mind, what mistakes do you feel you might have made in your life that you hope your children, grandchildren, or other young people don't make in their lives? [wait]

What mistakes are you thinking of? Could you say a little more about that?

## A TYPICAL DAY FOR YOU NOW

What's a typical day like for you now? You wake up, wash up, have breakfast, and so on. Can you describe a typical day, from the time you get up until the time you go to sleep?

# Holidays

## CELEBRATING CHRISTMAS/HANUKKAH WHEN YOU WERE YOUNG

When you were growing up, how did your family celebrate Christmas [or Hanukkah]?

Who would be there?

Did you always have a big tree?

Who would get the tree, where would it come from, and how was it decorated?

Was there any special meal that was always served?

Can you remember a particularly memorable Christmas/Hanukkah?

Why was that a memorable year?

What kinds of gifts do you remember giving and receiving? Any really memorable ones?

## CELEBRATING THANKSGIVING WHEN YOU WERE GROWING UP

What about Thanksgiving? What was Thanksgiving like when you were growing up? Can you describe an old-fashioned Thanksgiving for me?

Think back, and describe who would be there, what kind of food would be prepared, and in general, what that holiday was like for you.

Was it a religious holiday for you? Would you say a prayer, and if so, who would say the prayer?

## NEW YEAR'S

What about New Year's? What was New Year's like as a holiday?

Did you get to stay up as a child and make a lot of noise?

Do you remember any great or memorable New Year's parties that you have attended?

What happened? Describe the wildest and most memorable New Year's party that you ever attended.

## HALLOWEEN AND HALLOWEEN PRANKS

How did you celebrate Halloween when you were little?

What were some of the pranks you and the other kids used to play on Halloween?

What were some of the great pranks you have heard about being played on Halloween? Maybe by other kids?

Did you soap or wax windows?

What about the famous prank of overturning outhouses?

What about your kids? Do you remember any trouble any of them got into on Halloween? Or pranks they played while out on Halloween?

## THE 4TH OF JULY

What would you and your family do and where would you go to celebrate the 4th of July when you were young?

How did you celebrate the 4th then? Did someone always have a fireworks show?

## EASTER

Did you and your family celebrate Easter?

What would you do?

Are there any family traditions around the celebration of Easter?

What is the meaning of the Easter celebration, as you understand it?

## *Who Will Be The Next President*

**WHO YOU THINK WILL BE THE NEXT PRESIDENT**

Who do you think will be the next president?
  Why?
What do you think of the job this one is doing?
  Can you say a little more about that?
Do you plan to vote in the next election?
  Why, or why not?

## *People Will Miss You, Plans For The Future*

**HEARING OR SEEING THESE TAPES, PEOPLE WILL MISS YOU**

You know that people seeing or listening to these tapes in future years, after you are gone, might be feeling sad. They will be missing you—they'll hear your voice and see your face and they'll feel sad that you're gone. What can you say to them about that?
  Do you think they should be feeling sad if they are missing you?
    Why do you say that?

**A MESSAGE TO SOMEONE LIVING 100–200 YEARS FROM NOW**

Imagine for a moment your great-grandchildren or great-great-grandchildren who haven't even been born yet. If you can imagine them sitting around sometime in the future, listening to this tape, what would you like to say to them? [wait]
  What have you learned in this world? [wait]
Based on what you see happening in the modern world, what important things do you think might be lost by the time future generations are born that they ought to know about? What important values or ways of living are in danger of passing out of existence with your generation? [wait]
  I am thinking of things like individual rights in a highly organized society, or the loss of the wilderness areas, or the stability of families, or religion, or other values that you think are important. What is in danger of passing from the scene that future generations might want and need to know about? [wait]

## ANYTHING IMPORTANT ABOUT YOU THAT WE HAVEN'T TALKED ABOUT

Have I failed to ask you about anything that you feel is important about your life?

## ANY PROBLEMS I CAN HELP YOU WITH NOW

Do you have any problems now, or any worries that I might be able to help you take care of, or get taken care of?

## YOUR PLANS FOR THE FUTURE

What are your plans for the future?

# Special Questions For Jewish Narrators

**WHAT IT MEANS TO BE A JEW**

What does it mean to be a Jew? [wait]

    What else does it mean? [wait]

Does being a Jew in today's world mean the same thing as it did when you grew up?

    Why do you say that? Can you explain what you mean any further?

Do you think that being a Jew meant more to you when you were young than it means to young people today?

    Why do you say that?

**WHEN YOU WERE MOST PROUD TO BE A JEW**

What was the time in your life when you were most proud to be a Jew? [wait]

What is the thing now that makes you most proud to be a Jew?

    What are you most proud of about Judaism?

**MOST POSITIVE AND CREATIVE ACHIEVEMENTS OF JUDAISM**

In your opinion, what are the most creative and positive achievements of Judaism? [wait]

290

What are the greatest contributions that the Jewish religion and culture have made to the world?

Could you say a little more about that?

## WHY JEWS HAVE MAINTAINED THEIR IDENTITY FOR SO LONG

What do you think it is about Judaism that has enabled the Jews to maintain their identity throughout so much of recorded history?

Can you say a little more about that?

## IMPORTANCE OF JEWISH HERITAGE TO YOUNG PEOPLE

What would you say to young Jews about the importance of their religion and their cultural heritage? [wait]

Do you think that maintaining a strong identity as a Jew is as important in the modern world as it once was?

Why?

## INTERMARRIAGE

How important do you think it is for Jews to marry other Jews?

Why do you say that?

How would you feel if any of your children or grandchildren married outside of Judaism?

Do you think it is as important now for a Jew to marry another Jew as it might once have been?

Why, or why not?

## ANTI-SEMITISM

What was the first time you became aware of anti-Jewish feelings in other people? [wait]

Do you rememer an incident as a child when you became aware that some people were hostile to Jews?

What happened? Can you tell me that story?

Do you remember any other incidents of anti-Semitism in your life?

Can you tell me about some of them?

Which incident still stands out in your memory and still makes you angry?

What happened? What did you do and what did you think?

How did you feel about it?

Do you remember your parents telling you anything about anti-Semitism when you were growing up?

What did they tell you?

Do you remember ever hearing about anti-Semitic incidents from your parents' or grandparents' lives?

Do you know if any of your ancestors or relatives were victims of anti-Semitism before they came to America?

What stories are told in your family?

Did you ever hear stories about pogroms from your parents or grandparents?

## YOUR EXPERIENCE OF NAZISM AND ITS EFFECT ON YOU

What was it like for you during World War II when Jews in Europe were being imprisoned and killed? [wait]

Did you lose any of your relatives in the Nazi persecution?

Who was that? Do you know what happened to them?

Did Jews in America know what was going on with the Nazis, or was it unclear what was happening then, and only after the war that the full story of the holocaust came out?

Do you think that the Allied leaders bear some of the responsibility for the holocaust, because they did not consider saving the Jews who were being murdered a priority over the strictly military defeat of the German armies?

Could you say a little more about that?

What could have and should have been done, in your opinion, but wasn't?

## WHY ANTI-SEMITISM EXISTS

Why do you think some people are afraid of Jews and discriminate against them? [wait]

In other words, what do you think are the "causes" of anti-Semitism?

## IS ANTI-SEMITISM STILL A DANGER IN THE WORLD?

Do you think anti-Semitism is still important in the United States?
    Why do you say that?
    What do you think can be done about it?
Do you think anti-Semitism is still important in the world as a whole?
    Where does anti-Semitism seem to be a danger now, and what can be done about it?
Do you think that something like Nazism could ever happen in the world again?
    Why do you say that? Could you say anything more about it?

## COULD A JEW EVER BE ELECTED PRESIDENT?

Do you think a Jew could ever be elected President of the United States?
    Why, or why not?

## ISRAEL

How do you feel about Israel? [wait]
Do you remember the Zionist movement from when you were young?
    Were you very involved in Zionism when you were young?
    How important was the Zionist movement to Jews then?
        As you remember, did most Jews talk about and become interested in Zionism? Or was it a minority?
Do you remember when Israel gained its independence in 1948?
    What did that feel like for you?
    What did the creation of Israel mean to other Jews in the United States?
    What was the feeling about it in 1948?
Young people today take Israel for granted. Can you try to explain to them what it meant to you and to other Jews of your generation when Israel finally became an independent nation? [wait]
What do you think the future holds for the Middle East?
    Do you think there will ever be peace between Israel and the Arabs?

What do you think should happen to the Palestinians?

Do the Palestinians deserve a homeland of their own?

Why, or why not?

What do you think is a long-term solution to the problems in the Middle East?

Have you ever been to Israel?

What was your trip like?

What was its meaning for you?

Does your family have any relatives in Israel now?

Did you ever think about living in Israel? Did you ever feel the desire to move to Israel and become an Israeli citizen?

What would you think if any of your children or grandchildren left the United States and became Israeli citizens?

# Special Questions For Black Narrators

꒰ꕥꔛꕥꔛꕥ꒱

**BLACK PRIDE**

What was the time in your life when you were most proud to be black? [wait]
What is the thing that makes you most proud to be a black American? [wait]

**"ROOTS," BLACK HISTORY**

What did you think of the book and television show "Roots," about the African heritage of black people in America?
  Do you think it is important for young black people to be aware of their African heritage?
  Why do you think that?
What would you say to young black people today about the importance of their cultural heritage and history?
  Could you say a little more about that?

**GREATEST ACHIEVEMENTS OF BLACK PEOPLE**

What do you think are the greatest achievements of black people?
What do you think are some of the great contributions black people have made to culture and to mankind? [wait]

Do you think it is important to educate young black people about the creative achievements of their culture?

## FIRST EXPERIENCES WITH RACISM

What was your first experience with racial prejudice? What's the first time you remember as a child when you experienced racial prejudice? [wait]

Do you remember any other contacts with white society when you realized that something different was happening? Or when you realized that you were supposed to act in a different way around whites?

Tell me a specific incident from when you were a child.

Do you remember how you felt?

## OTHER EXPERIENCES WITH RACISM

Can you tell me about some of your other experiences with racism and racial prejudice? [wait]

What's the worst racial incident you ever witnessed or heard about when you were growing up?

Did you ever hear about a lynching?

Tell me that story. What happened?

Can you tell me about a time when someone cursed you openly with racial slurs, or called you a racist name?

What happened, and how did you feel?

What did you do about it?

Do you remember being warned about whites by your family when you were growing up?

What did they say? What did your parents tell you about white prejudice when you were growing up?

## THE KU KLUX KLAN

Did you ever hear about or see the Klan when you were growing up?

What was that like? How did the Klan act when you were growing up?

Do you remember any stories about anyone in your family who

was persecuted by the Klan, or did you yourself ever have any trouble or contact with them?

Do you think they are still a danger to black people in the United States?

Why?

What do you think should be done about them?

## HOW DIFFERENT YOUR LIFE WOULD HAVE BEEN WITHOUT RACISM

How different do you think your life might have been if you had not had to contend with racism and racial prejudice?

Can you say a little more about that?

Do you have any specific memories of lost opportunities because of racial prejudice against you?

What happened?

How do you feel about it now?

## ARE YOU STILL ANGRY ABOUT RACISM?

Do you still feel anger or bitterness about the prejudice and discrimination that black people have had to face in the United States?

What do you think can be done about it now?

If you have been able to avoid bitterness and anger, how have you done so?

## THE JOE LOUIS–MAX SCHMELING FIGHT

Tell me how you felt when Joe Louis knocked out Max Schmeling in 1938.

What do you remember about that night?

What did it mean to black people in the United States?

## THE CIVIL RIGHTS MOVEMENT OF THE 1960s

What did you think when the civil rights activists started demonstrating and riding buses and organizing voter registration drives during the 1960s?

What do you think the civil rights movement accomplished?

Can you say a little more about that?

Did you ever participate in any marches or demonstrations during that time?

Tell me about one of them that you participated in. Where was it, what happened, and what did you do?

## MARTIN LUTHER KING

What kind of a man was Dr. Martin Luther King? [wait]
Did you ever see him or meet him? Or hear him speak?
Where and when was that?
What do you think were Dr. King's greatest accomplishments?
Can you say a little more about that?
Were you influenced by Dr. King's philosophy of nonviolence?
What do you think of the philosophy of nonviolence as a means of protest and change?

## THE MURDER OF MARTIN LUTHER KING

Do you remember when Dr. Martin Luther King was murdered? [wait]
Where were you when you heard the news?
What happened where you were living on that day?
How did you feel when you heard the news that he had been shot down?
Do you think that the real killer of Dr. King was caught? Do you think it was really done by James Earl Ray, or do you think that there were others behind it who have never been caught?
In your opinion, who was behind the murder of Dr. King?

## WILL THINGS GET BETTER IN THE UNITED STATES?

Do you think that racial prejudice is going to continue unchanged in the United States, or do you think that, over time, things will gradually get better?
Why do you think that?

## CHANGES IN ATTITUDES

Do you think things have changed much in the United States since you were growing up with regard to the treatment and rights of black people?

Can you say a little more about that?

What do you think the main changes have been?

What do you think has caused the changes? What brought them about?

## COULD A BLACK PERSON EVER BE ELECTED PRESIDENT?

Do you think a black person could ever be elected President of the United States?

Why, or why not?

## WHY THERE IS RACISM

Why do you think that some white people are afraid of black people, and are prejudiced against them?

In other words, what do you think "causes" racial prejudice?

## MOST IMPORTANT BLACK WOMAN LEADER

Who do you think has been the most important or inspirational black woman of your lifetime?

Why do you say that? Who was she, and what did she do?

## BLACK LEADERS TODAY

What do you think of some of the black leaders today? [wait]

Do you think the black leadership in America is on the right track to best represent the interests of black people?

Why do you say that? What do you agree with, and what do you disagree with?

Who do you think was the greatest black leader of your generation?

Did you ever see him or her, or hear him or her speak?

# Special Questions for Hispanic-American Narrators

҈Ӂ҈Ӂ҈Ӂ҈

There are many different national origins of Hispanic-American culture and history: Mexican, Cuban, Puerto Rican, Central American, and South American. However, some general Hispanic American values and cultural characteristics are increasingly being recognized by both Hispanics and Anglos. Specific questions about the history or the country your narrator came from should be asked if applicable. For example, you would certainly want to ask any Mexican-American narrator eighty or more years old about his or her recollections of the Mexican Revolution of 1912. Or any Cuban-American over the age of forty or so should be asked to talk about the Cuban Revolution, Castro, Batista, The Bay of Pigs invasion, and so on. Puerto Rican Americans should be asked about issues of statehood and their feelings about further economic and cultural integration with the United States. Questions about childhood experiences, holiday celebrations, and values growing up, developed in the earlier chapters of this book, will have already captured some of the aspects of Hispanic culture you are preserving in these interviews. This chapter's purpose is to create an additional specific context within which American families with Hispanic background can begin to discuss and communicate some of their cultural heritage.

## HISPANIC COUNTRY OF ORIGIN

From what Spanish-speaking country did you or your ancestors come?

What would you say distinguishes [narrator's Hispanic country of origin] from other Hispanic-Americans?

For example, in your experience, are [Mexican/Cuban/Puerto Rican] people very different from you in their values and behavior?

What do you mean by that? Can you say a little more about how your culture is different from other Hispanic cultures?

## HOW HISPANIC CULTURE IS DIFFERENT FROM ANGLO CULTURE

How are Hispanic-Americans different from Anglo-Americans, in your opinion?

Could you talk about that a little more? What do you think some of the basic differences are?

What do you most like, and most dislike, about Anglo values and culture? What are the best things and the worst things about Anglos?

Could you say a little more about that?

And what about Hispanic culture? What are the best and worst characteristics of Hispanic culture?

Could you say a little more about that?

## HISPANIC PRIDE

What was the time in your life when you felt most proud of your Hispanic heritage? When you were the most proud to be Hispanic?

What are you most proud of now about your Hispanic heritage and culture?

Could you say anything more about this?

## GREATEST ACHIEVEMENTS OF HISPANIC CULTURE

In your opinion, what are the greatest achievements of Hispanic culture? What would you say are the most important contributions of Hispanic culture to the world? [wait]

Can you give examples from art, literature, music and dance, philosophy, science, religion or politics of the most important Hispanic contributions to mankind?

## PRESERVING THE SPANISH LANGUAGE

How important is it to preserve the use of the Spanish language, in your opinion?

Why do you say that? Could you say a little more about it?

Do your children and grandchildren speak Spanish?

How do you feel about that?

[If narrator is not a native English speaker]:

How long did it take you to learn English? How long did it take you until you felt comfortable speaking English?

## BILINGUAL EDUCATION/BICULTURAL SOCIETY

How important is bilingual education in the schools?

Could you talk about that a little more? Why do you think it is important, or not important?

Do you think American society should be a "bicultural," or "bilingual" society? With Spanish and English being treated equally? Or should people living here strive to learn and speak English as soon as possible?

Why do you say that?

## DISCRIMINATION

Can you remember the first time you ever became aware of feelings or prejudices against you just because you were Hispanic? [wait]

Can you remember a specific incident when you were treated with disrespect because of your Hispanic background or your use of the Spanish language?

What did that mean to you? How did it affect you?

Has discrimination been much of a problem to you in your life, or do you think you have had plenty of opportunities in your life?

Do you have any specific memories of lost opportunities because of social prejudice or discrimination against you?

What happened?

How do you feel about it now?

Many Hispanic-Americans, especially in the Southwest, bristle at the notion that they are immigrants of this country, because in fact Hispanic culture and institutions long preceded Anglo culture there. What has this meant to you, living in the United States? Has this ever been an issue for you?

## ILLEGAL IMMIGRANTS AND THE INS

There are many millions of Hispanic-Americans living and working in the United States who are in danger of being deported if they are caught by the INS. What do you think should be done about this problem? [wait]

Can you say a little more about that?

What do you think of the job the Immigration and Naturalization Service does? [wait]

Do you think the INS has a fair system?

What do you mean by that? Could you talk about it a little more?

## BECOMING AN AMERICAN CITIZEN

If you are a naturalized American citizen, can you tell what you went through to become a citizen, and what it meant to you?

Can you say a little more about that?

What does it mean to be an American citizen?

## RELIGION AS A VALUE IN HISPANIC-AMERICAN CULTURE

It has been said that religion and religious values are very important to Hispanic-Americans. Do you think this is true?

How important is your religion to you now?

How important are religion and religious values to your family?

Some people say that the modern world is destroying religion and religious values. Do you think this is true?

[If yes]: Can or should anything be done about this?

Could you say a little more about that?

## HISPANIC MUSIC AND DANCE

Who are some of your favorite Hispanic musicians?

Who were some of your favorites when you were growing up?

Which Hispanic performers or bands do you think most accurately express the feeling of Hispanic culture and dance?

Are you a musician yourself?

What is your instrument, and what kind of music do you play?

What about dancing? How important is dancing to Hispanic culture, and how important is it to you?

What makes Hispanic dancing and dancers different from the dancing of other cultures?

Is there any danger that American rock and roll will drive out an appreciation of Hispanic music and dance among young people?

Why do you say that?

If you think there is a danger, can anything be done about it?


## HISPANIC CULTURE AND THE "CAPACITY TO ENJOY LIFE"

Sometimes people say with admiration that one of the greatest strengths of Hispanic culture is the "capacity to enjoy life." Do you agree with this? Do you think Hispanics know how to enjoy life?

What do you mean by that? Could you say a little more?

What does a person have to know in order to enjoy life?

A Hispanic-American writer has commented on the Hispanic "sense of leisure and celebration" as one of the achievements of Hispanic-American culture? Would you agree or disagree?

If it is true that Hispanics know about celebrating life, why do you think that is?


## HISPANIC-AMERICAN FAMILY VALUES

It has also been said that to Hispanic-Americans the family is the most important focus, and that family values are the most important. Do you agree with this?

Is the Hispanic family different from other families in this respect?

Could you say a little more about that?

How have some Hispanic families been able to resist and survive some of the forces of modern life that have destroyed others' family values?

What about care of and respect for the elderly? Is this an important part of Hispanic-American family life?

If Hispanic-Americans tend to value their older people more than other groups, why is that?

Is there a danger that respect and care for the elderly in Hispanic culture might decrease? Or do you think it is one of the enduring virtues of the Hispanic heritage?


## WHAT CAN OTHER CULTURES LEARN FROM HISPANIC CULTURE

What can other cultures and groups learn from Hispanics?

What important values and skills do Hispanics have to teach Anglos and others? [wait]


## THOUGHTS ON POLITICS IN LATIN AMERICA

What do you think of the political and social unrest in some Latin American countries such as El Salvador, Nicaragua, Guatemala, and other places? [wait]

Should the American government be sending military supplies to one side or the other in any of these countries?

Why do you say that?

What do you think the American government should do, or not do, in these countries?

Could you talk about that a little more?

Should the American government ever send its own soldiers into Latin America?

Why, or why not?

Under what circumstances do you think such a thing might happen?

Would you ever be in favor of such an action, or would you protest against it?

Could you say a little more about your ideas about wars and revolutionary movements in Latin America?

Do you think Hispanic-Americans should be more concerned about American policies in Latin America than any other Americans?

Why?

## HISPANIC-AMERICAN LEADERS

What do you think of Hispanic-American leaders? Do you think they are doing a good job of representing your interests in the United States?

Who are the ones doing the best job, in your opinion?

Who are the ones doing the worst job, in your opinion?

## COULD AN HISPANIC BE ELECTED PRESIDENT?

Do you think an Hispanic-American could ever be elected President of the United States?

Why, or why not?

## WHAT ELSE IS IMPORTANT ABOUT HISPANIC HERITAGE

What else can you say to younger people about the value of their Hispanic heritage? What have we not discussed that you feel is important for younger people to know?

# Further Reading

Baum, Willa K. *Oral History for the Local Historical Society*, 2nd ed. Nashville: American Assn. for State and Local History, 1971.

Buhler, C., and F. Massarik, eds. *The Course of Human Life*. Springer, 1968.

Butler, Robert. "The Life Review: An Interpretation of Reminiscence in the Aged." *Psychiatry*, Vol 26(1), 1963, pp. 65–76.

Davis, Cullom, et al. *Oral History From Tape to Type*. Chicago: American Library Association, 1977.

Dollard, John. *Criteria for the Life History*. New Haven: Yale University Press, 1935.

Dundes, Alan. "The Native Speaks for Himself," in *Every Man His Way*, Alan Dundes, ed. Englewood Cliffs: Prentice-Hall, 1964.

Eisenstadt, S. N. *From Generation to Generation: Age Groups and Social Structure*. New York: Free Press, 1964.

Jeffrey, Kirk. "Varieties of Family History." *The American Archivist*, Vol. 38 (Oct. 1975), 521–32.

Langness, L. L. *The Life History in Anthropological Science*. New York: Holt, Rinehart & Winston, 1965.

Lichtman, Allan J. *Your Family History*. New York: Vintage Books, 1978.

Mead, Margaret. *Culture and Commitment: A Study of the Generation Gap*. New York: Natural History Press, 1970.

Mead, Margaret, "Grandparents as Educators." *The Family as Educator*. Pp. 66–75. New York: Teachers College Press, Columbia, 1974.

Rosengarten, Theodore, ed. *All God's Dangers: The Life of Nate Shaw*. New York: Alfred A. Knopf, 1974.

Terkel, Studs. *Hard Times: An Oral History of the Great Depression*. New York: Pantheon, 1970.

Watson, Lawrence. "Understanding a Life History as a Subjective Document," *Ethos* 4: 95–131.

Watts, Jim, and Allen F. Davis. *Generations: Your Family in Modern American History*, 2nd ed. New York: Alfred A. Knopf, 1978.

# Index